RED SERGE
AND STETSONS

EDITED BY

Donovan T. Saul

Horsdal & Schubart

Horsdal & Schubart Publishers Ltd.
Victoria, B. C., Canada

Cover painting, "The Old Mountie" by Arnold Friberg, Salt Lake City, Utah, with the kind assistance of Studio Graphics, Salt Lake City, Utah.

Typesetting by Donovan T. Saul, Victoria, B. C.

This book is set in Basset.

Printed and bound in Canada by Kromar Printing, Winnipeg, Manitoba

Canadian Cataloguing in Publication Data

Main entry under title:
Red serge and stetsons

Includes index.
ISBN 0-920663-21-4

1. Royal Canadian Mounted Police — Anecdotes.
I. Saul, Don.
HV8157.R43 1993   363.2'0971   C93-091623-9

CONTENTS

INTRODUCTION

This book was spawned from *The Way it Was — 50 Years of RCMP Memories*. Briefly, a committee was formed and primarily through the efforts of Alan Pennock, stories were forwarded from members, their wives and their families, (even some civilians). We had 5,000 copies printed in 1990 and it turned out to be an outstanding success, the copies being sold out in less than a year. Some thought was given to a second printing, but we decided to publish a second book instead. There were insufficient stories submitted to make a good book, so permission was obtained to use any stories we needed from the *RCMP Quarterly*. This permission is much appreciated and we are grateful to the RCMP for this. The editor of the *Quarterly*, Paul Hughes, was particularly helpful. I had all the *Quarterlies* from the first edition in 1933, and selected stories I thought would fit the theme we had in mind. We also received permission from Frank Spalding to use selections from his book *100 Years in the Saddle, or Stop the Musical Ride, I Want Off*.

One of the complaints about the first book was the use of terms unfamiliar to civilians: "OC", "CO", "NCO" and "time expired". The OC is the Officer Commanding a Sub-Division, the CO is the Officer Commanding a Division, and an NCO is a non-commissioned officer — all ranks from corporal to sergeant-major. Members engaged for a fixed period of time, initially five years, then each re-engagement was three years or less. The end of an engagement period was termed "time expired", since if one left before that, he was required to pay five dollars for every month short of the expired period, called "purchase of discharge". I've probably missed some, but this explanation should make this book easier to read.

The cover of this book is a story in itself. Arnold Friberg, a well-known painter from Salt Lake City, Utah, painted pictures of Mounties for many years for the annual calendar of The North West Paper Company, and most of my contemporaries have one or more copies in their dens. I got to know him in 1973 and he was kind enough to send me the calendar for 1959, which is this book's cover. He graciously let us use the painting.

Robert MacNeil of *The MacNeil-Lehrer Newshour* was sent a copy of the first book. He felt there should be more about the Marine Section in which his father was a commissioned officer. I accepted his advice, even to paraphrasing from his book, *Wordstruck,* and using the insignia his father had on the bridge of the *Dauphin,* of a member of the Force riding a German submarine with a revolver in his hand.

I would be remiss if I didn't express my appreciation to Marlyn Horsdal for the labour in editing to make it readable. Also to my wife, Lyn, who assisted me in many ways.

The maximum strength of the Force until 1950 was approximately 3,000. By the mid-1970s, it reached a strength of about 8,000. The rate of pay during the 1940s commenced at $1.50 per day and there were many one-man detachments. Members serving today would have difficulty visualizing the Force that existed during those times, much as the veterans and their families who were the contributors to this book experience difficulty visualizing the Force as it is today.

Donovan Saul, Editor

Chapter One

Small Towns and Rural Areas

FROM RESORT TO RANCHING COUNTRY

One bright spring day in Calgary in 1933, I was called into Inspector Ernie Bavin's office, where a sergeant, acting as if he was handing out a medal, announced that I was posted to Banff. This was a disappointment, as I had volunteered for northern service and fully expected to join the illustrious band of adventurers with names like Stallworthy, Millen, Joy and King. When I suggested the Banff posting was probably a mistake, the NCO was not amused.

I boarded the next train going west, struggling through a packed day coach in red serge and stetson. It was a cent-a-mile excursion and I stood with my kit, trying to keep my spurs from tripping people, the car redolent with the pungent aroma of orange peel and tobacco.

This proved to be the start of an adventure, entirely unexpected, by someone barely able to vote. Here I was, signed up for five years, earning $1.50 a day, about to receive an extra dollar a day to eat out in restaurants in Canada's most fabulous resort. Banff was at its apex as an international resort, attracting world-wide celebrities before the day of the jet set. The CPR had railway sidings able to cope with special trains from Chicago, New York and Minneapolis. Majestic in the distance stood the Banff Springs Hotel.

My arrival in Banff was not momentous as I stood on the station platform surrounded by magnificent scenery. No one expected or greeted me. I stored the kit bag and, carrying a haversack, hiked a lonely mile by a back road to the old Banff Detachment which stood, with stables, by the bridge over the Bow River. Behind the barracks was the zoo with its polar bear, and wolves that howled in reply to every train whistle.

Dick Lea, the driver, cranked up the OC's Buick and we drove to the station for the kit bag. Banff was a small division headquarters and the OC then was Inspector W.V.M. Bruce, a gutsy little hero of northern service. As a corporal in 1915 he had caught the murderers of two priests near Great Bear Lake. Red Cantrill was the sub-division orderly and Sergeant Taylor ran the detachment with hard-nosed efficiency and a tight rein on his men. He had daughters. We were young, athletic and full of the juices of youth. The good sergeant had to protect not only his daughters but the entire national park swarming with lovelies from California, Carolina, Georgia and New York. We could place them by their accents.

We wore red serge all summer and rode Sundance Canyon, the golf course and the many trails around and about, stopping for buses and Brewster Packards so the tourists could take pictures. We had to meet the trains, the specials coming from the south and the transcontinentals bringing visitors from New Zealand, Australia and Europe. It was heady stuff in the days of Nelson Eddy, Rose Marie and Co.

Looking back, they were golden years and I had four of them. The Banff Springs Hotel was a magnet for the rich and famous, out of which grew many stories and legends. The one I liked best concerns Denny Mighall who is remembered as a fine horseman, a great gentleman, a fine revolver shot and one of the smartest men to wear red serge. He was selected to represent the Force at the coronation of George VI in 1936.

Mighall served in Banff in the 1920s and was on duty the night the Prince of Wales disappeared from the vice-regal suite. Denny had just entered the detachment half-way through the night, had loosened his belt and was sitting quietly at the desk when the door burst open. A large, frantic, Scotland Yard detective croaked out, "He's gone!" The prince had taken a powder.

Denny calmed him, telephoned the sergeant and roused the troops, who woke up the horses, and they rode off in all directions. With Irish intuition Mighall crossed the bridge at the top of Banff Avenue and took a dark trail through the woods behind the large homes of prominent families. Horse muffled, spurs quiet, he came upon a romantic scene in a garden. After making sure there was no threat to the throne, Denny made a quiet retreat and hastened to the barracks to calm jittery nerves. Without surrendering details, Mighall gave his personal guarantee that His Royal Highness would soon be safely back in the arms of officialdom. No names, no pack drill, the horses and troopers went back to bed and Denny, the gentleman, completed his tour of night duty.

That was not, however, the end of the incident. Some days later a lovely young lady, prominent in Alberta society, caught up with our boy marching smartly down Banff Avenue. She invited him to join her over a cup of coffee in Gus Baracas' Banff Cafe.

"Denny," she said when they were settled, "by any chance were you riding up the trail to the Upper Hot Springs the other night?"

"Of course not," he replied. "I was on night duty in the village, checking stores and such."

"I know you are lying in your teeth," she said with a smile, "but I love you for it."

Later, I was transferred to Manyberries and came under the avuncular interest of the late, great Leo Hester who was born at Zephyr, Texas, in 1884. Coming to Canada in 1903 he began punching cattle when he was 19 and for the next 20 years he followed the chuck wagons of the famous ranches along the border. He joined the Alberta Provincial Police in 1923 and was absorbed into the RCMP in 1932.

It was a sad day for Manyberries and the ranching fraternity when I took over the detachment and Leo was moved to Lethbridge as district stock detective. Leo didn't have much time to train a newly appointed novice stock inspector, so designated by an unwitting government. However, he did try to ingrain in me his particular brand of warmth and kindness and cowboy savvy that combined an outward gentleness with hard-nosed ability to survive. There wasn't enough time for all the important lessons.

"Don't worry," Leo had said. "If you play the game, these folks, good or bad, will help you survive. You know you can't read a brand and they know it. So play it smart. Go through the drill. When you get to the corral, climb the rails, push your stetson back on your head and shout to the boss to run 'em by. Get the count right, the brand on the forms, collect the money. Nothing to it. You'll get by."

The dust had barely settled on the trail to Lethbridge when my first challenge came up. An important rancher named Murray, running the Top Hat brand, drove up in a large car. He was shipping 750 head of yearlings from a distant siding to Saskatchewan. I grabbed the brand book, tried to remember what Leo had told me, sneaked another look at the form and followed Murray across the prairie.

The siding was busy with cowboys riding herd and cattle milling, the train waiting patiently. All eyes were on the greenhorn. I can remember climbing the rails, doing it just like Leo had suggested, but when I shouted "Run 'em by!" the cowboys stopped and stared. Murray held up his hand, shrugged, jumped into the corral and stood as pivot so the steers raced past me one at a time. I had a good tally, carefully marked the brand on the certificate, remembered to check for horns and worked out the total. Murray wrote out a cheque and handed it over.

"Powerful good brand reading," he said dead pan. "The Top Hat brand happens to be on the other side of the critters."

Gray Campbell

* * * * *

THE SUN NEVER SET ON THE ONE-MAN DETACHMENT

To the wives and the telephone operators must go a word of thanks, when readers ask how it was possible to operate a one-man detachment, providing so many services throughout a large area. The area might have a population of 2,000 or more people, covering a thousand or more square miles and extending at times, as circumstances dictated, into the neighbouring detachment area. To my knowledge, the detachment boundaries were never firmly established except where there was a lake or river. For example the Oak Point Detachment was located on the east side of Lake Manitoba and extended to Eriksdale on the north, Woodlands on the south and about 20 miles to the east, where it bordered on the Teulon Detachment. There was never any dispute or discord in this respect. It was acknowledged courtesy, however, that if you were in another detachment area you would contact your neighbour.

Most often, when you visited the neighbouring detachment office, the member(s) would be away but the second man (his wife) would answer the door. She would know where her husband was and what he was doing. At the same time she would make a note on the blotter that you had visited and the reason. The wife was usually there to answer the door, the telephone, and in latter years, the radio. When the wife was away and there was no one at the detachment you would simply call the telephone operator. She would know, or it seemed so anyway, where the members were and in most cases what they were doing. There is every reason to think that the telephone operators eavesdropped on the police calls.

Those telephone operators of old, God bless them, I'm sure they did eavesdrop on police telephones, and why not? They were there, late at night when you were typing a report and didn't know how to spell a word, and if they didn't know how to spell it they would call the girl on the neighbouring exchange. It went on and on late at night. I recall at Strasbourg Detachment there were, at times, as many as ten or more friendly female voices on the line at one time. You can make "conference" calls today, but to be sure, they were invented 50 or more years ago by lonely Mounted Policemen and the girls on the telephone lines.

Something has surely been lost with the invention of the dial and touch-button telephones. In those days, a call to the telephone operator would bring assistance from miles around to fight a fire or search for a lost child. If the message came to the detachment office through the telephone, you did not have to waste time with explanations -- they knew all about it and while you were on your way they spread the request for assistance.

The telephone of yesterday was a very necessary means of communication and, were it not for the telephone operator, it would have had a very disturbing effect on the whole family during the night. The telephone operators were very understanding and considerate, and they surely knew from experience the disruptive effect of an unanswered phone. I'm sure they measured the interval of the rings at night to allow a member to get from his bed to the office. We were never, in my years, provided with an extension telephone beside the bed. It may be that that was a blessing as a ringing telephone in the bedroom would have wakened the whole family. The policeman was wide awake, like a mother with a new baby at the first whimper (of the phone), be it midnight, two, three or four in the morning, in the middle of winter when a blizzard was blowing and you were in your soundest sleep. When the phone rang at such an hour it meant there was someone in trouble, someone needed you and you were wide awake. It did not matter that you had just gone to bed after being out all night the night before and had not slept for many hours.

On one such occasion at Oak Point at about two a.m. on a Monday morning, I was called from some much-needed sleep. Down the stairs I tumbled, pulling on a pair of trousers, to find a young lady from one of the Winnipeg radio stations on the line asking for some information about a fatal accident on the Friday night, a rape in the same vicinity on Saturday and a breaking, entering and theft from a store in Eriksdale on the Saturday night. The intruder at the store in Eriksdale turned out to be a transient and I had been fortunate in locating him with all the stolen goods in somewhat record time. This did not shorten my day, however, as I had no lockup and the prisoner had to be taken to the Vaughan Street Detention Centre in Winnipeg. When I arrived home in Oak Point, 60 miles north of Winnipeg (Eriksdale is 30 miles farther north) at about midnight, my wife had a hot meal ready for me. Don't ask me how she was able to keep it hot and ready (without micro-wave) but there it was, and off to bed I went -- to be awakened about an hour later.

The girl on the phone wanted just a bit more information about the man I had lodged in the detention centre a few hours earlier. I guess I was just too tired, and yes, too angry to be annoyed, not that it would do any good, but as I recall this is how the conversation went.

RCMP Oak Point Detachment.

This is C.K.Y. radio station and I would like some information about the breaking, entering and theft at Eriksdale.

What did you want to know?

Do you have the name of the store etc. etc.?

Well, just a minute, I'll have to get my notes -- and (half asleep) what time is it?

Two a.m.

Did you not phone our headquarters for this information?

Oh yes, but I wanted to get just a bit more information about the fatal accident and the rape at St.Laurent, and --

I have just arrived back from Winnipeg, just got to sleep and I'm a bit tired.

You must have had a long day.

What time did you come to work?

Midnight.

What time do you finish work?

Eight a.m.

(All this time, I presume she thinks I'm thumbing through my notes so I can answer her questions.)

Well, I guess you'd get to bed about nine or ten a.m.

Yes, I should be sound asleep by ten.

Would you mind giving me your telephone number?

The number here is ---

No, I thought you would give me your home phone number.

Why do you want my telephone number?

Well, I just thought I would call you about ten or 11 in the morning and give you this information.

You're a nice guy.

You're a nice girl.
A somewhat curt but friendly voice said "Goodnight" and I responded "Goodnight" and went back to bed.

A.H. Clark

* * * * *

FINEST JOB IN THE FORCE

In 1935, the Alberta provincial government had requested that two members of the Force be assigned to two forest reserves for the sole purpose of game observation. The designated areas, which ran from the heights of the Rocky Mountains east to the foothills and beyond were previously part of the national parks, but when the federal government turned over natural resources to the provinces it included this country, which the Alberta government resolved to keep intact as a forest reserve.

Within this vast tract of land every type of big game animal except bison could be found. It was the only spot in North America where a hunter could make one camp and find moose, elk, caribou, deer (mule and white tail), grizzly and black bears, big horn sheep and mountain goats. It was also rich in such fur-bearing animals as marten, mink, fishers, otter, lynx, beaver and muskrat, not to mention an abundance of red squirrel. Many of the owners of registered trap-lines in the reserves also trapped cougars, wolves and coyotes. All of which testifies to the fact that a good game country without roads remains a good game country. There were no roads in the Brazeau Forest Reserve.

I was stationed at Coutts, Alberta, just north of the Montana border, when I was asked if I would proceed to take over this particular patrol area. I emphasize "asked" because that is not the usual procedure when transferring RCMP personnel from one detachment to another.

The brass first inquired whether I could ride well, pack horses, drive dogs, handle a canoe, and generally survive in the outdoors, and when I volunteered an emphatic "Yes!", I soon found myself in the heart of the Brazeau Forest Reserve and the Rocky Mountains of Alberta. After a considerable hassle with the desk people at headquarters over saddlery and equipment, I was given a free rein to proceed to Riley-McCormacks in Calgary.

I ordered what I felt was necessary. I also made a deal with the Blackfoot Indians at Gleichen, Alberta, for some exceptionally fine diamond hair cinches. I supplied my own clothing -- except chaps and spurs -- and took over a police saddle horse, Bob (Reg.No.2196), and two pack horses, Old Bill (Reg.No.2402), and Kate. The one-roomed cabin I took over came complete with two fine pack dogs (half wolf) called Bruce and Buster, donated by a local trapper. When I said goodbye to Harold Elvin, a fine horseman and RCMP stock detective who had been holding the fort until I got there, I was on my own.

I was anxious to get away on my first patrol! Anxious? Perhaps frantic would be a better word because I fully believed it was all too good to be true and it would be called off before I even got under way. It was too much: no uniform, a first-class outfit, plain clothes allowance, no schedule and hundreds of square miles of wildlife country to explore. And THEY were paying ME!

My first patrol more or less provided the pattern for all the subsequent ones except with respect to the speed with which I got away from the camp and up into the hills. It was also a fairly short first day as I was anxious to feel out the outfit, and stopped early to spend the night at the Beaver Dam cabin. The first concern of this trip and every one thereafter was the horses. It became routine to alternate between grief, worry, fear, and the taking of many an oath never to trust the "hosses" again, especially after a two-hour chase.

But they had routines too. As soon as a horse is unpacked the first thing he does is roll. No matter where, the ritual is always the same: smell the ground, paw a little, turn around a few times, then down in the dirt, dust or mud, and roll; then up again, a good shake and begin to feed. With pack bells ringing and hobbles adjusted they could be depended upon to eat without looking or selecting for about 20 minutes. After that, they would start to wander to their favourite feeding ground or, failing that, set out in search of one. It never changed.

In the meantime, I would move into the cabin if there was one or find a good camp spot if there wasn't. The tent, of course, was for only really bad weather. Then the pack boxes had to be unpacked, the saddlery put away safe from the porcupines, and a fire started. I would have to get water, start supper, check the horses, make up a bed, eat, check the horses, clean up, get kindling for the morning fire, take a walk and watch game, check the horses and go to bed. It was a life governed more or less by the tinkle of pack-horse bells.

But wasn't it terribly lonely, I'm often asked. The answer is I don't know. I was always too busy and too interested in everything there was to see and hear to be lonely.

It was off to Grave Flats the next morning, or to the Southesk, Rocky Pass, the Pembina or even Jasper National Park where I could spend a few days back in civilization with my fellow foresters, the park rangers. These men were employed for only five months of the year and I worked closely with them. During the other seven I had the reserves all to myself. The rangers were an exceptionally dedicated and competent few, grossly underpaid. They had to supply their own horses and equipment and tried to do in five months what really needed a whole year. I travelled with them on many a job, fixing bridges, fighting forest fires or simply patrolling an area, and I had a key to every forestry and ranger cabin there was. I was also welcome at every trapper's cabin and many a time I was very glad to crawl into one in the middle of a winter patrol, notwithstanding the inevitable "lynx stink"-- the scent lure trappers prepare for their traps.

None of them hid any game meat on my approach, and the small minority who were undesirable from the point of view of wildlife conservation were soon weeded out. In fact, the average trapper did more for conservation in many ways than he did harm by trapping. I hauled several out in winter (by dog sled) and summer, who had been injured or become ill, or had gone "off the trail".

Although it wasn't part of my job, I also checked lakes and streams for fish and game clubs on behalf of the fisheries department, and hauled in fry and fingerling to stock certain lakes in my district.

It was all part of the finest job in the Force. During my three years I took many a "passenger" along too -- quite contrary to regulations. But I could do just as good a job for the government with a Percy Millet, Bob Barry, Dominique Bernard, Lionel Foster (my brother) -- or a very choice co-educational party from the state of Washington along. All in the line of duty, of course!

Looking over some old game patrol reports I read: "Patrolled via S-H Reg.No.2196 and pack outfit to the headwaters of McKenzie Creek...and overnight there. Four moose and two mule deer observed. Miles 14. Continued patrol across country to Squaw Lake, checking Fallis Creek en route, overnight at Medicine Lick Lake. Three elk on gravel bar, with calves. Two moose, a black bear with cubs. Miles 16. Remained in camp forenoon and left on foot for small unnamed lake south of the Lick. Horses left to graze. Harlequin with brood noticed on lake, also merganser with brood on small unnamed creek. Miles (on foot) 9.”

Every patrol was a holiday and every mile an adventure, and so it went until late fall when the pack horses had to be taken to the Brazeau Flats where they wintered. The saddle horse was wintered at the home cabin because, not being a range animal, he likely could not have foraged for himself. The pack horses had been born on the range and wouldn't stay anywhere else.

The drill was to set out with Rangers Harold Parnell and Jim Irvine, picking up trappers Dino and Johnson on the way, and head for the winter grazing. This, like all the others, was a fun patrol. We would pack a few dogs with grub and some cooking pots, plus some oats for the saddle horses, which we rode back after turning all the rest out to range. When the trip was over Harold and Jim would turn their saddle horses loose as well, and they lost no time in returning to the pack horses on the winter range.

It wasn't very long before I acquired a good dog team, adding three good animals to the original two wolf-dogs. After considerable correspondence with headquarters, I was granted 25 cents per diem allowance for each dog and was therefore able to continue patrolling by dog team throughout the winter. Sometimes in the late fall or early spring I had to make patrols when there was too much snow to take all the horses, but not enough snow to use the sled. So I had to patrol with three pack dogs, one of which carried 35 pounds of oats for the saddle horse which carried me, my sleeping bag and other essentials. With the snow covering the grazing, three horses would have been too many because we couldn't carry enough feed for them.

The early spring patrols were the most interesting because from them I could develop a general idea of how the game had come through the winter. Once I found seven dead elk, or what was left of them, lying in a gully. They had apparently been trying to feed on the steep south slope and had slipped off the ice to their death.

I observed starved moose and loco ones. Some had become so infested with ticks, and so weak from cold and hunger, that they had died. Often animals in a similar state were boxed in by wolves and killed. I found a large bull moose with only his rack showing above the ice in a river; a dead man in a cabin; a trapper “off the trail”(as he put it), waiting to be taken out for care and treatment; an abandoned spring hunt camp with the dogs dead where they were tied and their owner missing. All that was left were two birds, a whisky jack

(Canada jay) and a dipper (water ouzel). No matter how cold and lonely a place could be, they seemed always to be there, welcome friends in a quiet world.

Time spent in caring for the horses and dogs was as rewarding as it was necessary. The dogs especially were of constant interest, each one a distinct personality. To travel day after day with such animals makes one realize how little we really know about them and how they react under so many conditions.

The behaviour of horses, however, is quite another story, as I have indicated already. Bob was a saddle horse, police bred and trained, a beautiful animal but in no way competent to understand the outdoors. He had been groomed, fed and stabled all his life and was, like most police horses, accustomed to goofing off, a natural slacker. He was terrified of moose and scared stiff of all types of muskeg.

The pack horses, on the other hand, were born on the range and knew all the angles, and then some. Faithful steeds! Not on your life! Knowledgeable? Yes, but beyond understanding in some ways. Once, when I had lost all direction and the outfit was enmeshed in a tangle of windfall with nowhere to go, I let Old Bill loose to find the way. He ploughed off in what I was certain was the wrong direction, and in no time at all we arrived at a plateau from which the way was obvious. He definitely had his good points.

When approaching muskeg, Bob, who didn't know good from bad and was afraid of everything anyway, would become frantic. Although he was trained to go in if ordered to, it was better if I booted Old Bill ahead to check the situation. And away he would go, stopping just short of the bog for a good sniff, dropping his head and snuffling the ground. If it was all right he wouldn't miss a step, heading straight through, but if it wasn't, no power on this earth could make him move into it.

The other pack horse, a buckskin mare called Kate, also had her quirks. There was a good forestry bridge on the way to Ruby Mountains, and every time we approached it during those three years the same thing would happen. Dozing along in the rear she would suddenly become alert, stop dead in her tracks, and with a terrified look dash off down the canyon a quarter of a mile, where she would ford the river with considerable difficulty, plough through brush and over windfalls, and catch up with the rest of us on the other side. Sometime in the past that bridge must have failed Old Kate, and she wasn't about to forget it.

I usually had to take two or three of my dogs along on pack-horse patrols as there was no one who would care for the whole team while I was away. They were very obedient and loved these free trips because they had nothing to carry. I have already mentioned Bob's jitters (a ruffed grouse exploding to wing right under his nose would send him into a terrified sideways fling that could send me sprawling), and he was no better when the dogs were around.

Travelling from Jasper with the outfit one quiet evening we found ourselves in the heart of grizzly country, a part of the park where these bears seemed to congregate. The horses, of course, scented them instantly, and displayed a marked reluctance to be first in line. The dogs were trailing behind and were quite uninterested, as they usually were in late evening. Bob's ears were sticking up like a rabbit's as he craned his neck, periscope-like, around every corner. It seemed as if the horses were trying not to breathe lest the bears hear them, and they walked as if every hoofbeat was a dead giveaway.

Sensing Bob's nervousness, I called for Dane, a big, black, Siberian husky who was the wheel dog in winter, and sent him up front. He poked along up to me, hoping I would change my mind and let him stay where he was, when Bob reached back, got his nose behind Dane's backside and actually "nosed" him up ahead! You could almost hear him saying; "Dane, brother, he told you to go first!"

Of course, I also goofed off now and then, but I would always find justification -- in my own mind. To find good grazing was the most important part of keeping horses in good shape for months on the trail, and coupled with all the other things that had to be done, I suppose I really didn't have much time off. I carried shoes, rasp, farrier's hammer and nails, and I could shoe the horses whenever a shoe was lost, but grazing was always the problem and always an excuse for a bit of a rest.

To find a beautiful lake in alpine country with lots of feed was a fine occasion to lay over for a day or two to allow the horses to rest and get fat. Such tranquil stopovers were really the highlights -- or at least some of them -- of my three years. I remember one place where the grass was so rich the horses were dozing with full bellies all afternoon, and the dogs exhausted themselves chasing rock rabbits.

But all good things come to an end, and this end came on September 3, 1939. That day I was at a small party when we all suddenly realized Neville Chamberlain was on the radio -- "and we are now in a state of war with Germany." I remember hurrying back to my cabin, well knowing that this was the end of a very peaceful existence. I knew the good life was gone for a while, so I hastened to catch a last look at the country I had enjoyed for so long.

Gathering up the horses, I packed as though I was jumping a board bill and took off to salvage a final three weeks. Far and away we went, to many of the known and even to some unknown places, just wandering and camping, hating to return. When I did, there it was, the telegram: "-- until further instructed -- discontinue all game patrols --."

Alan R.Foster
RCMP Quarterly - Volume 46, Number 1

Editor's Note: This article is reprinted courtesy of the *Times-Colonist*, Victoria, B.C.

*   *   *   *   *

THE GRAVE ON THE HILL

The year was 1947, the month was March, the locale was the village of Telegraph Creek situated on the banks of the Stikine River, in northern British Columbia.

I received a call from W.P. "Bill" Thorman, magistrate, coroner, local doctor, trader and friend and general confidant of the Tahltan Indians. Bill, then nearing 70, had been visited by one of the Indians who reported that Pete Curran, a trapper over 70 years of age, was missing.

Pete, well known to everybody in the Stikine area, had left for his trap-line at Grassy Creek, 40 miles east of Telegraph Creek, in September 1946. This was his yearly routine. He would make the trip to a point as near as possible to his trap-line with pack horses supplied by an old friend of many years, Ira Day. Grub and equipment were brought to the cache and from there transported, when convenient, to the trap-line cabins by sleigh and pack dogs, these too supplied free of charge by Ira Day. The horses were taken back to the Day Ranch at Wards Hill, 16 miles east of Telegraph Creek; it was understood each year that Pete could keep the dogs for the winter and bring them back on his return to the outside in the spring. Transporting all the equipment to the cabins was a difficult chore for the old man and it had become a practice of his friends, the Tahltan Indians, to deliver, during the winter, some of the food supplies which Pete would leave in his cache ten miles from his main cabin.

Deep snows and extremely severe weather had prevented the Indians from getting to the Curran cabin during the winter and the food at the cache had not been picked up. This seemed to indicate that Pete was either dead or in desperate straits for want of food. March in the Stikine area is break-up time and any quest to find the old man would have to leave soon. This was the reason I had been called to Taku Traders by Bill Thorman. He was too old to go; would I make some attempt to locate and save his old friend?

In the north country one does not question a request of this type. Preparations were made immediately, grub secured, bedrolls checked; tents and most other equipment would have to be left behind. The snow had disappeared near the river and as our only transport would be dog sled, the river ice would be our road. Snow-shoes were a necessity because the snow at Grassy Creek would still be deep. Some extra food was taken along in case Pete was still alive; matches, axes and ropes were the only other extra equipment.

One could not travel alone on a search of this type so I enlisted the services of Fletcher Day, son of Ira, who knew the country and was a long-time friend of the missing man. We left that afternoon for the Day Ranch, a trip that would take us up the river on ice that was breaking up, through the fabulous Stikine Canyon. This was an unforgettable trip. The Stikine is a large and deep river, one of the fastest on this continent, and the canyon is second only in depth and size, I believe, to the Colorado.

It was dark when we arrived at the ranch; the dogs were fed and bedded and the equipment stored in the bunk house. Then we retired to the main house to eat a meal which only a northerner could devour. The first course is always moose stew with rice which is not too hard to take, but when dining with Ira Day, a man is expected to eat three times as much as he would normally. Then comes the home-made bread with local blueberry jam, butter by the pound and numerous cups of tea -- tea as only a northerner can make it. After this we had the usual evening of chatter in front of the crackling birch fire and made plans for an early start. Early in this country is four a.m.

Three a.m. -- a lusty call from Ira and everyone in the country is wide awake -- a wash in ice-covered water, then to the kitchen again. Breakfast consists of three helpings of porridge cooked to perfection over a wood fire, moose stew again, toast and coffee.

At four we were on our way, sleds lightly loaded, morning frost on the snow and the dogs frisky. They lost some of this after the first three miles though, which were all up steep hills with not too much snow. On the top of the hills it was deeper and snowshoes were the order of the day. Then the snow was crisp and travelling fairly easy, and it was not many hours before we came to Pete's cache. Checking, we found his winter supplies untouched and secure. Only one conclusion -- Pete must be dead. Apparently the snow had been too deep for the old man to traverse because in the cache were sufficient supplies to last a man two months at least. With dread, we carried on to Pete's main cabin.

The country began to open out and we were now in the vicinity of Grassy Creek. With binoculars we could discern Pete's cabin and our fears were confirmed -- the door of the cabin was swinging on the hinges, and standing near the door were two guns. Near the guns were Pete's snowshoes. We knew he must be in the cabin; no trapper would leave in the winter without his snowshoes.

The scene that met our eyes at the cabin was one of horror. On the porch were the remains of the dogs' legs, several owl heads and legs and portions of ravens. Starvation was the certain fate of this old-timer. Entering the cabin we found the earthly remains of Pete on his bunk. His mattress was grass pulled from the swamps and made into hay. Over this was a thin and worn blanket, and covering our old friend was a piece of canvas. This was his only bedding. He was frozen stiff, curled up and his hands in a clutching position. No doubt he had fought death to the last, the victim of starvation and bitter cold.

Examination of the cabin showed there was no fuel, the flour barrel had been scraped on the inside with a knife, feathers of owls and ravens were in abundance and dog hair and skin was on the floor. There were no matches, a desperate plight in a northern winter. The most pathetic sight of all was what was to have been a last meal on the stove in a cooking pan, frozen solid. The old fellow had cut the babiche (thongs) from a pair of snowshoes into small pieces with an axe and was attempting to boil it. Obviously he had run out of fuel and matches, then with the bitter cold overtaking his meagre strength, he had gone to his bunk, pulled the canvas over his body and lain down to die. Pete was a man of the north and one can be sure that he was well aware that there was no hope. I often wonder about his last thoughts -- he was a confirmed atheist.

We searched the cabin but there was nothing of value except one mink skin which had been placed in a tin container to avoid damage by mice. This was the entire product of a winter of trapping and the price of the life of an old man. The coroner had suspected that we might find the old man dead and had issued instructions that should this be so, the body was to be returned to the Telegraph Creek area to be buried.

We built a fire to thaw the old man out so that we would be able to place him on one of the sleds. We wrapped him in his piece of canvas, re-searched the cabin for valuables, set it on fire and started for home. Travelling most of the night on the frost, we reached the Day Ranch the next morning. Old Ira met us as we came through the gate and his first question was, "Where is Pete?" I pointed to the sled and the eyes of another old man filled with tears.

We contacted the coroner who said that if we were positive of the cause of death, we could bury our old friend near the Day Ranch, the summer home that he had always loved. We were sure and arrangements were made. Fletcher Day and I took a team with a stone-boat and the required tools and drove to the highest hill that we could locate overlooking the Day Ranch and the Stikine Canyon. Here on the brow of the hill we dug a grave and returned to the ranch.

Then, accompanied by Ira, Amy, Fletcher and their two small daughters, we placed the remains on the stone-boat and with a wreath of paper flowers made by Mrs. Day, went to the grave. While the family of friends stood with bowed heads I read the burial service and committed Pete to the ground. We returned to the ranch and, leaving my sled and harness there to be picked up later, I continued on to Telegraph Creek on foot. The dogs did not mind this in the least.

It was a sad day for this little outpost. The effects taken from the cabin were turned over to the administrator as were several pension cheques picked up from the post office. There had been no reason whatever for the old man to be away from the village but it was his own wish to be on his trap-line. He knew the dangers and decided to accept them. He was the master of his own destiny. He decided to take the chance and the result was that he gave his life for a mink skin.

Later in the spring, accompanied by Reverend Godfrey Bird of Telegraph Creek, an Anglican minister, I returned to the grave on the hill. There, in the presence of many old-time residents of the area including Indian friends, Reverend Bird carried out a full burial service and blessed the grave of his old friend who had always denied any belief in God. We raised a rough wooden cross over the grave on the hill and there, for time eternal, old Pete will lie, looking down on the things that he loved most in the land of the Tahltans.

G. Redhead
RCMP Quarterly - Volume 26, Number 2

*   *   *   *   *

WATCH THE STOVE

It was late in the 1960s when the last detachment in British Columbia had a sewer system (in this case a septic tank/field system) installed. For those involved, it was a red-letter day, whereas today a sewer system is the norm.

This brings to mind an incident that occurred to me in the early 1950s while I was stationed in the Peace River Sub-Division. Being a senior constable (over five years service) and single (a not uncommon state in those days), I found myself relieving at various detachments, i.e. temporarily replacing a member who was away for an extended period.

Early in January the member in charge of a detachment, which must remain unnamed for obvious reasons, was sent to Fairmount Barracks in Vancouver to attend a training course for six weeks. His family went out with him and they were going to take three or four weeks annual and accumulated leave at the same time. The second member was transferred out and was not going to be replaced during this period, as the powers-that-be were of the view that the work load would be light during this coldest period of the year. They were very wrong -- but that is another story. The member in charge graciously allowed me to use his attached married quarters for the duration of my stay. (On reflection I don't know he had any choice in the matter.) The town in which this detachment was located was regarded as modern since it had electricity. Alternative power was supplied by a most unreliable community diesel plant that seemed to work for a maximum of two hours, likely during daylight hours. Water for the detachment was purchased by the pail from a vendor who came around once a week.

There was no sewer system, so the facility was an outdoor biffy. The detachment didn't have a normal basement, but it did have a dug-out area that was about 20 feet square. During the worst of the winter weather a chemical toilet was located in this dug-out area, which was unheated, but not quite as cold as the outdoor toilet, and, of course, out of the wind. The chemical toilet consisted of a stand on which a standard toilet seat was mounted, and a receptacle consisting of a five-gallon paint can. Lime was generously added to the contents periodically.

Thanks to the combination of the lime and cold weather this chemical toilet was quite acceptable, though the contents usually froze in the container and had to be thawed out before being emptied into the outdoor biffy. (It was surprising how quickly one person can fill a five-gallon can.) Being young and lacking somewhat in patience I felt it best to thaw the container and contents on the stove and turn on the element for a time rather than have it sit on the kitchen floor to thaw out over several hours. So, place it on the stove I did, and to hasten matters I turned the element to high with every intention of returning to check it in a matter of minutes. Unfortunately, I became distracted with other duties and forgot about the stove until a rather pungent and tell-tale odour permeated the office from the open door of the married quarters. The contents on the stove had not only thawed and simmered a bit, but had boiled a lot and boiled over -- everywhere. You had to see it to believe it.

One would have had to participate in the chore to appreciate the clean-up job that followed. I never did tell the wife of the member when she returned some weeks later, and as far as I know I must have disposed of all the evidence of failing to watch the stove.

Anonymous

* * * * *

A DIFFICULT ESCORT OF A MENTAL PATIENT

In April 1934, at Melfort Detachment, Saskatchewan, I was detailed to proceed to the St. Brieux District to apprehend a mentally ill homesteader and take him before a justice of the peace for committal under the Mental Diseases Act. Travel would be by train and hired horse livery as the roads were largely impassable due to thawing.

My day started with an early breakfast at seven a.m. and I boarded the train for Meskinaw at eight a.m. A livery team met me at the train upon arrival. The liveryman had a lively team hitched to a closed-in "caboose" that sported a wood stove, something new for those days. All went well during the first part of the morning while the road was still frozen, and we made good travelling time.

At the homestead, several people were walking around the yard. The obviously violent patient stood with an axe in his hand amongst smashed furniture in a house with the windows broken out. I did my best in various ways to gain the confidence of the patient, and to converse with him, but to no avail. After a scuffle, the handcuffs were applied and he was trussed up with the issue blanket straps which I had brought along. The patrol continued on to St. Brieux where the patient was taken before the justice of the peace and committed to the provincial mental hospital at Battleford.

It was on the road between St. Brieux and the railway stop at Meskinaw that trouble developed, when the patient broke out of the restraining straps. In the struggle that ensued the wood stove was knocked over. The horses ran out of control when the caboose upset, and they broke away. Fire from the wood stove set fire to the caboose. The fire was promptly put out, but not before the patient took off across the field with me after him.

After quite a struggle, the patient was returned to the caboose. The liveryman caught up with his horses and found their torn and broken harness tangled in trees off the road. With the help of a nearby farmer, he patched the harness up. A good piece of rope was obtained from the farmer and took the place of the broken blanket straps, and the patrol reached Meskinaw in late evening. The only shelter available was in the livery barn where we stayed until the arrival of a freight train at eight a.m. on its way to Melfort. At Melfort the patient was held in the courthouse cell until the arrival of the provincial escort, complete with restraining equipment which made my blanket straps look as puny and inadequate as they had proven to be.

I received treatment for the many bites to my arms and legs, and the scratches to my face. A welcome bath soothed my aching body and removed the mucus spat into my face by a violent and powerful mental patient.

T.S.Guthrie

*   *   *   *   *

WHAT GOES BUMP IN THE NIGHT

Security control of a crime scene is a basic fundamental. The first step is to ensure that nothing is disturbed until photographs, fingerprints or other technical examinations are done. If the scene is some distance from the required specialists, the area may be under guard for hours or days. This thankless but vital task usually falls to the junior man, the reasoning being that he can be most easily spared, leaving the more senior, experienced members for investigational matters.

The year was 1950, the location was the B.C. interior and this was my maiden experience in this important duty. We had the suspicious death of a backwoods hermit in the sleeping loft of his ramshackle cabin. The downstairs living area comprised one room, sparsely furnished, with an open stairway leading up to a combination sleeping and storage loft under the gable roof. The body lay at one end of this loft. Technical assistance was not available until at least the following day and I was elected to stay and guard the scene. The corporal regretted he could not leave me the car. He cautioned me that he would prefer I stay outside, but in consideration of the cold October weather I might go in if I was careful not to touch or disturb anything. With that and a kindly wave goodnight, he drove off into the sunset.

A long, lonely night loomed ahead. Whether to shiver in the dark outside or sit quietly in the musty, dank, but slightly warmer inside was the only decision that faced me that night. About midnight, shivering got the better of me and I elected for the slightly warmer interior.

Mindful of the corporal's instructions, I hunkered down in a corner far from anything even remotely resembling a clue. It is paramount that no policeman sleeps on the job, but I do admit lapsing into deep thought, probably about better times, when it suddenly occurred to me I was hearing the loud footsteps of someone rapidly descending the stairway from the loft above me. In much less time than it took you to read this line, my flashlight beam swept the area, but nothing moved in the empty space between me and the stairway.

There now seemed sufficient cause for an alert mind to ponder, beyond the obvious "What the hell was that?" I even considered shivering outside again. I couldn't see my watch in the dark but I knew it was suddenly ticking much slower than usual as it didn't compare at all in frequency with my perfectly normal pulse rate, and both seemed much louder. Maybe darkness makes one's hearing better?

As these and other philosophical problems were receiving due consideration there was another footstep, but now at the top of the stairs and to the left. I was quicker this time, probably the practice, and my flashlight caught the glow of two beady little eyes retreating to a corner.

Not wishing to unnecessarily disturb any part of the scene, I carefully took the stairs about four at a time and he was cornered! He was a pack rat and he had been into a bag of potatoes. One teetered precariously on the top step while another lay where it had thump, thump, thumped its way to the bottom.

Good morning corporal -- yes it was a quiet night.

Jack White

* * * * *

THEY NEVER SAY GOOD-BYE

The arrival and departure of members of the Force at various postings is often a matter of routine to the communities concerned. This had been the case at Hazelton, a small community in north-central British Columbia, until a different incident occurred. The interesting aspect was the fact that the people concerned, in the majority, consisted of the residents of the Hazelton Indian Reserve.

The scene was the Hazelton Ice Carnival, being held on an open-air skating rink. The unannounced arrival of four hereditary chiefs, attired in traditional ceremonial regalia, resulted in the request for the attendance of RCMP Corporal and Mrs. A. Borodula. The following address was made by Chief William Wale:

"I am very pleased to have been asked to extend, on behalf of the Young People's Educational Association, their deepest thanks and appreciation to the Borodula family for their interest and cooperation in our community affairs. They especially thank Mr. Borodula, not only for the efforts which he has shown in the field of sports, but for his efforts toward creating a better feeling of cooperation between our people and his Force. The goodwill which he has created will always be remembered. We of Hazelton will be forever grateful for his contributions to our Club. May he and his family enjoy an even brighter and more successful future as they move on."

Following the presentation of gifts, which included a miniature totem pole, two of the chiefs reverted to the past. In Gitksan dialect, to the accompaniment of ceremonial rattles, they evoked the spirit of goodwill with words from the remote history of their ancestors. The following is a translation of one of the presentations:

"Those who are leaving will walk in the clearness
of the sky,
If shadows fall, the sun will soon rise again,
To shine on all, whether rich or poor, strong or
feeble,
I will lead you through the clearness of the sky,
I will lead you through the clearness of the sky."

Although to some the foregoing might appear ostentatious, those who know the Indian will appreciate the sincerity and solemnity embodied. That a chief of such prominence was selected to make the presentation is a reflection of the people's esteem for the Borodulas. As far as can be ascertained, this is the first ceremony of this nature in Hazelton history wherein the principal was a member of the Force.

The Young People's Educational Association, mentioned by Chief Wale, is the equivalent of organizations sponsoring social functions and sports activities in other communities. Corporal Borodula and his family had associated themselves with the Y.P.E.A. in promoting sports and activities for the youth of the community, and through this association a mutual feeling was fostered. The ice carnival was an appropriate setting as it was through Corporal Borodula's efforts that the first Hazelton carnival was organized.

This was the gesture of people who, in their native tongue, do not have a comparable term for "good-bye".

Anonymous
RCMP Quarterly - Volume 27, Number 2

*   *   *   *   *

OUT OF CIGARETTES

Late one winter evening in the early 1940s, the Moosomin Detachment received a report that a bachelor of the district had not been seen for some time. The members proceeded to his farm to sort out the problem. Upon arrival, they found he had died alone in his shack while sitting upright in his chair, and was now frozen stiff. After conducting the usual preliminary investigation, the members sat the body in the back seat of the police car. In those days, the police car was often used as an ambulance or hearse, when other, better means were unobtainable.

On the way back into town, they passed a lone Indian walking along the road. Since it was a cold and blustery night, they stopped and offered him a lift. He got into the back seat. After a while the Indian turned to his fellow passenger and asked if he had a cigarette. Hearing no reply he took a closer look. Suddenly realizing his companion was a corpse, he let out a yell, flung open the car door and disappeared into the night. Many Indians are very superstitious regarding dead bodies.

No report was ever received about a missing Indian, so the members assumed he had arrived at his destination.

P.A. Anderson

*   *   *   *   *

A WINTER PATROL

I was stationed at Hanley, Saskatchewan, in 1942. In February of that year there was a very heavy snowstorm with blizzard conditions which blocked all roads, including the highways. We had received a request from out in the country, necessitating a patrol to the area. As soon as the wind let up enough so that we could see our way, Corporal Dixon and I took a railway hand-car to the next town. Although the wind had abated somewhat it was -35 degrees Fahrenheit, with a wind-chill factor making it much colder. Pumping the hand-car kept up our circulation but our faces and hands went numb. We thawed out in the hotel and then rented a team and cutter for the balance of the journey. Some of the snow drifts were quite deep, making it tough going for the horses. At times they would stay on top, then they would sink down and flounder. A number of times we nearly tipped over, but we finally arrived at our destination where we were given a hot cup of coffee before proceeding with our business. In retrospect, the patrol couldn't have been all that urgent as for the life of me I can't remember the reason for the trip.

The return journey was no better and, to make matters worse, it was getting dark. We finally arrived back at Hanley without mishap. There, a warm room and a hot meal were a welcome sight.

Trips like this were not uncommon on the prairies and I dare say other members can relate more harrowing stories. However, in the light of society today, it was a little unusual.

H.C. Shepherd

* * * * *

THE CASE OF THE VANISHING CORPSE

This is a sad and macabre story which happened in the early spring of 1948 when I was stationed in a small town in southern Saskatchewan. Two brothers, in their early 20s, lived with their parents on the family farm. Both young men were quite good musicians and, consequently, were in great demand to play in the local dance orchestra. On the night of the tragic happenings related here, they were to play at a dance on the far side of the river from their home. They left the farm in the early evening, and, despite the fact that ice was still running in the river, they crossed in a small row boat. Apparently all went well at the dance and the brothers left, intending to ferry themselves back across the river in their little boat. They never reached home.

An alarm was raised by the parents the next morning and the local RCMP detachment commenced a search. The boat was located downstream, near the confluence of the Red Deer and South Saskatchewan rivers. There was no sign of the brothers.It was obvious that the missing persons had met with an accident.

A few days later the body of one of the men was found washed up on the south bank of the South Saskatchewan River. There was no trace of the second person. Spring passed into summer and all efforts to locate the missing man proved fruitless. As southwestern Saskatchewan sweltered in a heat wave, the search became intermittent, and it appeared likely that the body of the missing brother would never be found.

Early in July a rancher whose land bordered the South Saskatchewan River, some ten miles downstream from the confluence, came to my detachment and reported he had found human remains partially buried in a sandbar near the south bank of the river. The rancher advised me that a trail led down to the river and it would be possible to drive a truck across a gravel bar to a point close to the body. He agreed to guide me to the site.

A local implement dealer, who owned several trucks, provided a pickup and came along to assist. This man had the foresight to pick up several yards of heavy kraft paper from his grain elevator. This paper, together with a length of rope and an old tarp which I kept at the detachment for similar unpleasant occasions, was eventually most useful for wrapping up the recovered remains. At the site we found a badly decomposed and unrecognizable body. The clothing matched that of the person missing since April and the wallet recovered from the trousers contained identifying papers. We wrapped the body in the tarpaulin and, as there was no tailgate on the truck box, we tied the feet securely to the front of the box. Later events proved this to be a vital move.

On our arrival back in town we left the truck and body with the implement dealer who had agreed to lock them in his machine shop while I went to the telephone office and contacted the detachment nearest the home of the deceased, requesting they contact the young man's parents to arrange disposition of the body. I then returned to the machine shop and was gratified to note the truck and body were gone. I presumed they were safely locked in the machine shop. Gratification turned to horror when the implement agent came around the corner of the shop and asked me what had become of his truck containing the body.

As it turned out, the agent found his employees had locked up the machine shop and left for home prior to his arrival. He didn't have an extra key on him so he waited for some time for my return. He finally decided to walk over to his residence and pick up the extra key. In the meantime, the truck with the body had disappeared. We now had the case of the missing corpse.

I should note the implement agent was a very busy person. Not only did he deal in farm machinery but he was also a grain buyer and mayor of the town, and he owned two farms and a ranch in the area. He assumed that one of his employees had hopped in the vehicle and taken it home. All his trucks came complete with keys in the ignition and in the dark the cargo in the box of the pickup wouldn't be noticed.

The search began. A check was made with the two employees who resided in town. Enquiries were also made at the two farms and the ranch, but all the employees and their families denied having seen either the truck or its contents. As there were no telephones in any of these locations the enquiries entailed considerable driving, which was time consuming. The night wore on with no results.

When I returned to the detachment office in the wee small hours, my wife informed me she had received a call from the parents of the deceased, saying that they would be arriving early in the morning to make funeral arrangements. I was not looking forward to meeting them, nor attempting to explain the disastrous turn of events.

I went back to continue the search. I stationed the agent in his machine shop and patrolled all the streets and back alleys in town. Nothing. I finally stopped the car in front of the detachment to contemplate my next move. Dawn was breaking when I heard a motor vehicle approaching from the neighbouring town to the east. The vehicle turned into town and proceeded along the main street. As it came into view I saw it was the missing truck. I took off in hot pursuit. The truck pulled up in front of its home port, the machine shop. The young man driving the truck turned out to be a neighbour of mine who lived with his parents across the street from the detachment. He was accompanied by a young girl.

I placed the driver under arrest and subsequently charged him with taking the truck without the owner's consent. At this point the whole story was told. Apparently, the young fellow wanted to take his girl friend to a dance in the neighbouring village. She lived on a farm about 30 miles away. The lad's father refused to let him have the family car, so the son decided to borrow another vehicle. He came upon the implement dealer's truck and without looking in the back, drove off. The girl friend was picked up, the two of them danced the night away after parking the truck beside the dance hall and then drove back to town. Nobody noticed the gruesome cargo in the back of the truck, despite the fact the wrapping paper and tarp had blown away sometime during the night.

All's well that ends well. Needless to say, I didn't feel it necessary to inform the parents of the deceased of the untoward happenings.

G.R.Engel

*   *   *   *   *

A GIFT FROM THE BIRDS

Many years ago in a small coastal town in British Columbia that shall be mercifully unnamed, the proprietor of the local hotel was given to filing numerous complaints, generally unfounded, about the local police detachment. He was also in the habit of serving liquor to intoxicated patrons and ignoring the requests of the local RCMP personnel to mend his ways.

He had booked a trade union convention that was to be the major event of his summer season and the opening ceremonies in the main floor lobby and convention room started on a gala note. The area was awash in well-dressed guests.

An anonymous miscreant, who has never been identified, made his way unobserved to the roof with a loaf of bread and a bottle of rum. He spread some rum-soaked crumbs around the roof and very soon collected an extremely conscientious group of noisy seagulls. After the clamouring flock had achieved a suitable state of intoxication, he led them over to the elevator, which fortunately went up to the observation level on the roof. They eagerly rolled and scrambled into the elevator which he had also liberally sprinkled with the delicious morsels. He next pushed the lobby button and left the uninvited guests alone for their trip down. They arrived and commenced a raucous diversion for the startled guests below.

The proprietor took some time to dispose of his uninvited intruders, and commenced a clean-up of the various deposits left behind by the boisterous merrymakers. He then phoned the police to complain about the lack of protection and demanded an immediate investigation by the top authorities.

It has since been cruelly rumoured that the first member to arrive on the scene had traces of bread crumbs on his slacks, and a vague odour of rum on his hands. This went unnoticed, however, in the overall confusion and the variety of fragrances permeating the lobby. The crime was never solved.

R.W.Morley

*   *   *   *   *

TRANSPORTATION OF CADAVERS

The early summer of 1955 was unusually wet. The Peace River country was always known for its mud and gumbo, but early July was even worse as it rained constantly for the first two weeks. I was as green as they come, having been transferred straight from Regina to Manning in October 1954, and thence to the two-man detachment of Fairview in the spring of 1955.

About the middle of July word was received that a young male had gone off into the bush some 60 miles northwest of Fairview and about 20 miles from the nearest settlement of Hines Creek the day before and had not returned. The information we received was that he was depressed after breaking up with his girl friend and the family suspected he could be contemplating suicide.

The corporal and I left the detachment early the next morning in our standard, two-door 1953 Chevrolet. After about three hours of driving through mud, water and gumbo, constantly slipping from ditch to ditch, we finally arrived at the location where the subject had gone missing. It was still pouring rain, so hard we had to stop and dry off the spark plugs when the car sputtered to a sudden stop.

The lad's family pointed in the direction he had gone the day before. We started looking for him and were joined by two male relatives. After searching for several hours we came across the body of the missing young man, hanging by a rope from the branch of a tree.

After taking the necessary photographs for the inquest we decided to take the body out right away. We had no stretcher, but the body was stiff so the four of us carried him out, one on each side lifting an arm and one on each leg until we got him to the police car. We had to place him in the back seat, which was quite a chore due to the weight and stiffness of the body. The front seat had to be pushed forward to get the corpse into the back. He was over six feet tall and barely fit across the seat. The feet protruded out the side so it required one of us to hold up the legs from the inside in order to close the door. By the time we had a cup of tea and took the required statements it was evening and getting dark.

We pulled out onto the highway heading back to the detachment. If the roads were bad when we went out, they seemed even worse on the return journey. The corporal was driving and how he stayed out of the ditch was a miracle. Many times the car slipped and fish-tailed from the edge of one ditch to the other. The area was sparsely populated, mostly heavy bush. Fortunately, as we got closer to Hines Creek the bush gave way to homesteaders' fields. As we continued to plough on slowly the motor suddenly started to sputter and eventually stopped altogether. We pushed the car over to the shoulder and tried to determine the problem. The engine was covered with mud but the spark plugs, carburetor etc. seemed to be working. We soon found out that no fuel was getting to the carburetor and that the fuel pump was missing.

It was quite dark by this time and we could faintly make out the lights of Hines Creek some ten or 12 miles away. Taking stock of our situation, we realized that there was no point in waiting for help as no one in their right mind would venture out under these conditions. Our only hope was to find a farmer with a tractor to tow us into town, or else walk all the way to town to pick up a new fuel pump. This, of course, would mean that whoever was left would have to "baby-sit" the corpse, probably for most of the night. We decided to flip a coin to see who would stay with the body. The corporal won the toss and elected to hike into town.

Needless to say it developed into a very long, long night. At first I sat on the passenger side, but found that every time I got out of the car the legs of the corpse would fall out the door. This meant that every time I got back into the car I had to reach back with one hand to hold up his feet and attempt to close the door with the other. This was most awkward, not to mention disconcerting to a young constable spending "time" with his first body. I finally solved this by sitting in the driver's seat. To set the scene again one would have to imagine what it was like, stranded alone with only a corpse for company, miles from anywhere on a very black night with not a sound in the car but the rain on the window and the beat of your heart. You must also remember that there were no radios of any kind in the police cars in those days. As the hours slowly ticked by I tried to think of anything but the body resting peacefully in the back seat. There were no blankets so the body couldn't be covered. It was probably my imagination but I thought I detected a strange odour in the air. Trying to sleep was impossible and I was cold, damp and hungry which added to the situation being altogether miserable.

I sat there alone from about eight p.m. until after daylight, waiting for the corporal to return. Finally about nine a.m. I saw a tractor approaching with the corporal standing on the back. I was never so happy to see anyone in my entire life. He had walked all the way into town, stopping several times to look for a homesteader with a tractor. He was almost into town before he found one with a tractor willing to drive him back. He managed to get a fuel pump from a garage in town early in the morning and walked back to the homesteader and his tractor where he got a ride to the disabled police car.

Within a very short time he had the fuel pump changed, the car was fired up and we were on our way. The homesteader followed us in his tractor for a while but by this time the rain had stopped and we had no further trouble.

Needless to say this is a story that would be hard for anyone to forget, let alone a young constable spending the night with his first body. This story typifies detachment life in remote areas in those years. There were no ambulances or hearses and it was necessary for the police to transport corpses who had died from other than natural causes as part of their job.

Ed Cook

*   *   *   *   *

THE TEENAGER GETS HIS MAN

When I was growing up I lived with my family four miles west of Smoky Lake, Alberta. My father was a hard-working and respected farmer. He liked strong drink and was a frequent patron of the village beer parlour. At home he drank whisky as well as illegally made liquor, commonly known as "moonshine".

There were quite a few illegal distillers in the Smoky Lake district and the RCMP officers were diligent in their efforts to catch the guilty parties. Every so often a bootlegger or moonshine distiller would be caught and, upon appearing in court would be fined, or sentenced to three, six or 12 months in gaol.

It was common knowledge in the Smoky Lake district that my father was a frequent imbiber of illicit liquor and therefore a constant suspect. However, although he bought lots of moonshine, he never brewed any. During my youth I can recall the RCMP coming to our house with search warrants at least half a dozen times and spending hours searching everywhere, but they never found any moonshine.

One Saturday in April 1936, the RCMP drove up to our farm in a 1935 Chevrolet sedan. As my father wasn't home, they presented my mother with a search warrant. They spent 2 1/2 hours searching the buildings but they were unable to find anything illegal. The raiding party consisted of two RCMP members and one civilian interpreter to translate, English to Ukrainian and vice versa. The roads in 1936 were not gravelled and on this particular day the dirt road was terribly muddy with mud holes getting deeper as the ground thawed. About 20 minutes after the RCMP left, one of the Mounties returned on foot and asked me if I could harness a team of horses and tow their car to Smoky Lake. He said they had got stuck in a mud hole a quarter of a mile from our house and while they were trying to get out, the drive shaft broke.

I said: "O.K." I jumped at the opportunity, as I could visualize the bicycle I wanted very badly. This was a heaven-sent opportunity for my dreams to come true.

We had very good heavy draught horses and I harnessed our best team, hitched them up to a doubletree, a clevis and a 16-foot logging chain and hooked the chain to the car bumper. I pulled the car out of the mud hole, sat on the hood, braced my feet on the bumper and away we went. Meanwhile, the Mounties sat in the car, relaxing and having something to eat. It took me about two hours to tow them to Smoky Lake which gave me time to think and plan my strategy. I was 15 years old at the time, somewhat brash no doubt, and I remembered that they had forgotten to make a deal with me before I hitched the team to the car. Price was never mentioned. Sitting on the hood of the car in tow for an hour, I realized that I had my bike. I knew that the bike cost $35, and I also knew I had the RCMP over a barrel for that amount. I just decided this was the price they would have to pay me for the tow.

When we arrived at Smoky Lake in front of the Chev dealer, the RCMP corporal got out, came up to me and said, "O.K., son, how much?"

Without hesitation I said, "Thirty-five dollars."

He said, "You must be kidding, that's a lot of money."

I replied, "I agree, but that's exactly what I'm worth, so pay up."

The corporal said, "Hey, wait a minute, that's more than half a month of my wages."

I answered, "I agree, but that's my worth for half a day for two horses, doubletree, clevis and chain."

The corporal was getting a bit exasperated trying to reason with this cocky, single-minded teenager, so he said, "I'm not getting anywhere with you. I'll go to the beer parlour and settle the account with your father."

I said, "No, I'll go with you; I'll tow the car to the hotel and you get my dad outside and we'll discuss it." I refused to unhook the car. Reluctantly he agreed and I towed the car to the front of the hotel. The junior RCMP went into the bar and brought my dad out. My dad tried to reason with me but I wouldn't listen. I refused to be swayed.

By this time a crowd had gathered around us, mostly half-drunk patrons from the beer parlour wondering why the RCMP had escorted my father outside. My conversation with my dad was in Ukrainian and the RCMP did not understand what we were talking about, but they saw that I was not giving any ground. Finally, in an aside to my dad I said, "Look dad, suppose they had found half a bottle or so of moonshine at the farm and the judge said 'six months Mr. Starchuk,' you would have had no choice. This is the same situation. I want my $35."

I convinced my dad and he said in broken English, "I did not make no deal with you RCMP. I'm not going to try to settle it. You solve your own problems. My beer is getting stale." Then he left. I was so proud of my dad that he was on my side.

The crowd that had gathered started to heckle and harass the RCMP, calling them cheapskates, etc. The corporal went into a huddle with his two assistants and finally paid me the $35. I towed them back to the Chevrolet dealer, about two blocks away, unhooked the chain, mounted one of the horses and rode home with the $35 in my pocket. Two days later I bought my bike.

Steve W. Starchuk

* * * * *

RED SERGE AND SIRENS

In summer, the population of Banff, Alberta, multiplies. One reason for the influx appears to be the northward migration of Americans, particularly unwed schoolteachers from California. Another is probably the temporary transfer of numerous members of the Force from various provincial detachments. Many of these men were forced to wear red serge, breeches and boots throughout the hot summer for the edification of the California schoolteachers, cameras and all. However, this punishing duty had its own rewards.

One of these scarlet-coated entrepreneurs whom we shall call George, because that's his name, quietly rolled a police car into the parking lot of the Banff Springs Hotel at the pre-arranged hour of two a.m. He flashed his headlights and shortly thereafter a female tourist scuttled quietly out of the shadows into the front seat. George didn't have time to remove his spurs. His stetson was hurled to the back seat in his eager manoeuvring.

In those ancient times the button that activated the siren was located on the floor near the dimmer switch. Push it once -- it's on; push it again -- it's off. You guessed it. George pushed it once. In his mad thrashing to kick the button again he unfortunately caught a spur in the horn ring, thereby activating a series of intermittent blasts.

The lady then formed a single, firm resolution. She had to get away from this crazy red-coated so-and-so and return with a certain amount of dignity to California at the earliest possible moment. In her eagerness to present a respectable appearance to the onlookers who were now flooding to their hotel windows, she tripped the switch on the dash that activated the roof flashers.

The scene in the hotel parking lot was now reminiscent of a squad of drunken bagpipers putting on a fireworks display. George did his level best. After breaking the horn ring, he left a trail of rubber in the asphalt of the immediate area and returned to less spectacular duties.

R.W.Morley

*   *   *   *   *

DOUBLE MEANING

In view of the many Canadians of French ancestry at St. Paul Detachment in Alberta and because the francophone minority wanted to ensure they could be served in the French language, a French-speaking member was always posted to this detachment when one was available. In 1938 Constable Jacques D.... was posted to St. Paul for general duties. Jacques was very good-looking and had a pleasant personality. He cut quite a figure in uniform and was a favourite with the local girls. It must be said that he was overly affectionate with them on occasion and they constantly warned him not to get fresh with them.

Jacques could not speak or understand English very well but he was eager to learn the language and liked to practise at every opportunity. He was sent to investigate a complaint of non-support by a young French-Canadian girl with a small baby. She lived in a shack on a local farm. Her husband, who was also French Canadian, was never home and was usually just bumming around with little or no money. The cupboard at the farm was bare and the young wife was destitute. A charge of non-support was laid. The magistrate and the defence counsel were French Canadians. As all the participants could speak fluent French the trial could have been held in that language but our hero insisted he was fluent in English. His evidence was that there was no food in the house and the woman and her baby had nothing to eat.

When he was cross-examined by the defence counsel he was asked, "Constable, was there a cow on the farm?"

Jacques replied, "Yes, there was a cow there."

The next question was, "Was the cow fresh?"

Jacques dropped his chin in his hand, pursed his lips, knit his brow and recalled the girls continually telling him not to get fresh with them. Finally he replied, "Well, the cow didn't get fresh with me."

After the laughter subsided the magistrate found the accused guilty and said that even if the cow was fresh the wife should receive other provisions as well.

Chris Forbes

* * * * *

NOW IT CAN BE TOLD

Before I had completed training at Depot in 1932 I was posted to Edmonton in a hurry with five others. One was a World War I veteran, Lionel Broadway (who wore ribbons), and the others had previous service. We boarded the train with our kit, appearing in red serge for the first time and excited at the prospect of getting into action. Vaguely we knew there was trouble brewing and we were to fill in some gaps.

We were on the milk train that crawled through the night with many stops. One of them was Saskatoon, the home of our war veteran, and he had a plan. Lionel Broadway had been a member of the famous wartime concert party, the Dumbbells. We could jump off the slow train, join Broadway's coming home party, catch the express five hours later and reach Edmonton as ordered. It was a great escape from the discipline of Depot and a memorable party, but our arrival in Edmonton was something less than grand. We stumbled off the train carrying a hangover, rumpled, and lugging our kit bags, and were greeted by a sour driver who forced us into the back of the black maria.

We joined a quickly assembled mounted squad to break and train horses brought in from pasture. Sergeant Baker, just out of the north, marched as if he was wearing snowshoes. We hardened the horses and ourselves with long rides. When the temperature dropped and hovered at -20 degrees Fahrenheit we changed to buffalo coats and moccasins. We built an outdoor riding school and realized there must be signs of trouble because a dismounted squad from Vancouver arrived to fill the barracks. It was an interesting mix of Maritimers, men from the old country and members from central Canada and the west. Names like Tony MacKenzie, Buck Jones, George McLellan, Doug Forrest, Scotty Morrison and Chuck Colvin come to mind. When we schooled the horses in the riding school the dismounted squad helped in the riding ring by playing rioters, trying to spook the horses with noise makers and missiles. We lived with those horses when we weren't catching up with lectures, and writing exams on the criminal code given by Superintendent Cadiz.

When we had an evening off and could afford it, we would hike downtown in uniform to take in a movie. At times, we wondered why people around us would get to their feet, mutter imperceptibly and move away. It took several incidents to help us realize that our heavy fur coats and caps were redolent of the stables, sweaty horses and leather, a delightful mix from the hours of stable duty.

These memories came flooding back when I read an account of the Alberta Hunger March of December 20, 1932. Published in *Western Report* September 1986, this exaggerated account made me wonder if the writer had done his research in a communist paper of the time that called us "Cossacks of the North" in headlines. This is their version:

> "...'All right comrades, let's go,' exhorted the last speaker as the crowd pressed on to the streets. The City Police on foot, backed up by some 150 RCMP reinforcements on horseback, charged in. They knocked people down and the horses trampled them under foot. A total of 29 were arrested, among them active members of such left wing groups as the

Ukrainian Labour Farm Temple Association, the Workers
Unity League and the Young Communist League."

I wondered what the late Clive Holbrook would have thought
about this bit of journalistic nonsense. He stopped a rock in the face
which left him groggy, but he remained in the saddle. Little Charlie
Colvin in the dismounted squad, his Irish up because he didn't care
for people who throw bricks, chased a couple of rioters up a blind
alley. With the Irish buzz-saw in hot pursuit, they dived through the
plate-glass window of a hardware store.

As for the mounted troop, we walked slowly in two ranks,
through the crowd and back again as the mob quietly and slowly
evaporated from the market square, with Holbrook the only visible
casualty. It had been a job well done, smoothly and efficiently. The
magazine in question would have been very disappointed with the
truth for we had gone into action with less than two dozen horses. The
next day six of us returned to the scene, making a quiet patrol.

Toward spring there was another dust-up in Calgary that had
been handled by the city police at a site called Mission Hill. That night
we were on the train with our horses, headed south. From Lethbridge
another troop was on its way. The horses filled the Pacific Cartage
stables beside the railway tracks and we bedded down on the top floor
of the post office.

When we had settled in and were resting the first morning
someone said, "Too bad Happy Skelly was left behind. He wanted to
come in the worst way."

Skelly, across the room, rolled over. "I came in the worst way,"
he said. "I came with the horses."

There was good-natured rivalry between the troops. We were
jealous of the Lethbridge horsemen. They had better looking horses,
already in their summer coats, and we worked hard to get ours looking
as sleek. It was probably Lionel Broadway, the ingenious old showman,
who paid a social call at the Calgary Brewery. Word leaked out that
we had a stash of beer, compliments of the brewery and the
Lethbridge troop apparently moved most of the hay in the loft looking
for it. The rest of our stay we rode through the streets of a Calgary
without skyscrapers, making eye contact with the girls, and riding
drills on the prairie.

Gray Campbell

*   *   *   *   *

INSTANT EXTRADITION

As a young constable serving in British Columbia, I received an early practical lesson in international jurisdiction from a senior constable in our force and a sheriff from the United States. This negotiation of jurisdiction over the custody of a murder suspect took place right on the 49th parallel.

The suspect, the object of an extensive manhunt, was wanted in Canada for murder. Information was received that he was in a barn in a remote area near the Canada - U.S. border. Discreet enquiries and observation convinced the constable that the man was in the United States. The sheriff, having jurisdiction, was contacted and all proceeded to the barn. On arrival the sheriff said "Hell, that barn is in Canada". The senior constable said "Like hell, it's in the United States."

When the barn was lined up with the border slash, it appeared to the Canadians to be in the U.S. but to the Americans to be in Canada.

The sheriff's strong argument was that wherever the barn was, the culprit would end up in Canada, so it was lucky that the barn was in Canada; we could have him in our "bucket" that day instead of waiting weeks and months for "that international court stuff".

We sort of agreed that he had a point. He told us to go ahead and get the fugitive while he covered us from the U.S. side. We did so, only to find that the barn was empty.

George Reed

*   *   *   *   *

PROMOTION

Until recent times, promotions in the Force resulted from a recommendation by the sub-division officer commanding on an individual which was forwarded to the division commanding officer for his consideration or rejection. There were usually far more recommendations than openings, so the division commanding officer had the unenviable duty of making the decision. His was not the final word, as his list had to be approved by the commissioner.

On one occasion in "F" Division, Saskatchewan, the commanding officer noted that a senior constable stationed at a northern detachment had many years of service but had never been recommended for promotion. He wanted to know why, and was told that this member, although stationed at the same detachment for 15 years, had never had a court case. The CO stated, "If any member of the Force is able to keep law and order in his area for 15 years, he deserves to be promoted." And so he was -- to the rank of corporal, much to the surprise of everyone concerned.

I.C. Shank

*   *   *   *   *

RCMP SHOW BAND -- THE UNSEEN ENFORCERS

On October 3, 1979, Staff Sergeant Chuck Hendricks and his RCMP Show Band came to Midway, B.C., to entertain the local residents -- and entertain them they did! Approximately 400 locals slapped, stomped, bounced and sang along with the band during their most enjoyable and impressive show. Next day, the words "RCMP Show Band" brought pleasing smiles to all locals -- all except one.

Midway is a logging community and where there is logging there are many logging trucks. Mr. Logger was a local contractor who owned more than 12 such trucks, the largest private owner in this area. He also created the largest problem for detachment members enforcing the Motor Vehicle Act and Motor Vehicle Regulations because of the many defects in his fleet. Jack Keswick, the local weighscales operator, had given Mr. Logger written warnings and tickets in vain, in an attempt to have him replace the many bald tires, repair the broken lights, attach the required mud flaps and take care of the many other problems that were constantly noted on his trucks.

Then it happened! Approximately two weeks before the RCMP Show Band came to town, Mr. Logger called the local motel to make reservations for a grader operator he was bringing into the area to upgrade many of the logging roads. A motel employee said there were no rooms available for that night. The RCMP had made reservations for them all. Nothing else was said, but Mr. Logger must have been living with a terrible guilt complex.

Mr. Keswick advised me that during an approximate ten-day period before the band arrived, he noted that the trucks belonging to Mr. Logger were steadily and rapidly showing a reduction in the number of defects. Bald tires were being replaced with new ones. Not only were burned-out or broken lights being repaired, but the trucks were looking like Christmas trees with more than the required amount of lighting. Mud flaps were being attached where required. By the time October 3 rolled around, not one defect could be found on any of the trucks. Keswick was thrilled, though bewildered, by this chain of events. Why was Mr. Logger spending so much money on his trucks in such a short period of time?

On October 4, the answer to this question was revealed. One of the first truck drivers to cross the scales could keep it a secret no longer. When Mr. Logger had been told the RCMP had booked the local motel, he apparently reasoned that a task force was being brought in to enforce the Motor Vehicle Act and Regulations. I am told he thought he would have the last laugh, because even with our secret task force we would find no defects on any of his fleet. Rumour has it that he spent over $7,000 in less than two weeks.

To the RCMP Show Band -- thanks for the enforcement, many thanks. But don't mention the word "band" to Mr. Logger.

B.A.Tidsbury
RCMP Quarterly - Volume 45, Number 2

*   *   *   *   *

WALRUSES

When I was stationed at Lethbridge in the 1940s I assisted the sub-division clerk in the performance of his duties for a short period. He had been born in England and had a dry sense of humour, together with a quiet chuckle.

In those years there was a complete list of all official forms in use throughout the Force, one of which was an "Annual Walrus Return". When the clerk spotted this return he gave his quiet chuckle and muttered, "I must demand this return from Corporal Shaw in charge of Manyberries Detachment." Manyberries is in very dry cattle country southeast of Lethbridge, about the last place one is liable to find a walrus. The clerk promptly sat down and typed a memo to that effect, requested an immediate reply, and an explanation as to why the return had not been submitted.

About a week later, back came a reply, to the effect that due to the extremely dry weather in the area of Manyberries during the past few years, all traces of *"Trichechus Rosmarus"* had disappeared.

None having been found in the area it was not considered necessary to submit the return. However, the matter would be kept in mind, and should any of these animals re-appear in the future, an immediate return would be submitted.

The clerk was very happy with the success of his practical joke which he greeted with his usual chuckle. It must be stated that no walruses ever appeared thereafter.

C.R.C. Peters

* * * * *

DISPENSING JUSTICE IN NORTHERN MANITOBA

In 1945, I volunteered for the one-man detachment at God's Lake in northern Manitoba. The detachment building was a three-room clapboard shack on an island, perched on stilts in muskeg and lined with discarded boards from dynamite boxes, which didn't keep out the bitter wind. There was a wood stove and a kerosene lamp. In the immediate vicinity on the island were 15 jerry-built shacks, several warehouses and two abandoned mine shafts, all in various stages of disrepair as the mine had closed in 1942. When the wind blew there was a noisy cacophony of slamming doors, metallic clashing of corrugated roofing and the creaking of loose boards, along with many other eerie sounds in the deserted buildings. The streets, overlain with cyanide tailings impregnated with iron pyrite (fool's gold), glittered in the sun as if they were lined with gold. Caving-in of the mine below caused the streets to buckle; one house had fallen completely over on its side and was being "devoured" by the muskeg. Apparently the previous inhabitants had been airlifted out on short notice, leaving everything but their most treasured possessions behind.

Two itinerant white men had remained behind and with me were the sole occupants of this weird and lonely cluster of buildings. A mile away, across the bay, was a free trader and an Indian village of about 200 somewhat intemperate natives who, through association with the mining personnel, had picked up many of the white man's bad habits.

The detachment's judicial area encompassed about 35,000 square miles of hinterland, sparsely populated by scattered bands of Indians plus a few trappers and prospectors. Besides three local communities on God's Lake, there were two outlying settlements, a Swampy Cree Band at Oxford House, 100 miles to the northwest and a Saulteaux tribe at Island Lake, 100 miles to the southeast. They spoke a different language and little English, making it necessary for me to hire a local interpreter at each settlement. White-water rivers, dangerous rapids and miles of rock and muskeg separated all these communities. The region seemed to be situated in a corridor from Hudson Bay which kept it cold and we had open water for only about four months of the year.

According to RCMP regulations, only those north of an imaginary line known as the 60th parallel of latitude could be deemed to be in "Northern Service". Compared to my situation, I couldn't help but feel they were molly-coddled and pampered with all the amenities it was possible to provide. Quarters, fuel (local wood chopped by detachment members) and rations were supplied, along with the services of a permanent "chauffeur" by way of a native hired as a special constable to handle the dogs, man the boat, etc. Northern detachments were staffed by two men for moral support and often situated in a regular community with other white people to associate with -- and they were allowed extra money to compensate for the hardships they endured!

None of these amenities were available to me as I was situated south of that imaginary line in the "Banana Belt" and not entitled to the luxuries of Northern Service. I had to learn to cope with "once a year shopping" -- a year in advance -- as all my supplies came in on the tractor-train during winter and there were only two official mail days a year. The few non-freezable goodies I purchased came in at double the cost and had to be stored under the ice in the lake. When taking over from the previous member I had to find $400 to buy out the stock of rations he had on hand. Arrangements had to be made to have my wood cut and hauled. Except for a canoe and outboard engine which were provided, I had to find my own transportation, which was sometimes a problem as dog teams were not always available.

I was in a vast wilderness, surrounded by Indians, with no means of obtaining help. I knew that in order to keep everything under control, all complaints would have to be pursued to the limit of my resources, regardless of how minor the offence or what inconvenience the investigation might entail. The natives in the region were in the habit of brewing and consuming bean juice, and getting intoxicated on it. I felt strongly that liquor was the root of all evil with the natives and that if intoxication was not nipped in the bud, more lawlessness, including murder, would follow. It was not long before my views were put to the test.

Investigating a local report of intoxication and public disturbance, I determined that one of the five involved was the son of a subchief who, in broken English, warned me of the dire consequences should any action be taken against his son. This was obviously an attempt to intimidate "the new boy on the block" and it was apparent that an immediate precedent must be set. The five offenders were notified that charges would be laid against them, but the magistrate was 250 miles away at Norway House and the problem was how to get them there. There were also two male witnesses who would be required to testify. The cost to prosecute such minor offences seemed ridiculous, but I was mindful of one of the Force's precepts over the years that "Crime will be dealt with, no matter how remote the place, how dangerous the journey or how great the cost."

The police canoe was an 18-foot cruiser with a five horse-power outboard engine, which wasn't adequate, so I borrowed an 18-foot freighter and loaded the two canoes with eight men, rations for five days (which I provided) and 50 gallons of gasoline (extra gas was carried to cache along the way for the return journey). With the freighter in tow, we left for Norway House.

First we were held up by wind, then about 100 miles out of Norway House the bottom gears went out of my engine. We started paddling and the last 25 miles were against the current of the mighty Nelson in a rain storm, where whirlpools capable of devouring our little craft seemed to dance about and were hard to avoid.

Because of delays en route we ran out of rations and had nothing to eat for the last two days except for a rabbit that one of my passengers killed with a rock. He was rewarded with the eyeballs, a delicacy, which he devoured with relish. The crunching of those eyeballs turned me off tapioca forever.

It was a seven-day journey and the accused were taken before the magistrate, convicted and sentenced to a period in the RCMP lockup at Norway House. Leaving them behind, and with only the two witnesses as passengers, I returned to God's Lake.

I made a similar trip the following summer, but this time I had seven prisoners to escort. Initially there were 14 prisoners to be escorted to Norway House. In June 1946 I was detailed to escort the

Treaty Party, making treaty payments, within my detachment area. The party was headed by the Indian agent who was also, ex officio, a magistrate. This gave me the opportunity of bringing all my outstanding investigations before the court.

The first stop was Oxford House and two natives charged with a shooting incident were convicted and sentenced to hard labour at Norway House. No time could be taken to escort them out then so they were simply told to hold themselves in readiness to make the journey in due course.

The Treaty Party moved on to God's Lake Narrows and here ten more Indians were sentenced to hard labour at Norway House. Two more outstanding charges at Island Lake were expected to result in convictions and sentences to Norway House, adding up to a total of 14 bodies to be escorted to Norway House. The sheer volume of numbers was a big problem as I felt seven was the most I could handle by canoe. Canadian Pacific Airlines was serving the Treaty Party with periodic flights as required and one evening when the aircraft arrived it was going on to Norway House that night and returning the next morning. There was room for three on board, so, taking two of the prisoners, I escorted them out to Norway House and returned the next morning in time to resume my duties with the Treaty Party. The aircraft was going back to Norway House and would not be returning to God's Lake. Again, there was room for three passengers. I took advantage of the opportunity to send three more prisoners out on the aircraft, giving the warrants of commitment to the pilot who agreed to deliver them to the RCMP at Norway House. Another opportunity presented itself at Island Lake after treaty payments were concluded there and the aircraft was making several trips transporting personnel and equipment back to Norway House. On one trip there was space for me to take the two prisoners from Island Lake to Norway House to serve their sentences. This reduced my escort responsibilities down to a manageable seven prisoners by canoe.

My second escort of prisoners to Norway House by canoe was a 300-mile trip, with many terrible portages and dangerous rapids between God's Lake and Oxford House. On the basis of 16-hour days, we estimated the trip would take five days, provided we were not plagued with unfavourable weather or misfortune. Rations for 98 meals were packed (from my stores). This consisted mainly of canned goods, plus flour, lard and baking powder for making bannock, some beans and ample tea. Along with 50 gallons of gasoline, it added up to a fair amount of weight to pack over the first two portages.

Our troubles started 20 miles across God's Lake at Bayley Portage, which is two miles of deep muskeg and was known as "The River of Mud". Sometimes the canoes could be dragged through liquid mud, but mostly they had to be carried. I had only gone a few steps when I went down to my thigh and a sapling that had been cut off just below the surface caught me at the ankle and ripped my leg open to the knee. The wound was soon sealed with mud and stopped bleeding.

In this low-lying muskeg, insects of every description attacked voraciously and they were so thick as to impede breathing. I was carrying the engine and once, when I fell, it disappeared into the mud. After being cleaned, it condescended to run again. Upon reaching Bayley Lake, I walked straight out into the lake, fully clothed, to wash off the mud which had engulfed me to the ears. Crossing Bayley Lake into Wolf River, we had to portage three times around rapids before reaching Knee Lake about ten p.m. We camped there for the night. Next day, Knee Lake was a bit rough but we managed to keep going into the Hayes River where the first eight miles was fast water with many rapids, some of which we negotiated with poles. We had to portage at Trout Falls and Knife Rapids, reaching the Hudson's Bay post at Oxford House in the late afternoon.

The gash in my leg was cleaned up and dressed at the post. Two more native prisoners were picked up and early next morning, with the five God's Lake Indians in the canoe being towed and the two Oxford House boys in my canoe, we set out for the 200-mile journey upstream to Norway House.

There was a high chop on Oxford Lake, but we kept going by hugging the south shore, entering the Hayes River at Wipanipanis Falls, where we had to portage. Continuing on to Windy Lake, we were held up by strong winds so we camped for the night. My five horse-power engine was being overworked and it started to give trouble; consequently it had to be pampered and this put us behind schedule.

The fourth day out we crossed Opiminegoka Lake, then back into the Hayes River again, where we portaged twice around rapids before entering Logan Lake. Between Logan Lake and Robinson Lake there was a mile-long portage circumventing rapids where the river dropped 56 feet. Crossing Robinson, we entered the Hayes River again and followed it to its source at the height-of-land called Painted Stone Portage. There we camped for the night and the fifth day portaged into the headwaters of the Ichimamish River, which is a weed-strewn, sluggish stream wending its crooked way through about 40 miles of muskeg before reaching Hair Lake. This murky waterway often turned right back on itself and in other places was so thick with vegetation that we had to paddle and push our way through. Here again, the insects descended in such thick hordes that we appeared to be surrounded by an ever-changing mist and they also looked like clouds in the sky. The shore for almost all of this 40 miles was nothing more than floating swamp land and landing places were few and far between. Fortunately, we were near one of these dry outcroppings, with tree shelter, when a terrific storm could be seen approaching, so we landed, put up the tent and crowded in before the storm struck.

I was lying on bare rock and swear I could feel it shake when claps of thunder went off over our heads. In the flashes of lightning, I could see that my prisoners were all on their knees praying. When the storm passed, we found that a tall poplar right beside the tent had been shattered by lightning. I couldn't help but think that perhaps the aborigines' prayers had saved the day after all. We camped there for the night.

The next day we struggled through the mud of the Ichimamish again and it was night before we reached Hair Lake. This body of water is unique in that it is completely covered by long-stemmed bulrushes. Five miles across, the lake is only about four feet deep and these bulrushes grow to about 12 feet all over it. Entering this heavy growth, one can become completely disoriented without a compass or taking a bearing from the sky because the plants, on their long stems, open up to let the canoe through and close in again behind, so that the only view is straight up.

We camped at this lake and the Indians dug up some bulrushes, eating the roots, which proved to be quite palatable and filling, much like parsnip. They also revealed another trick of theirs to obtain food. When there is a breeze on Hair Lake, the wind in the bulrushes makes such a noise a duck is unable to hear a canoe approaching. When you paddle fast against the wind, any ducks in your path do not see you until you are almost upon them. Their only escape route is straight up and if you are quick enough the ducks can be grabbed by the legs. So we had "parsnip" and duck for dinner that night, which supplemented our meagre larder, as this was our sixth day out and we had started with only enough food for five days.

Next day we emerged into the mighty Nelson River at High Rock and between there and Sea Falls it churns down between narrow chasms against which we seemed to be barely making any headway. I tried to help the engine by paddling and thought my passengers would take the hint, but they all sat stoically staring straight ahead, completely ignoring my initiative.

Making a landing to portage around Sea Falls is rather a tricky manoeuvre, as one must come in fast through turbulent water to the base of the falls and depend upon an agile bowman to leap ashore and hold the canoe from going under the falls. As we approached, the Indians in the towed canoe seemed unconcerned and did not follow our example in the lead canoe, assuming, I suppose, that I was going to forsake my canoe and pull them safely to shore. That, however, was not my intention. As soon as my lead canoe struck shore, I dropped the tow rope and a whirlpool caught their bow and they went into a spin. Amid much whooping and ki-yak-ing they found their paddles and managed to paddle out of it and to shore. It certainly brought them out of their lethargy in a hurry. Sea Falls is considered rather a dangerous spot; although unconfirmed, a rumour had it that years ago an Indian agent drowned there and his strong box containing $20,000 treaty money was still at the bottom of the falls.

We carried our equipment over the rocks, launching the canoes into the river above the falls and fought our way up to Playgreen Lake where some engine trouble developed. While we were working on the engine, an ominous-looking thunder storm was threatening from the west. This was about 11 p.m. and, being only six miles from our destination at Norway House, we took a chance on crossing, hoping to reach it before the storm struck. We were still about a mile short when we were caught in a violent rain storm with lightning and high winds. The canoes were being buffeted and jerked about, the tow rope creating a very serious situation for us all. Fearing we would all be swamped, I cut the tow rope loose. The five prisoners in the canoe being towed disappeared into a maelstrom of huge waves and darkness, while the two prisoners and I in the lead canoe were fortunate, making it to the safety of the RCMP dock at Norway House.

At early light next morning, just as Constable Betts of Norway House and I were preparing to go in search of my other charges, they nonchalantly came paddling in, none the worse for their experience. They had managed to gain the shelter of an island and had camped for the night. All's well that ends well and that brought to a satisfactory conclusion the execution of 14 warrants of commitment that had been causing me no little concern.

I made many more trips by canoe, dog team, tractor and aircraft, all of which had their share of perilous moments, but no lasting scars were sustained. God's Lake was an interesting detachment, with a variety of investigations. Keeping the consumption of liquor under control meant there was no crime, other than some alleged illegal beaver trapping. Things were not always done "according to Hoyle", but I felt the end justified the means. Sometimes it seemed as though I had stepped outside the bounds of civilized society and perhaps life was passing me by. After three years of that spartan existence, I decided I'd had enough and made a request for a transfer, thus bringing to an end my experiences and adventure in maintaining and dispensing justice in a far-flung reach of our great domain.

Jerry Bradley

*   *   *   *   *

MS. GALAHAD?

Along with other changes within the Force in the recent past, members of the Terrace Detachment in British Columbia are doing their best to overcome the notorious reputation of being male chauvinists.

At nine p.m. on January 5, 1975, a young constable had occasion to stop a carload of young people and charge the operator for driving without "due care and attention." While the constable was sitting in his vehicle writing up the traffic violation, the passengers from the offending vehicle milled about. In due course the traffic violation was issued and the young people proceeded merrily on their way.

The illustrious guardian of the law started to continue his patrol, but found to his dismay that persons unknown had been tampering with the clasps on the tire chains, and when he drove ahead the chains remained behind. The constable, a city boy, was not familiar with the proper attachment of tire chains. While he was pondering the situation, an attractive young lady about 20 years old happened along and offered assistance. The constable advised her of the problem.

She, without hesitation, came to his aid, crawled under the car and put on the chains while our "hero" directed traffic out of concern for her personal safety.

The Force once again acknowledges the equality -- superiority? -- of women.

Anonymous
RCMP Quarterly - Volume 40, Number 2

* * * * *

Chapter Two

The Wide Variety of Police Duties

DUTIES NO LONGER PERFORMED
RECEIVER GENERAL'S OFFICE

After completion of training, one of the first duties I was given was guard duty at the receiver general's office. This entailed walking around during office hours, accompanying the clerk to the various banks with money, and guard duty during the silent hours. All these duties were performed in red serge, breeches and boots; the logic behind this completely escapes me. I was assigned to guard the Bank of Canada office. They had offices in the main centres, the one referred to in this story being on Scarth Street in Regina.

My first experience on this duty was most embarrassing. I had never been in downtown Regina in uniform, and was somewhat shy at wearing review order. I had taken the street-car to the receiver general's office, and not wanting to wait for the next stop which was some distance from the office, decided to hop off the car while it was in motion and get into the office as quickly as possible. I was not used to wearing spurs and as I jumped off my spurs got entangled and I fell flat on my face. I had some trouble getting my spurs unhooked and recovering my stetson, much to the amusement of the pedestrians in the area.

One time I was on duty from midnight to eight a.m. My midnight lunch had been delivered to me and the streets outside were quiet. As I was eating I heard a strange noise downstairs. It sounded like someone playing around at the window in the lane, which ran past the building and was quite dark. I crept downstairs and did not put on any lights as I felt this would warn the person or persons trying to break in. I again heard a rasping, scraping sound at the window and assumed it was someone tampering with the bars on the window. I took out my service revolver and fired a shot at where I thought I could see a man's arm reaching towards the bars. I then called the city police and they came over to check as we were not allowed to leave the building. The officers who attended came to the door laughing and invited me to take a look at what I had shot. It was a big tom cat and it was his stretched-out body I had mistaken for a man's arm. All the cat was doing was sharpening his claws on the window frame. I was sorry I had shot the cat, but was pleased that I had heard something and that if it had been an intruder I would have wounded him on the arm.

This guard duty was very boring and in an effort to give myself something to do I got into trouble with the manager. He reported me for spending my time doodling on a piece of paper and not attending to what was going on. He did not speak to me about it but complained to Depot, and the result was I was paraded before Inspector Mercer. He asked me what I had been doing. I asked the officer if I could get my page of doodles which I brought back. When I took the sheets to him he saw that every time I had been on duty, I looked over each person who had come into the bank and listed a description of them, height, weight, clothing etc. In other words I had been making a list of all possible suspects who might have been casing the office with the intent of holding up the place. The manager was informed and the next time I was on duty he apologized for not asking me personally what I was doing.

J.H."Joe" Armstrong

*

Editor's Note: Joe forwarded a great deal more material, mainly police cases, and there were two police aids in the stories he submitted that are worthy of note. One was the use of confetti in wheat to identify the source of wheat suspected of being stolen. This is a fairly common practice today, but back in 1929 it was unique.

The other was an aid to identify a stolen horse. Some horses were stolen from a rancher, and the investigation failed to locate them. Joe Armstrong spoke to the rancher and arranged to get some new dimes from the mint and insert them in certain parts of the horse's body to provide absolute proof of the ownership of the animal. Three places on the body of the horse were used to insert the coins. On the near side when the front foot is lifted and pulled forward there is a length of skin which is not muscle. A slit was made, the dime inserted and the small hole stitched up. When the tail is lifted there is again a stretch of hide which has no muscle and a dime can be placed there. The same procedure was done on the off side of the horse. The owner knows where to feel and can easily detect the coin, but a stranger could work with the horse for months and never discover this.

One of the coined horses came back to the ranch and the rider was questioned about where he had bought the horse. As a result all the stolen horses were eventually accounted for.

*   *   *   *   *

KINGUALIK AND THE CORONATION MEDAL

After I arrived at isolated Baker Lake Detachment by boat in a typical September snowstorm during the fall of 1953, my first task was to unload one year's supply of food, fuel and maintenance materials. When this was properly stored, my second responsibility was to familiarize myself with what was required of an operational and administrative nature at the detachment. Uncovered in the detachment safe was a sealed, registered, official OHMS envelope.

Inside was a Coronation Medal and scroll which identified the recipient as E2-109, Ooyoumut, an Eskimo believed to be living somewhere in the Back River area. The Force had been asked by the Director of Indian and Northern Affairs to make an official presentation in ceremonial dress to Ooyoumut, take photographs, and send the photos to Ottawa. Ooyoumut was described on the accompanying parchment as being "an outstanding hunter and provider amongst the native people". Not knowing who this soon-to-be-honoured Eskimo might be, I asked E2-4, Special Constable Ooyoumut, if he knew who he was.

"That's a relative of mine," he said, "but he's been dead for a long, long time." Checking the death certificates which were maintained by the Force, as Registrars of Vital Statistics in the Northwest Territories, I learned E2-109, Ooyoumut, had indeed died ten years earlier. E2-110, Kingualik, his wife, was still alive, however, and believed living somewhere along the Back River. She was not known to have ever visited the settlement of Baker Lake, and it was highly unlikely she ever would.

I communicated this revelation to the Commanding Officer "G" Division at Ottawa, who, after conferring with the Indian and Northern Affairs Department, agreed with my suggestion to award the medal posthumously to E2-110, Kingualik. Correspondence in reply reiterated the initial dictate to perform the ceremony in red serge, forwarding the photographs to Ottawa.

I wasn't quite sure how to go about undertaking the arduous

200-mile trip to the Back River area by dog team in the dead of winter, and complying with instructions to the letter. My dilemma was resolved the following spring when an RCAF single-engine Otter dropped into the settlement on a training flight. The pilot asked if I wanted to visit any of the more distant, remote camps to check on native conditions. It took me about 30 seconds to remember the ceremonial presentation to Kingualik. The RCAF crew agreed to try and find the Back River camp, affording an opportunity to visit other isolated camps as well, and check on native conditions in general.

Enquiries conducted at a camp near Pelly Lake led us northeast along the Back River towards Chantrey Inlet, where we finally located Kingualik's camp. In the nomadic life of these inland caribou Eskimo, survival depended primarily on individual resourcefulness. Although they may have lacked material wealth, they possessed an abundance of sociability, greeting us in a very friendly fashion.

It was still quite cold, and you may be able to appreciate the astounded expressions on the faces of young and old when I took off a long outer caribou parka, revealing the red RCMP serge tunic, boots and breeches. As I put on my stetson, I told Special Constable Ooyoumut that what I wanted to do was stand with Kingualik long enough to take a photograph, then perhaps we could join them in their igloo for a cup of tea, during which I would explain what the occasion was all about.

The Eskimo started laughing. The RCAF crew were doubled over with laughter to such a degree tears were actually flowing. The more they laughed, the more Kingualik laughed and it indeed became difficult to gain control of the situation long enough to capture the significance of the occasion on film. That finally being accomplished, everyone -- ten Eskimos, Special Constable Ooyoumut, four RCAF air crew and myself -- crammed into the igloo and assumed as comfortable a position as possible while tea was brewed.

With Ooyoumut interpreting, I tried to explain to Kingualik what this once-in-a-lifetime occasion was all about. I related to her that she could indeed be proud of her departed husband who had been selected amongst all Canada's Eskimos to receive the Coronation Medal commemorating the crowning of Princess Elizabeth as Queen of England. Her husband had been recognized as an "outstanding hunter and provider" amongst his people.

At this precise moment, and without any hesitation, Kingualik raised her hand denoting silence and boldly stated, "Wait a moment! That's not true! Many winters I was hungry."

After recovering from her candid expression I tried to impress upon her that she should treasure this medal, and that with the passing of time, handing it on from grandparent to grandchild, it would increase significantly in personal family value.

Departing from Kingualik's camp some two hours later, after shaking hands once again with everyone, including all the children, I felt richly rewarded to have shared the emotion, compassion, and joy of meeting these friendly, proud people. I thought too, that this would probably be my one and only encounter with Kingualik. This proved not to be the case!

One year later, the following spring, Sandy Lunan, a 35-year northern veteran and Hudson's Bay manager, cranked up our detachment land-line and demanded, "Dent, what the hell did you tell Kingualik up on Back River?" Lo and behold, Kingualik had made the trek into the settlement from the Back River with her son and was at that precise moment in the Bay store to trade.

She had entered the Bay warehouse and, acting like an experienced customer, had commenced telling Mr. Lunan what she wanted. First on her list was a 22-foot Peterborough freighter canoe and outboard motor. She also wanted a .250/3000 rifle and a case of ammunition. That was followed by a request for a case of tea and then tobacco.

Realizing the sizeable sale, Mr. Lunan enquired where her fox pelts were, and how many did she have. Much to his astonishment, Kingualik pulled her Coronation Medal out of a small duffle bag and, as she pushed it across the counter towards him, said "The policeman told me the medal was very, very valuable." She explained to Lunan that she hated to part with it, but the supplies were needed more than the medal.

The intrinsic value of the medal was soon explained to Kingualik. Fortunately, her son did have some fox and caribou skins to trade which, coupled with Family Allowances, enabled them to purchase most of the items they required. Kingualik returned to the Back River after I had had the opportunity to reinforce the proper significance of the medal through the able interpreting abilities of both Mr. Lunan and Canon W.J.R. James, the Anglican missionary.

Caribou did not migrate through the Back River area during the fall of 1956 or the spring of 1957, resulting in severe hardship for all and death by starvation for 15 of the Eskimo scattered through this area.

When I returned to Baker Lake again in 1958 after a two-year absence, Kingualik and a grandson, 14-year-old Ooyoumut, were living at the post. A school had been constructed during my absence and Ooyoumut, for the first time in his life, had the opportunity of attending. Very much the proud hunter following in his grandfather's footsteps, he rushed excitedly home from school one day in mid-October, telling Kingualik that he had heard there were caribou about four miles northwest of the settlement. Although unfamiliar with the terrain he was confident of his hunting abilities and desperately wanted to kill a caribou for his grandmother. She told him to let the teacher know and, if he was given approval, it would be all right to go hunting.

He returned home that night elated with his hunting success, telling Kingualik and the teacher that he had shot a caribou and would return to it the following day with his dog to back-pack the meat home.

Three days later he had not returned -- three days during which the winter's first serious snowstorm reduced visibility to zero. Kingualik went to Special Constable Seeteenak's home and told him that her grandson had failed to return with the caribou he had shot three days before. Up until this moment we did not know Ooyoumut was missing.

The task ahead was next to hopeless, considering weather conditions and Ooyoumut's unfamiliarity with the countryside around Baker Lake. Commandeering every available experienced adult Eskimo living on the post we organized a fan-out search of the area north of Baker Lake. Temperatures had been well below zero, and, with the wind-chill factor, survival was doubtful.

When we failed to locate Ooyoumut on that first day's search, the result was inevitable. At headquarters we reconstructed what probably happened. When Ooyoumut went back to recover the caribou kill, a southwest wind began blowing. Snow, coupled with wind, dimmed visibility to inches. Ooyoumut must have thought, "If I keep the wind on my left shoulder as I walk I will reach the north shore of Baker Lake within a few hours." Once he encountered the shoreline it would be a simple matter to continue west until he came across the canoes wintered along the shore, oil barrels, buildings and home. Good logic.

What he didn't realize was that the wind had shifted very gradually from the southeast to the southwest. This would then cause him to walk in a semi-circle and pass north of the settlement.

Exhausted and freezing, death would have been inevitable. In all probability his body would be found northwest of the post.

During the evening, as exhausted searchers returned and were accounted for, the wind and snow subsided. Clear skies set in and the temperature plummeted. At noon the next day one of the searchers, scanning hillsides about four miles northwest of the settlement, spotted slight movement. Zeroing in with his telescope he identified Ooyoumut's dog sitting up. When he reached the site, he found Ooyoumut's body partially covered with snow, lying on his back, hands crossed over his chest, frozen like granite.

Rather than relate his find first to the police he went to Kingualik and told her that he had found O oyoumut, dead. He then came to tell us. By the time I got to where Kingualik had been living, she had gone. Her friends told me she was in a state of emotional shock and had wandered off over the hill by the cemetery. I immediately sent one of our special constables to find her and bring her back. The other special and a local Eskimo were dispatched to bring in Ooyoumut.

Special Constable Seeteenak brought Kingualik back towards the settlement by dog team. Rather than permit the sled to bump across a steep hill I picked her up and, carrying her, walked to the Anglican mission. I almost made it. I slipped and, rather than let Kingualik strike the frozen ground, I tried to cushion her fall by clutching her in my arms at the last moment. My back cracked. I was left motionless and could not move or straighten up. Kingualik walked to the mission, and I was taken home lashed to the komatik, carried into the house and put in bed.

The special constables attended to funeral arrangements, making a coffin and taking the body to the church for service, then to the cemetery overlooking Baker Lake for burial.

Kingualik came to the detachment office some two weeks later with one of the special constables to act as interpreter. With tears flowing freely, she produced the Coronation Medal and, pushing it across the desk towards me, said, "I cannot keep the medal any longer. Were my husband alive, Ooyoumut would not have perished. I do not deserve to have it."

Considerable time was spent convincing her she must keep the medal. No one could have prevented what happened. "*Ajurnarmat*", I said to her, an Eskimo word that covers a multitude of misfortunes regardless of circumstances. "It cannot be helped". This fatalistic perspective she accepted.

However, Kingualik once again surprised me. From her duffle, purse-like bag she produced a small ball of something green, similar to a small marble. She painstakingly took it apart, eventually unfolding and flattening out a one-dollar bill. Where on earth she came into possession of currency, I do not know, as it was only shortly after this incident that the Hudson's Bay converted from tokens to money. Currency had not been used. Probably some white person had paid her for sewing, or domestic chores, with this legal tender. Whatever its origin, as an alternative to my accepting the Coronation Medal she felt obliged to pay the police for the services of searching for and locating the body of Ooyoumut, and for assisting so much with the funeral.

Kingualik's emotion and pride were so evident it was indeed difficult not to join in openly shedding tears with her. The matter of payment for services rendered was resolved when Kingualik agreed to write a letter to one of the Baker Lake Eskimos confined in the Clearwater, Manitoba, sanatorium, putting the letter and money in an envelope, and mailing it.

Today these northerners are called Inuit. To me, with all the warmth, compassion, and recollection it is possible to muster, they are still Eskimo. My life, and my wife's, have been significantly enriched through our exposure to, and dealings with, these Eskimo of by-gone decades.

Clare Dent
RCMP Quarterly - Volume 46, Number 1

*   *   *   *   *

"I MUST HAVE THE WRONG NUMBER...."

The green lights of the Canadian Police Information Centre machine are winking merrily as I open the office door to begin a new day. The sun shining on the harbour sends a shaft of light across the desk, and over the two-way radio and computer, and glances off the bookcase containing its red-covered statutes, blue administration manuals, and assorted reference books of many hues. It is a colourful morning.

The phone jangles.

I answer, "Good morning, RCMP Detachment. May I help you?"

"Oh, I must have the wrong number."

"What number were you calling?" She gives the correct one. "Then you have the right number, madam."

"I do? Who are you then?"

Here we go, another day like others in the past 12 months.

Dear Public: I am here, breathing and working and doing my job. Why can't you accept me? Try to give up the long-held image of the Mountie dashing off to get his man single-handed, for there are females working in the office now -- women who are being trained to answer your questions, operate the two-way radio, cope with the idiosyncrasies of computers and generally give administrative assistance to the Mountie who goes forward to get his man!

But change comes slowly on the south shore of Nova Scotia. One does not expect to hear a female voice when phoning the Mounties, nor is one prepared to bare one's soul to a gal at the desk ready to take particulars of an accident report.

The accumulation from last night's shift is on the desk. There is plenty of work to be done. Change of venues. And remember the notes hastily written in the shorthand book? They are waiting to become the written message, or the complaint that will send a policeman out to solve another problem.

The door swings open. A burly six-footer stands there.

"I want to see someone."

(Don't say it. Hold back the quip, "Well, who do you think I am? No one?")

"Fine. May I help you?"

"Don't expect so. I want to see one of the men."

Further questioning reveals he has been issued a parking ticket. Out come the ledgers: fill in the necessary particulars on Form 19G, complete the voluntary penalty form, accept his money, issue his receipt. It is all over and done with. Painless. He is on his way. Score one!

Now, let's see. A liquor exhibit to attend to -- exhibit forms to be completed; motor vehicle infractions -- informations to be typed. Everything is well documented. These RCMP are a joy to be associated with. Seldom do they leave loopholes.

The phone again.

"Is there anyone in?"

(Anyone in? Of course there is someone in. I'm here. Who do you think answered the phone? One of the horses, long distance from Regina?)

"Yes. We have members in. May I help you?"

"Well, I really want to talk to a man. I want to know if I can run my old truck. Somebody said you can't run it after the end of January. The registration runs out."

Sounds familiar. I've heard the sergeant dispense this information before.

"It has to be registered again after the end of January."

"Oh...you knew? Good-bye."

The problems take care of themselves one by one. The sergeant is at hand most times unless he has been called out. The community makes many demands on him.

The ticklish problems for me, when he is out, are the guns to be registered. There is something about a strange man coming to the counter with a gun for registration that strips me of my professional facade. A shiver of fear courses through me. Has he a record? Guns and crime -- to me anyway -- are synonymous, in spite of the mild-mannered members of the local gun club.

But I don't know this man. Please don't give me a hard time, I pray. Common sense comes to the fore. Go to the counter and take the particulars for the application; be careful to note the type of gun, serial number, calibre, number of shots, length of barrel, full name, date of birth of the applicant...

Then look him in the eye, smile sweetly and say, "I have to have one of the members sign this. Would you come back, say in an hour?" As soon as he leaves you dash to the computer, send off an inquiry to Ottawa and Crime Index to determine if he has a record or has been prohibited from carrying a gun. Thus you have bought yourself time in case he is indeed a felon, and you can call in one of the members.

Who is approaching the counter now? I remember him. Used to be a gateman at the local newsprint mill. Flinty type.

"I want to see a male member," he demands. Fine. A corporal comes from the rear office to the counter in response.

"I had this here accident about four months ago. Halifax tells me I should have reported it. Damned foolishness."

The corporal reads the letter. He is on his way to a fracas, but answers calmly, "I'm sure our secretary can handle this for you, sir."

Abashed, "Flintstone" turns to me: "Oh, so you're one of them Flora MacDonald kind of girls. Takin' over everythin'. Well whatya want t'know?"

"If you will give me your licence, your motor vehicle permit and insurance card, please, I will fill out the necessary accident report." Sure enough, Halifax had prodded him to come to the office, pointing out his negligence in not doing so. As the report is being completed, his antagonism shows signs of weakening. We reach the end. Amicably.

"Is that all?"

"Yes, all I need to know. You are required, however, to answer the query from Halifax." This presented an additional problem to him. "Would you like me to do it for you on the typewriter?"

"Sure would."

Report finished. Envelope addressed. Mission completed, all but the purchase of a stamp. He turns to go.

"Sorry if I offended you -- about that Flora MacDonald thing, girls takin' over and all that. I'm a Liberal, but damned if you didn't do a good job!"

Score two!

Don't get the impression this is a one-gal show. Not at all. The NCO is on duty daily: the members are in and out as they cover the policing of both town and county. The detachment functions smoothly. However, the men can't be desk bound and that is why we are here, as public servants, to carry some of the load.

It is the amount and quality of training given by the NCO that determines a public servant's efficiency and help to the Force. It takes a great deal of patience on his part to train a neophyte to think on RCMP lines, make you capable of handling administrative details and mastering the interwoven system of ledgering. If he can do this and, with a minimum of supervision, let you handle the public and act as liaison, then your function has been established and fulfilled.

It leaves the NCO free to handle administrative details of a more sophisticated nature. You learn by mistakes. too. Believe me, I know -- they are great teachers. You try not to make them twice. Which reminds me: I wonder why the boss has that placard in his office which says, starkly, "PATIENCE." Is he trying to tell me something?

Your NCO trains you, and should you meet or surpass requirements, the credit for this accomplishment should rightly go to him. And in time, the public will accept our role.

Back to the desk again: last night's court material awaits final recording, letters to be filed, some to write, two reports waiting. But take a minute to look at the view from the window. The sea has turned from silver to blue, and a ship enters the bay. A beautiful sight. I like it here!

The radio crackles. "Car 113, Mrs. P, will you query N.S. licence...as soon as possible?"

The phone rings, electric typewriter hums away waiting for you to finish the sentence you started. But you must do the query on the computer at once!

R.r.r.ring! Oh, not now, Please! I must do the query!

"Good afternoon, RCMP, may I help you?"

The voice answers, "Huh? I must have the wrong number. I wanted the Mounties..."

Beryl Pitblado
RCMP Quarterly - Volume 40, Number 3

*   *   *   *   *

FIRST DAY ON THE JOB

A member of Surrey Detachment General Investigation Section had arranged to pick up a newly arrived recruit on the lad's first morning on the job. He did so, in an unmarked car. On the way back to the office they were diverted by the dispatcher to check on a lady in North Surrey who was reportedly causing a disturbance.

They drove to the area and discovered that it was "Lena", a prominent local lass. She was swinging smartly along the sidewalk, wearing nothing but ankle socks and sneakers, looking like a cheerleader at a Sons of Freedom barbecue. She was gathering a curious retinue of school children en route to classes, so the members decided they would have to get her into their car. Since she weighed close to 200 pounds, the logistics of this were awesome.

By virtue of some friendly persuasion, judicious handling and polite pushing, the lady was finally trundled into the back seat of the car. Asserting a degree of authority, the senior constable directed the recruit into the seat with her and they left the area. His next communique to the dispatcher was along the lines of "Now that we've got her, what are we going to do with her?"

Trying to drive along as inconspicuously as possible, they still attracted a modicum of attention on the way, as Lena soon decided that incarceration was not a viable alternative and she repeatedly made attempts to resume her march. Dismissing a fleeting temptation to float her into the Fraser River, the harassed pair finally got their passenger to the office.

An early-morning gathering of solicitous onlookers at the office commenced various offers of sage advice when the parade arrived there. The dishevelled driver, a crafty devil, drove up, parked the car, and tersely announced to the spectators before walking away, "I got her in -- you guys can get her to hell out."

R.W.Morley

*   *   *   *   *

FRESH PORK(ER)

Members of the Force have often been called upon to perform duties that have little or nothing to do with police work. I imagine several have been awakened by the persistent ringing of the telephone only to have some hysterical person demanding that you find a dog or cat which has wandered away. In most cases, depending upon the degree of your chagrin, you will either pacify them or get very upset and tell the poor caller your personal view on the subject. You can probably imagine the reactions of Constable D.M. Ferguson and me when we received a call that a pig was wandering down one of the principal streets in Campbellton, New Brunswick.

Constable Ferguson and I were stationed at the Campbellton City Detachment, and we worked shifts. At the time of this incident, we were working the night shifts from ten p.m. to six a.m. and midnight to eight a.m. Everyone who has ever worked those shifts finds that time drags by very slowly, and any excuse to relieve the monotony is welcomed with open arms.

The call was received about two a.m. on March 3, 1970, and since we were in the vicinity, it was only a matter of minutes before we arrived on the scene. No pig was to be seen, so we tried to find out where it had come from. In the area where it had been sighted, there is a meat-packing plant, and it was there that the trouble had originated. A large van had been unloading pigs, and about ten of them decided they didn't like the accommodation and left in a rush. Only one man was on duty, and he managed to recapture two of the truant pigs, but had no idea where the others had gone. He was greatly relieved when the Mounties arrived on the scene.

A request for assistance was radioed to the office and

confirmation was received within a few minutes that the manager of the plant and some helpers were on the way. Constable Ferguson and I continued our patrol, but did not find any pigs. We made another visit to the plant to see if any had been recovered. As we pulled into the parking lot, a taxi turned off the road and parked behind us. The taxi driver ran over and said, "There's a pig running down the highway near the Iron Bridge." A few minutes later, the pig was sighted and that's when the fun began!

I herded the pig into a service-station lot with the car, and in another minute the chase began. Neither of us had ever wrestled pigs before, and we didn't even know at which end to start. After a fruitless chase, we decided the situation called for a length of rope. We ransacked the trunk of the police car but the only suitable item was a grey issue blanket. This pig was a really big one and if it was captured, then and only then would we decide our course of action. How do you go about apprehending a pig? We were soon to be experts (?) on the subject.

While Constable Ferguson called the office, I chased the pig down the road, brandishing the blanket like a matador at a bullfight. I succeeded in entangling the pig in the blanket, but it was soon out again and on the run. I finally grabbed one of its hind legs, and while it struggled, I grabbed the other and began to walk it back to the car wheelbarrow fashion.

By this time Constable Ferguson and I were almost hysterical with laughter. I would have given a week's pay for a camera. As stated before, this pig was a real whopper; it was doing everything in its power to shake me loose, and when we got reasonably close to the police car, I was pretty well exhausted. Constable Ferguson retrieved the blanket and put it over the pig's head. The pig sat down and I sat on it. During our little show, a number of cars stopped to see what was happening. It wouldn't take much imagination to figure what was running through their minds.

Constable Ferguson drove the car to where I was sitting on the pig and opened the rear door. The pig was gaining strength by the minute and was getting boisterous again, and I was in no condition to handle it if it ran off. I managed to catch hold of the pig's hind legs again and when I wheeled it close enough to the car, I flipped it into the back seat and closed the door. It was too big to move around much. The pig was taken to the detachment where it was photographed.

Then it was returned to the plant. The men on duty were asked if all the pigs had been recovered and they said yes. I told them we had something in the back seat that would interest them. The door was opened and the men had a good laugh while they herded the pig into the pen. Thus ended one of the most amusing capers that had happened in the area for some time.

The Mounties always get their man -- or pig.

M.J. Seliske
RCMP Quarterly - Volume 36, Number 3

*   *   *   *   *

HELP ME

When Floyd Richards, a service-station employee in Rosetown, Saskatchewan, opened the flap of a car bearing Alberta licence plates to fill it with gas shortly after 11 a.m. on September 22, 1968, he noticed a slip of paper fall to the ground. Curious, he retrieved it and read: "Help! To whom it may concern. This man is posing as my husband. He is forcing me to act accordingly. Please find some way to help me. The lady of the car. Thank you."

Richards hastily conferred with the proprietor of the business and they decided to call the police. Meanwhile, Richards returned to the car and the driver paid in cash and left without saying a word. He drove south. The owner decided to follow the car to check its direction, but when he reached the town of Thrasher and still saw no sign of the fleeing vehicle, he concluded it must have headed east on Highway 15 towards Outlook.

RCMP at Rosetown notified all surrounding detachments as well as Saskatoon Sub-Division. Richards had supplied a good description of the car, plus the Alberta licence number, and all patrols were on the lookout.

Finally at seven p.m., Rosetown RCMP were advised the car had been intercepted by the highway patrol near Maple Creek, Saskatchewan, and that the couple had been identified as a pair of newly-weds on their honeymoon. They had been married the day before at Alsask, Saskatchewan.

Hearing this, of course, police laughingly knew the answer-- nothing more than a practical joke with a new twist on a pair of newly-weds!

Anonymous
RCMP Quarterly - Volume 35, Number 1

*   *   *   *   *

A LITTLE OLD TYPEWRITER

On August 20, 1970, I attended the funeral of one of my very best friends, ex-Sergeant L.H. Yeomans of the RCMP, at Smiths Falls, Ontario. Among the many relatives and friends present, there were quite a number of pensioners from the RCMP Veterans' Association including several who had served in the eastern Arctic in the 1930s with "Hammy" and me. When all was over the vets split up in small groups, which is not very unusual, to talk over old times and happenings in the Force since we had gone to pension.

I was with one group, all of whom had spent time in the eastern Arctic. When I turned around, I noticed my wife was engaged in conversation with another group which included former Commissioner L.H. Nicholson and his wife. They were all looking in my direction while listening to the commissioner, who seemed to be telling a story. From the expressions on their faces, it seemed to be something funny and about me. Curiosity getting the better of me, I hastily left my group and joined them.

Commissioner Nicholson said, "Paddy, I was just telling these folks about the typewriter I sold you and how you used to carry it around with you on your patrols by saddle horse."

I replied, "I sure did. I also carried it all over the Arctic including Ellesmere and Devon islands by dog team. It's still in working order. I've had to replace the roller several times, but it never let me down."

This is the true story of a little Remington portable. It all began in 1926 when I was a recruit in Regina. I had not finished the training course, but for some reason or other I was sent to Balcarres, Saskatchewan, for temporary duty to relieve Constable L.H. Nicholson who was about to take his discharge, time expired. I persuaded him to sell me the new portable typewriter which he had ordered some time before and which had been delivered while he was away. Incidentally, I remained in Balcarres, did not finish my training course, and was never in Regina again during the 26 years I served in the Force.

Now I will tell you why I carried that little machine on patrol. The NCO in charge of that detachment was, I would consider, about as cantankerous a person as I have ever met, and he thought that he and only he knew it all. He would not allow me to practise typing in the office. When I took my typewriter to my room and practised there, he did not like that either.

I therefore conceived the idea of taking it with me when I went on patrol, and I practised in the evenings in my room in the little prairie hotels where I put up for the night. I am sure my old horse, Ginger, did not mind the extra weight as I used the universal saddle which was much lighter than the stock saddle.

After much hard work, I became a fairly good four-finger typist. Of course, it was the typewriter which could not spell and made terrible grammatical errors. In fact, no matter how much I belaboured it, it never did overcome these faults. A large quantity of RCMP paper was wasted in correcting innumerable errors in order to have the finished reports acceptable at headquarters.

In 1928 when I was posted to Dundas Harbour Detachment in the eastern Arctic, my typewriter went along. Three years later my faithful companion went with me to Bache Peninsula, and it was from there that we were parted for a number of years.

In the summer of 1932, the annual supply ship was unable to break through the ice and bring us our yearly supplies. During the winter we received a radio message through station KDKA in Pittsburgh, Pennsylvania, telling us to close the detachment and proceed by dog team to Craig Harbour where the ship had left supplies for us. We took our trunks containing uniforms, other clothing and personal effects -- which in my case included my typewriter -- to Fram Haven and stored them in an old wooden shack, hoping the ship would call in for them after it had picked us up at Craig Harbour.

In April, we closed the detachment and travelled to Craig Harbour by dog team. In the summer the supply ship picked us up at Craig Harbour, but would not go to Fram Haven for our trunks. If it had not been for ex-Corporal Bill Kerr loaning me his civilian suit after he came aboard at Pond Inlet, I would have arrived back in civilization still wearing my polar-bear patrol pants.

Several years later, an Arctic scientific expedition picked up our trunks and took them to Copenhagen, Denmark, from where they were shipped to Ottawa. My little old typewriter and I finally got together again when I opened my trunk at Rockcliffe Barracks upon my return from Craig Harbour in 1937.

It is now 1970 and still works. Its spelling has not improved and its grammar is poor. Recently, I have been thinking about a condemning board for it. I hope you remember the evidence: "unfit for further use through fair wear and tear". The question which bothers me is which should I condemn, the machine or the owner?

Paddy Hamilton
RCMP Quarterly - Volume 36, Number 3

*   *   *   *   *

RESPONSE TIME

One of the important hallmarks of an efficient detachment is a prompt response to citizen complaints. A watch commander in Surrey had developed an immediate response system that was exemplary -- most of the time. On a quiet Sunday morning at about three a.m. everything had been reasonably tranquil for about an hour. A full moon actually made headlights unnecessary and a silent radio lent itself to the quiet ambience of a beautiful night. Citizens were slumbering and late revellers from the drinking palaces of Blaine, Washington, had made it home more or less unscathed.

This interlude of harmony apparently lent itself to Constable Tommy's dozing peacefully away. This in itself would have attracted little attention were it not for the fact that Constable Tommy was the sole occupant and pilot of a police car. He cruised casually through a stop sign at a "T" intersection and rolled over everything into a citizen's front garden.

Hearing an unusual noise, possibly the result of the emergency roof equipment squirting across his grass, the slumbering taxpayer glanced out his bedroom window and saw four tire tracks newly relocated between his rhododendrons and his dahlias. Headlights were illuminating the roots of other flora, and the set of four tires had rudely plowed new furrows across his carefully nurtured lawn. Transformed instantly into a raging bull, he groped for his bedside phone and dialled the emergency police number. Meanwhile, summoning a hitherto-untapped reserve of bleary-eyed dignity, Tommy groped for his forage cap and marched up to the front door, rehearsing his opening statement. Dignity and a certain presence, mingled with a confidently quiet yet capable authority, would probably be the most successful opening gambit. He rang the doorbell.

The householder, actively supported by a voluble wife, opened the door a few seconds after he had hung up his telephone. He stood back admiringly as he saw the uniform. "Officer, that's what I admire -- efficiency. This is the quickest response to an emergency that I've ever seen."

R.W.Morley

*   *   *   *   *

NEW POLICE TRANSPORT SYSTEM

It is not easy to keep a good story to yourself, especially if it contains a few chuckles. That is my reason for telling this little gem.

It happened many years ago when the headquarters of "G" Division was in Edmonton. In the January 1934 issue of the *RCMP Quarterly* there appeared a cartoon by Harry Taylor depicting the arrival of the Christmas mail at a northern outpost. A copy of this eventually arrived at Fort Reliance where Constables Jimmy Robinson and Leslie Fyfe were then stationed. This cartoon appealed in no small fashion to these "guardians of the right." In fact, it tickled them so much that when, some time later, they found a dead and frozen caribou near their detachment they decided to produce their own "living" cartoon.

With sturdy poles, the dead caribou was propped up in a standing position. Behind it the artistic constables placed a Yukon sleigh and, with the aid of bed-roll straps, formed a harness. To record the occasion of this historic moment, photographs were taken. The story might have ended there except that during the long winter months, nothing was stirring at Fort Reliance but a rather fertile Irish imagination.

A report prepared for the attention of division headquarters found its way to Edmonton. Long and detailed, it dealt at great length with winter transportation in the north, pointing out the difficulties of carrying sufficient food for dog teams on prolonged patrols, and the time involved in looking after dogs in the summer.

The report went on to say that in Finland, the problem had been overcome by the Lapps in their use of reindeer, and that since the nearest approach to this animal in Canada was the caribou, the men at Fort Reliance had gone to work on one. This type of animal, it was suggested, would be of great value: the winter patrols would only have to carry food for the men as the caribou could forage during the evenings, and at night, if the teams were properly selected, a supply of fresh milk would be available for the tea. Furthermore, in the case of direst necessity, caribou meat was a more palatable diet than dog flesh.

"G" Division, it seemed, liked the idea and engaged in the big caribou hunt, aided by the supporting photograph sent with the report. However, they wished one or two points cleared up.

In their memorandum to Inspector B.B. Curry, O C Fort Smith Sub-Division, they requested further information and trusted that the Wildlife Branch of the Department of Northern Affairs would have no regulations that would interfere with further experimentation, and capturing and breeding the caribou. Unfortunately for the members at Fort Reliance, the Sub-Division O C was a little wiser in the ways of the north and a sudden visit to that detachment from Sergeant Frank Cook made them aware of this fact.

Sergeant Cook, with traditional NCO diplomacy, observed that since these two men were most versed in "bull" they might wish for immediate transfer to Regina, a place where the last-mentioned animal was conspicuous by its absence, but whose place was taken by multitudinous horses which were well fed and required continuous attention by volunteers with the usual stable implements. The idea was most repugnant to the members concerned and no further caribou suffered a similar fate -- at least not publicly.

S.J.B. Kirby
RCMP Quarterly - Volume 30, Number 4

*   *   *   *   *

INGENUITY PLUS

Members of an RCMP highway patrol in B.C. came up with a novel idea in an attempt to halt the ever-increasing highway fatalities. They painted their "ghost" cars with water colours, then placed a store mannequin beside the driver, in order to give the "Sunday drive" effect.

One irate motorist complained to the Officer Commanding that the ghost-car members were entertaining females in their cars, on duty. The usual investigation was undertaken and a patrol member was interviewed. He admitted carrying an additional passenger and promptly introduced a shapely, blond-haired, blue-eyed female mannequin to the bemused investigator.

Anonymous
RCMP Quarterly - Volume 29, Number 2

* * * * *

LAW SCHOOL -- 1936

A telegram came to me where I was stationed at North Battleford in September 1936. "Vacancy in Law School, New Brunswick. Advise whether willing to attend at own expense and state amount of savings. Commissioner." The wire, direct from Ottawa, puzzled me, so I checked with the OC North Battleford. He advised me to reply to the commissioner and send copies of both telegrams to him so he could notify the Commanding Officer "F" Division. It was not until about three years later that I got the answer to this puzzle.

I arrived in Saint John in October and was met at the railway station by Jim MacBrien who took me to his boarding house where he had rented an adjoining room for me at seven dollars per week. Jim explained to me that a Member of Parliament had raised the question in the House of Commons: "How come the son of the RCMP Commissioner is being put through law school at government expense?"

My salary was $2.05 per day and I was granted one dollar per day living-out allowance. This latter amount paid my board, and my salary paid for tuition, books, law-society fees and articling costs. I was required to perform duties on the detachment; the sergeant in charge put me as telephone orderly from five p.m. to midnight on weekdays and assigned me to highway patrol on Saturdays. These duties permitted me time in the office to type my notes and do study assignments.

Somehow Ottawa found out that I was articled to a law firm (as required by the university). I received a memo from the adjutant to cancel the articling. Jim MacBrien told me to hold the memo as his father was visiting him the next week. Jim explained this requirement to his father when he arrived, so two weeks later a memo arrived permitting me to carry on the articling, provided this was not used as an excuse to leave the Force within five years after graduation. This was contained in a paper I was required to sign prior to commencing the course.

The course proceeded smoothly for the three years and I spent the summers lecturing to reserve squads in Fredericton or doing detachment work out of Saint John. On one occasion I was required by the lawyer to whom I was articled to prepare a defence brief in a case arising from a seizure by the RCMP. I received my law degree in May 1939 and was transferred to the Criminal Investigation Branch at Headquarters, Ottawa, as a reader. Fred Regan, who had taken his law course at Dalhousie University, and I were promoted to the rank of Acting Lance Corporal at the pay of $2.35 per day on July 1, 1939.

The puzzle surrounding the initial telegram was cleared up a few months later. The file messenger "accidentally" dropped my personal file among criminal investigation files on my desk. I found out the commissioner had given my name and that of another constable to the CO "F" Division as holding university degrees and eligible to take a law course. The CO had advised the commissioner that I was not suitable as I had an inferiority complex and would not make a good showing in court. Therefore in 1936 the commissioner wired me direct.

In October I was summoned to Fredericton to be admitted to the Bar. Though the war was on and leaves were cancelled, I was given a weekend pass. On my return to Ottawa I submitted a rather cocky memo saying that I had been admitted to the New Brunswick Bar as "Barrister, Solicitor, Commissioner for taking affidavits, etc." and was therefore permitted to practise law in any court of the Province of New Brunswick. Fred Regan and I were promoted to the rank of Acting Corporal in October 1939, and confirmed 2 1/2 years later. I believe Frank Lindsay, Fred Regan and I were the first three to be sent to university by the Force.

Ed Brakefield-Moore

*   *   *   *   *

WHERE'S THE BIBLE?

And it came to pass, many years ago in the Province of British Columbia, in the Municipality of Burnaby, the wheels of justice came to a screeching halt. The courts had to close down -- because the Bible had been lost. Bibles are not a common item around your average police detachment, and a frantic search was unsuccessful. A junior constable arrived at an acceptable solution. He scratched around until he located a firearms catalogue that was of suitable size and consistency. He next placed an acceptable plain brown cover on the book, and adorned it with a cross and suitable inscriptions. It was placed in the witness box and court reopened.

The witnesses continued to testify in appropriate fashion, and the good book was used with satisfying results. Maybe it's still there.

R.W.Morley

* * * * *

A NIGHT TO REMEMBER

For almost three weeks in 1935, residents of Regina were patient but somewhat disturbed over the presence of more than 1,000 relief-camp strikers who came to the city on freight trains. The strikers had left relief camps in British Columbia several days earlier and, of course, gained strength en route. Their intention was to continue the trek to Parliament Hill, Ottawa, in protest of unemployment. The group appeared to be well organized. During their stay in the city, the strikers were billeted at the exhibition grounds and welfare assistance was provided by the federal government. To encourage their existence as a group, the strikers held a tag day which proved productive and, of course, with the passing of time, they became more confident and less fearful.

Negotiations between the strikers and government officials had apparently broken down and a mass meeting was planned for the city's Market Square on the evening of July 1, 1935. Plainclothes members of the RCMP and Regina City Police moved silently in on this meeting to arrest the leaders. Uniformed members of the RCMP were transported to the scene in large, closed-in vans.

Two piping blasts on a whistle were the only audible warning as police moved with the rapidity of a summer shower. Several people were trampled in this human stampede, as three hours of chaos and terror started. The crowd fled, carrying everything before it. After the initial charge, the police had wheeled and returned to aid fellow officers against strikers who seemed to pick bricks to hurl from nowhere. At the outbreak, a mounted troop of RCMP rode silently in and assisted largely in dispersing the mob; they were supported by members of the Regina City Police, on hand from the outset.

A few yards from the hurly-burly immediately behind the fire hall, Detective Charles Millar of the Regina City Police slumped to the ground while a club-wielding striker rained blow after blow upon him. City and Mounted Police rushed to the unconscious officer and while some beat off assailants, others dragged the fallen detective through a rain of bricks and stones to the police garage. Detective Millar was unarmed and had little chance of defending himself. He had left the station after seeing a fellow policeman being attacked on Halifax Street. Detective Millar died in hospital without regaining consciousness. He had served 15 years with the force.

In the centre of Market Square police hurled gas grenades amid the strikers. A striker grabbed one and hurled it back while mounted men rode through the crowd, wielding truncheons as they went. Ambulance after ambulance dashed to various places to load up men covered with blood. Police cars were rushed to the lot and men -- police and strikers alike -- gory with caked blood, were piled in and driven away.

With foot police taking care of the disorganized men on the square, officers mounted on horses swung to the streets in groups of about eight to ten, riding three and four abreast. They rode up and down the streets and sidewalks, forcing men and women under cover for their own protection. As one fight was cleared, another sprang up. From Broad Street to Osler, the avenue was nothing but a mass of men and flying debris as the fight continued.

"Go ahead", called an officer at the front of a group of Mounties. He raced forward and his men followed. Stones were hurled in their direction, some bouncing from steel helmets. Rocks struck them in the face and body, but they tore into their adversaries and dispersed them for the time being; strikers verbally chastising the police were forcibly taken to cars and removed.

Idle curious jammed the surrounding streets. They raced before the police horses from one battle smack into another. Tear- gas fumes which floated across the square had telling effects. One street-car motorman, just after crossing Broad Street on 11th Avenue going east, saw a huge crowd on the tracks. They started to come toward the car and the driver, ringing the gong for all he was worth, shot on the power and headed straight for the mob. The strikers gave way and hurled stones at the windows as the car flashed past.

On one of their charges down 11th Avenue from the east, the Mounties rode their horses on the north sidewalk, jumped the small chain fence around the City Hall lawn and scattered a bunch of strikers gathered there. Market Square was littered with stetsons, caps and broken riding crops. The latter proved to have little effect on the strikers.

Abandoned autos at the intersection of 11th and Lorne impeded the work of police and had to be pushed aside. One car lay on its side with smashed windows. The sounds of battle continued with a striker being hit by bullets in both legs. He was taken into a restaurant on Cornwall Street where two striker Red Cross men attended him as he lay on the floor. He was given first aid and rushed to hospital. Again a lull in the fighting came. Police held the corner. Other mounted squads came up 11th from the west, exploring alley entrances and side streets off Lorne and Smith streets.

The corners of the Imperial Bank and the Canada Permanent blocks, examined later, clearly showed the white pockmarks of bullets, but curiously, not one window in either building was pierced. City and Mounted Police concentrated on Scarth and 11th and for one block radiated from this intersection. Mounted Police on horses cleared off hundreds who, despite the warnings, came back into the fighting zones and had to be removed time and time again.

After the riot had been checked, police patrolled the streets to prevent further looting of stores which had occurred earlier. By midnight most of the strikers had returned to their quarters at the exhibition grounds. Fearing another outbreak and in order to prevent one, the police were fully armed, and for the next day or so maintained order and prevented the strikers from organizing another demonstration.

During and following the riot many people were taken into custody. In fact, 117 violators and suspected violators were made available for an identification lineup at the RCMP barracks on July 2, resulting in many charges being laid. When all had calmed down, very few plate-glass windows remained intact in the city. In addition to the tragic death of Detective Millar, many strikers, police and sympathizers were injured, some seriously, from bullet wounds and flying debris.

Harold A. Johnson
RCMP Quarterly - Volume 35, Number 1

*   *   *   *   *

WHEN YOU GOTTA GO.....

Saturday nights at Golden, B.C., in the 1950s routinely called for the corporal and me to patrol several Columbia hamlets, checking country dances with their attendant problems of drinking and driving. This one was unfolding no differently than usual until we spotted three furtive figures in the business district of Parsons. (I should explain that the business district consisted of perhaps six or seven commercial buildings among a scattering of houses.) By their actions, the three clearly did not want to be seen by the police and our suspicions centred on a possible burglary of either a store or a garage.

With quick instructions to me, the corporal circled the block and dropped me off for foot patrol while he continued on for a similar patrol on the opposite side of the spread-out area. For the next hour or so I carried on a sneak-and-peak prowl through the quiet darkness until the individuals eventually proved uninteresting and all premises were found secure. Now to find the corporal and continue our normal patrol.

Eventually I saw him walking, or rather staggering, down the road towards me and as he drew near it was apparent he was much the worse for wear, with obvious scuffs and scratches, and a torn uniform.

I said, "What happened?"

He could only moan, "Go get the car, we're going home."

While we were driving the several miles back to the detachment, the story unfolded. Endeavouring to keep the target individuals in sight, he had been picking his way through the construction site of a new hotel. He couldn't use his flashlight as he didn't wish to make his presence known at this time. Sans flashlight he was carefully crossing the newly laid sub-floor, passing through framed partitions, when the next thing he knew he was in a heap in the basement some ten feet below! He had stepped off into the space of the basement stairwell where steps had not yet been built. Groaning out the painful tale he grumbled that the toughest part was not the fall, or even the sudden stop at the bottom, but rather trying to find some means of getting out. Eventually, groping around, he found his flashlight, and with the aid of some scrap lumber he had shinnied back up the wall, fortunately without serious injury except to his pride. He didn't realize anything was missing. End of the Saturday-night patrol.

Early Sunday morning I was awakened by the steady jingle of a persistent telephone. On answering, I was immediately assailed by one very irate and anxious woman. Get down to Parsons at once! were her instructions. Apparently her small son had just arrived home locked in a set of handcuffs. While she couldn't seem to describe the exact problem, it was clear he was in a bad way.

As I raced south my mind also pored over the possibilities -- where had he obtained the handcuffs and was a leg or an arm now suffering from lack of circulation from cuffs locked too tightly? Arriving, I found one little boy bouncing up and down with an obvious and very urgent call of nature plus one very cross mother threatening he had better hang on -- or else. Prominently in view was a gleaming pair of handcuffs locked through belt loops on either side of his brand new jeans; until they were unlocked, there was no way those pants could come down.

When the key had been turned and nature's crisis averted, it was time for questions and answers. A somewhat calmer mother explained there was no chance she was going to cut belt loops off an expensive new pair of jeans, and what were handcuffs doing lying around in a construction site anyway? Had they dropped from the sky?

Professing all innocence of their origin, I retrieved the handcuffs and begged a hasty retreat to other urgent duties.

Jack White

*   *   *   *   *

THE DYNAMITE CACHE

The report from headquarters was brief. Information had been received that just prior to World War I a German corporation had established a dynamite cache several miles from Thistle Creek, Alberta. Please investigate.

It was a pretty meagre description of the location, to say the least, considering the size of Canada, and this is why the report had travelled from one detachment to another until it reached the gates of Jasper National Park where our Hinton Detachment was located. The constable in charge hurried to shunt the investigation from his doorstep, stating that there was a Thistle Creek somewhere in the Rocky Mountains, bordering the Brazeau Forest Reserve. He suggested that Coal Valley Detachment ought to carry out the investigation because access was easier for them.

The source of the information might never be known, but the date, October 1939, a month after the outbreak of World War II, suggested at least two theories: an interned enemy alien may have offered the information, hoping for some consideration as a reward, or perhaps an appreciative immigrant of German descent who had settled in Canada after World War I was trying to do his bit to help his new country.

Whatever the source, I had a bit of a problem. It was getting late for travel by pack outfit; there was too much snow for any decent grazing for the horses and not enough for dog sledding. I had heard many stories of the "German outfit" that had hauled supplies and equipment into the area prior to World War I when frozen lakes and muskeg made for easy freighting, and I had made a patrol to this drilling site some two years earlier. I had been intrigued with the amount of equipment and stores that had been abandoned when the German outfit made their hasty departure at the outbreak of World War I. The stories of this supposed "drilling site" were also interesting.

There were few rangers' or trappers' cabins in the district which did not boast of kitchen utensils and other equipment taken from the site over the many years since it was abandoned, but I had never heard any stories of dynamite nor had I found any traces of explosives when investigating the property.

To make the best possible time, I "borrowed" one of the many range horses turned out for the winter, a fast walker called Snowball (because he was white), one of the few who could keep up to my saddle horse, Bob. I would travel light, using only one pack horse and two of the sled dogs, Bruce and Buster, who would each carry 35 pounds, mostly oats for the horses, and dog feed. Off I went in search of the cache.

In three days, I arrived at Dino's cabin in the Southesk area near Thistle Creek and, in spite of the overbearing stench of his special mink scent mix, I was glad to get out of the snow for one night and bed down on his dirt floor. It was a small price to pay for the information I expected.

As it turned out, he could tell me nothing about a dynamite cache and was much more interested in heading out early to check his traps. He had caught a female cougar and two kittens the previous day, and had set further traps, hoping to get the rest of the family.

We started early the next morning and found his traps had not been sprung. He decided to return to the cabin, taking a new route home, and I went along with him.

We had travelled several miles in fairly high country when I spotted a large game lick at the edge of a flat. I asked Dino if he knew the lick but he didn't so I surveyed the area with binoculars and saw a small cabin in the centre of the dark, churned-up circle. I decided to investigate.

Dino went on his way and I started to travel directly toward the lick over windfalls and through muskeg. Soon it was necessary to camp for the night and as usual with a pack outfit, where there is grazing there is no water, and if there is water there is no grazing. The horses were very spooky and did not like the place a bit -- too many game smells. The dogs, happy to get rid of their packs and eat, just curled up and had a good night.

The next day we made our way to the big flats and came to the cabin in the afternoon. It was a large lick, heavily trampled by game, fighting and pawing over the years, attracted by their favourite and necessary tonic, salt -- in this case saltpetre from dynamite. The cabin was sturdy with a sloping roof and a door on the high side. It had not been chinked nor had the corners been trimmed. The roof was made of cedar poles, but the centre ones had been pushed aside leaving an opening large enough for animals to exit through the roof.

I tied the horses up to the cabin while I investigated. The inside was stacked with boxes of dynamite marked "Canadian Explosives Ltd., Victoria, B.C., Jan. - 40% Dynamite, 1913." My official inventory as reported read: 60 boxes of stick dynamite intact and about 200 boxes broken open and scattered within the cabin.

The intact boxes were stacked against the walls; most of the broken boxes had been trampled, creating a sawdust floor. It was the "cache," but what do with it? I decided to return to Dino's cabin for the night. The next morning I talked Dino into returning with me. He was not a bit enthused, but agreed and we arrived there about noon.

The ground was frozen hard so burial was out of the question, and there was no way I could pack it out even if there had been a trail and many horses. The only way to dispose of this "exhibit" was to burn it, but first I had to get the necessary evidence for my report in order to justify the magic words "investigation concluded". I stacked as many full boxes as I could in front of the open door with some broken boxes scattered about and told the dogs to get up front for their picture, then asked Dino to take one with me and the outfit. It took some time because Dino was not interested and wanted to get back to his trap-line. As soon as he had taken a picture, off he went. I kicked some loose stumps out and packed them within the cabin's protruding corner logs and got a fire started, intending to move the horses as soon as the fire got under way. That didn't take long. There was a loud "swoosh" and flames shot out between the logs as if they had come from a flame thrower. Off went the horses as if they had been shot!

My knowledge of explosives at that time was very limited indeed. Years later as a demolition officer in the army I would understand the dangerous and sensitive qualities of explosives, especially old ones.

Alan R.Foster
RCMP Quarterly - Volume 47, Number 4

*   *   *   *   *

AN UNFORGETTABLE MOMENT

After I completed my RCMP training at Regina in 1930 I was posted to Dawson City in the Yukon. I was detailed for active duty patrolling the streets of Dawson. Shortly after my arrival a new officer took command of the northern district, then known as "B" Division. In uniform this officer looked most impressive; it was rumoured that he wore a ladies' corset.

One evening when I was patrolling the streets on duty, a gold prospector who had had too much to drink became violent and I had to arrest him. He was locked up in the RCMP guard room. The usual procedure was that the prisoner would appear before the Officer Commanding the next day at nine o'clock to be acquitted, fined or sentenced to a couple of days in jail. My instructions were that I was to notify the sergeant-major and he would advise the O C that he had a court case the following day.

The sergeant-major tried to reach the OC but was unable to do so. He turned to me, "Constable Olson, slip over to the O C's residence and inform him that he has a court case at nine o'clock."

"Very good sir," I replied, and off I went.

Before going I hurried up to the barrack room and shined my buttons and gave my shoes a quick brush. This was my first confrontation with the new Officer Commanding and being a recruit, I was most anxious to leave a good impression.

The OC's house was on the police grounds a short distance from the main barracks. It was with some trepidation that I rang the door bell. The officer's wife, a young and beautiful lady, opened the door.

"Good morning ma'am. I have a personal message for the Officer Commanding," I said nervously.

There was a slight hesitation. "My husband is upstairs, you can go up. The second door on the right."

"Thank you," I nodded with a smile, as I took the stairway near the door.

Hesitantly I tapped on the door, then quickly stepped back into position to give my O C a good snappy salute. I was most anxious to leave a good impression.

The door was suddenly pulled wide open and with his hands partly in the air, a man dressed only in his birthday suit shouted "Surprise!" Apparently he had mistaken my gentle tap on the door for that of his wife. With a changed expression on his face, he reached for something, most likely a towel but it could have been a revolver. I did not take chances. I made a dash for the stairway and with one hand on the railing, I went down three stairs at a time. I ran all the way to the sergeant-major's office.

As I was gasping for breath, I blurted out what had happened at the OC's house. After the sergeant-major had a good laugh he shook his head and said, "Married couples sometimes play some silly, crazy tricks on each other. I'll have a talk with the OC. In the meantime, if I were you I would not mention to the boys what happened."

As I was leaving the office, the sergeant-major asked, "You didn't see any corset, did you?"

"No sir," I replied.

Oscar Olson

* * * * *

SUPER SNIFFERS

During the late 1940s and early 50s in rural Saskatchewan, in addition to their regular policing duties, RCMP detachment members also gave drivers' tests by written exam, as well as testing the actual driving skills of applicants. One of the provincial statutes enforced was the Fuel Petroleum Products Act, under which farmers could purchase "tax-free" gas from a bulk fuel dealer for use in their farming operations -- but not for use in their private cars. This was commonly called "purple gas". There were, of course, always a few who would attempt to beat the system.

One balmy summer afternoon a father and son arrived at Vonda Detachment and while they struggled with the son's written test, the RCMP member surreptitiously tested their car for purple gas.

The test proved positive. Without revealing his finding at this time, the member joined the pair in the farmer's car for the driving-skills portion of the test. During the test, after a couple of approaching cars had passed, the corporal casually remarked that he could smell purple gas. When he asked the farmer and his son if they could smell it too, he received a red-eared but negative reply. As they disembarked from the car back at the detachment, the corporal remarked that he could still smell purple gas and proceeded into the office to mark the written test. (As the corporal told it, the father had given his son the wrong answers.) A routine check of their fuel tank -- because the corporal could "still smell purple gas" -- proved he was correct and prosecution followed in due course.

Some time later, the proprietor of the local garage related how he had been asked to fill two empty, clear glass whisky bottles, one with red and the other with amber gas from his pumps. Shortly after, he observed a group gathered in his shop seriously sniffing the contents of the two bottles he had filled and a third bottle filled with purple gas, trying to ascertain if there really was a difference. Obviously their noses weren't up to the task because the story did make the rounds that the RCMP corporal with the "super nose" could smell purple gas.

W.K.Barker

* * * * *

PRISON FACILITIES -- FORT RELIANCE

One incident of note when I was stationed at Reliance was the occasion when we arrested three members of the Dog Rib tribe for having a musk-ox hide in their possession at a time when these animals were protected. We took them to Fort Resolution for the trial. They were found guilty and each sentenced to 30 days imprisonment, the time to be served at Fort Reliance. I hastened to inform the magistrate that Fort Reliance Detachment was not equipped with a cell. The magistrate was adamant that they serve their time at Fort Reliance and directed they be taken back there, a distance of some 250 miles, to serve their sentence.

We returned the prisoners to Fort Reliance where we pitched a tent and kept them there until their sentences were served. Needless to say we were relieved when the 30-day period expired.

Robert W. "Tommy" Thompson

*   *   *   *   *

TRUCKIN' TO THE TANK

The staff of the liquor store in Revelstoke, B.C., were counting their cash following the close of business on a busy Saturday in the late fall. Suddenly a masked gunman crashed through the office window and, brandishing a sawed-off shotgun, relieved them of several thousand dollars before escaping into the evening darkness. He was soon traced to a local hotel and subsequently identified.

Several days later he was arrested in Vernon, minus the money, and returned to Revelstoke. When questioned he said that he had run into the woods after leaving the store, and concealed the money and his weapon in a plastic bag under a log. He later offered to recover it, and a constable (who had not been in the top ten of his graduating class) went into the woods with him. The suspect took off at a rapid pace into the tall timber after he had persuaded the solicitous constable to remove his handcuffs as they were impeding his progress through the bush.

The innovative corporal at Revelstoke was able to borrow a large tractor-trailer unit from a friendly trucker and commenced driving back and forth along the nearby highway. On about the third pass, a tired, cold and bedraggled bandit staggered out of the woods and lifted his thumb attempting to get a lift. The 18-wheeler stopped and he was accommodated.

R.W. Morley

*   *   *   *   *

THAT "SWEET" TASTE OF SUCCESS

In the late evening of November 12, 1969, a resident of Slave Lake, Alberta, contacted the RCMP and reported that his half-ton truck had just been stolen. The truck had been parked in front of the local theatre, unlocked, with the motor running. Taken along with the truck were items left in the vehicle, including two sealed bottles of an expensive Canadian rye whisky. Initial attempts to locate the truck were fruitless.

At 3:45 the following morning, A...., a local transient, was found wandering aimlessly around town. A.... was known to have a record for auto theft. While he was being interviewed regarding his actions, police found two sealed bottles of a similar brand of rye whisky in his possession. Only the mind of a policeman would know the investigator's thoughts at this point: with just a small amount of circumstantial evidence, you need to know more. The decision -- the sometimes disappointing decision -- had to be made as to what avenue of investigation should be taken.

A.... was quick to explain that he had purchased the whisky from someone at a party. His story was proved false and his attitude changed from bad to worse. Still, there was hardly enough evidence to take him to court. The task of obtaining conclusive evidence was becoming more frustrating by the minute. The first break came when the NCO in charge of the detachment radioed to report that he had located the stolen vehicle at the high school, about two blocks from where the suspect had been picked up. The circumstantial evidence was slowly building up.

When picked up, A.... was wearing gloves, presumably to avoid leaving fingerprints, something that would have assisted greatly in placing him in the vehicle. Nevertheless, a physical examination of the vehicle was made and there it was -- the missing link. The policeman couldn't hold back a grin; that "sweet" feeling of success rushed through him when his flashlight beamed down on a piece of chocolate bar melted to the driver's side of the front seat.

Sure enough, a check of A....'s trousers located a chocolate stain of the same size, and the chocolate found on the seat of the truck had cooled sufficiently to retain the pattern of his trousers. A.... pleaded guilty and received an 18-month prison term.

The piece of chocolate had to be held for the duration of the appeal period, after which came the unpleasant task of disposing of the bar.

J.B. Clover
RCMP Quarterly - Volume 36, Number 3

*   *   *   *   *

THE GAMBLING HOUSE RAID

When I was stationed in Kelowna, B.C., in the 1950s, the sergeant in charge had been on the receiving end of several tirades from local women demanding action. It seemed their husbands were losing their pay cheques in a poker game that supposedly continued every night. My role was to record licence numbers of cars frequenting the premises concerned as I went about my nightly rounds. I was also told to figure out the easiest means of entry for the time when a search would be undertaken.

After some days (or rather nights) the time, at last, had come. Several of us were called in one evening for a briefing on the roles we were to play in the coming raid. Midway through the session I was called on to outline the physical layout from my observations. I stepped forward and with chalk in hand outlined the target on the blackboard. I then emphasized that the search team must enter by the side door. I had reached this decision by the process of elimination. A small side window provided one narrow crack, not covered by the blind, where I had been able to see a portion of the room. I noted that the inside of the front door was well secured with bolts and locks. I presumed the side door was similarly barred, but to me this seemed like the best chance of entry as it was in the alley and removed from the view of passers by. I was thanked for my keen observations and the briefing continued on to the next phase.

Surprise was paramount. We were to get to the gaming table while evidence, in the form of cards and money, was still in place. Finally we were in position, lined up on either side of the door like a wedding arch while the biggest and strongest had been elected to break the door down. He stepped back a few paces for effect, then charged the door like a wild bull, to be followed by the rest of us once the door was open. He struck it shoulder first and they (he and the door) sailed into the room in one fluid motion, somewhat like a surfer riding the crest of a giant wave.

It was like a dream in slow motion. The spectators, both at the table and those of us peering through the gaping doorway, watched entranced as this large policeman slid past the card table on top of the door. When we finally recovered sufficiently to enter, not one of the players had moved even so far as to lay down either cards or cigarettes.

At this point the keen observation of which I had been proud dropped in the estimation of my superiors. Later examination of the door revealed that it had not even been locked and entry could have been effected by merely turning the handle.

Jack White

*　　*　　*　　*　　*

THE CRIME REPORT

My first detachment after completing my recruit training at Regina was Portage la Prairie, Manitoba. During our training our instructors had drilled into us that genius is an infinite capacity for taking pains and I was determined that all my investigations and subsequent reports would leave no stone unturned. My first case was a minor traffic accident and I threw myself into the investigation with meticulous attention to detail. I covered the vehicles involved, their mileage, condition of the tires, when they had the last oil change, time of day, width of road, condition of all the passengers, given names and nicknames, etc. etc. My report covered five pages.

The NCO in charge grew weary after the first page and sent it on to sub-division headquarters as it was. Several days later a terse little memo arrived stating that this constable should be instructed to make his reports more concise in future. Needless to say, I was somewhat crestfallen as it is always disturbing when you are expecting a pat on the back to receive a kick somewhat lower instead.

The next day I investigated a firearms accident where two youths playing with a rifle had accidentally fired it, wounding one of the lads. Remembering my choke-off, as a joke I typed a crime report as follows: "Two young lads took (a) a lunch (b) a rifle (c) a walk in the woods. Rifle discharged. One received a superficial injury in arm. Nice lads -- too bad. Accident. Won't happen again. Concluded here." I slipped the phony report in the In basket and awaited comments. To my surprise, the NCO, who liked a good laugh, did not mention it. I assumed he had not found it funny and had confined the report to the waste basket.

However, what had really happened was the report had got hooked on to another report by a paper clip and it was forwarded to sub-division headquarters unread.

A week or so later I escorted a prisoner to Winnipeg and I had no sooner arrived at headquarters than I was confronted by the sergeant-major. "The Officer Commanding has left instructions that you are to be paraded before him on your first trip to Winnipeg. I shall check with him to see if he wants to see you," he said.

A few minutes later he came out of the OC's office and said "The OC will see you now." In fear and trembling I was escorted in and came to a halt in front of the OC. On his desk was a report. I tried to see what it was but I was never any good at reading text upside down.

"Ah yes, Rolstone, is it?" he said and picked up the report. "Is this yours?" as he handed me the report. To my horror it was my phony report. I gulped and stuttered but no sound came out. "Rolstone," he said sternly, "brevity is the soul of wit, but let's not be too witty. You may go," and his face broke into a smile. As I tottered out I blessed Officers Commanding who had a sense of humour.

Ivan Rolstone

*   *   *   *   *

UNDERCOVER OPERATION

Just what are the qualifications an undercover man needs in order to penetrate the underworld narcotic ring in one of Canada's largest cities? The answer is personified in two members of the RCMP Drug Section who completed a highly successful undercover operation.

In October 1967, Constables Stewart Brown and Raymond Cardinal were engaged on general police work in the Vancouver area -- Constable Cardinal at Vancouver Town Station and Constable Brown at North Vancouver Detachment. The two were selected from a number of candidates as the most likely to fit the stereotypes of a hippie pot head or a pot head who has graduated to hard narcotics -- heroin. Their job was to gather information and make purchases of drugs used by the hippie element; then, when the time was considered appropriate, attempt to infiltrate the criminal element dealing in heroin.

First they had to learn the street jargon of these people: slang expressions such as "speed" (methamphetamine), "narcs" (drug squad men), "nickel or dime bags" (five or ten dollar purchases of marijuana), "stuff" or "junk" (heroin), "uptight" (frightened), "fix", "score", "hit" and so on -- it seemed endless. It really didn't take that long though, and these expressions formed a good part of their conversation.

Meanwhile, to create effect and to become more easily accepted, Brown quickly sprouted whiskers, which became a healthy beard in jig time. Cardinal's face, on the other hand, remained as smooth and hairless as a billiard ball, but his hair grew to near shoulder length.

Now was the time to enter the haunts of the hippie. Almost at once, the two were successful. On their first "buy" both were naturally anxious and a little nervous, but were pleasantly surprised to be so easily accepted by this element of society. Their close association soon earned them the nicknames "Tonto" and "The Lone Ranger" , an obvious reference to Cardinal's forebears and Brown's soft voice. It was during this period that both men witnessed a young user take speed for the first time.

Seconds after the injection into his veins, the young man ran about the room smashing at the walls with his fists, and, eyes wild with excitement, challenged everyone in sight to fight him. These excursions into the weird and drug-sodden lives of the lost brought the seriousness of their job forcibly home. They found that experience is the best teacher and later realized how inadequate words are in describing scenes they had witnessed.

Shortly after January 1, 1968, it was decided the "dynamic duo" should endeavour to purchase heroin. No change in appearance was considered necessary as a number of hippies had already graduated to hard narcotics and were frequenting the Hastings Street scene. On their first run into the dingy hotels and cafes of Vancouver's east end Cardinal met a "friend" from the other side of town -- Vancouver's West 4th Avenue -- who was quite happy to introduce the pair to people in the "know".

Cardinal's good fortune continued as he soon became the favourite of one of Vancouver's ladies of easy virtue. I say this knowing full well that his morals were never in danger, as a senior NCO 's eagle eyes were on his every move. This young lady greatly assisted entry to the "pushers' table" and within a month, every active heroin trafficker in Vancouver had sold to the undercover men.

On February 16, 1968, the two policemen were in Prince George, having just completed an undercover purchase of narcotics in that northern B.C. city. They were instructed to return to Vancouver immediately as the operation was to be concluded the following Monday morning -- two days away.

Hurried arrangements for their return to Vancouver were not entirely satisfactory as at Kamloops they were bumped from the aircraft by passengers who had previously booked seats. The kind cooperation of the Officer Commanding Kamloops Sub-Division resulted in a shuffle by highway patrol cars which facilitated their arrival in Vancouver at 9:30 that night. The long process of locating the transient hippies' whereabouts was started, and only concluded a few hours before the seven a.m., February 19 deadline.

The first arrest was made at 7:01 and the day finally ended with 48 people behind bars for offences under the Narcotic Control and Food and Drug Acts. Of the 63 cases made during this investigation only five persons remained at large, one of whom is now a resident of Europe.

In retrospect Brown and Cardinal agreed that although the hours were long and the three-month investigation cut drastically into their private lives, it was not without its amusing moments. For example, one of their long-haired friends, upon his arrest, maintained his inflated ego by stating that he knew all the time that the two were policemen. On another occasion their disguise was tested by two experienced Vancouver police officers who questioned the pair, then placed them in custody on an investigation into stolen property. The undercover men proceeded to headquarters where they requested that the arresting officers and their prisoners proceed to a private room. There, after a hilarious conversation, the suspects were released.

F.G. Kilner
RCMP Quarterly - Volume 34, Number 3

*

Editor's Note: The story doesn't end here. In the fall of 1972 I was in charge of the RCMP program celebrating the 100th anniversary of the RCMP. In order to publicize this historic event it was planned to have billboards spread across the country. A number of photographs were selected and placed on the walls of the centennial offices. I wanted to have the public relations depict an actual function of the Force so a picture of a member in uniform explaining the Canada Shipping Act to a pair of young girls by a boat on a lake in Nova Scotia was selected. The two young ladies were wearing lifejackets and the scene seemed ideal. After the decision was made to use this picture for the billboards, I received an urgent call from the Criminal Investigation Branch: the constable in the picture had been transferred out of plain clothes in Vancouver to uniform duty in Nova Scotia because a contract on his life had been made by the Vancouver drug element. I took a close look at the photograph and decided to go ahead with it, as the picture of the constable only showed his profile from the rear and it was deemed unrecognizable. The man in the photograph was none other than Constable Raymond Cardinal.

*   *   *   *   *

RURAL JUSTICE OR INJUSTICE

It was a clear, crisp, late February morning in the winter of 1940, the sun had returned to the little Arctic settlement of Norman Wells and Andy and I had just finished our breakfast. We were prepared for another quiet day at the detachment when the kitchen door opened softly, as only an Eskimo can open it. Sally came in, trying bravely to smile, with blood trickling down from under her black hair and tears on her cheeks.

My first thought on seeing Sally's face was that she had accidentally injured herself and had come to us for medical treatment, there being no doctor or nurse in the settlement. While Andy examined the injury, I said, "What happened to you, Sally?"

I was quite surprised when she replied, "Ben hit me with a snow beater and I don't want to live with him anymore," as any time I had seen Ben and Sally together they were always smiling at each other.

Sally, a 17-year-old Eskimo girl and 18-year-old Ben, -- (not their real names) -- an Eskimo working for the Hudson's Bay Company, had been married in the native custom the previous summer.

The injury was the priority here. The snow beater, a fairly smooth bone instrument used for beating snow from fur clothing on entering a house, had left more of a bruise than a cut. After clipping some hair around the wound we readily got the bleeding stopped and applied what we thought was quite a professional dressing.

This was an assault case, normally a simple investigation and court procedure. If Sally did not wish to live with Ben, this would be of no concern to the police; a social worker could attend to that. Andy and I talked the case over. This was not the "outside" and there were no social workers and no magistrates. In other words, this wasn't a routine case. The usual judicial procedure would require a special police aircraft flight to Yellowknife or Aklavik to take one of us, and Sally and Ben, to the nearest magistrate. Ben would probably plead guilty, a fine would be imposed which he couldn't afford to pay and he would be imprisoned in a territorial jail at Aklavik or Fort Smith. He would return to the settlement and the social problem would still not be solved.

This was a small settlement at this time of the year. There was the Hudson's Bay manager and his clerk, two RCMP constables, the native special constable and his wife, an Eskimo widow, Patoolik, and her three children and Sally and Ben, a total of 12.

Sally's parents lived at Coppermine, some 200 miles distant, and Ben's adoptive parents were at least two days away by dog team at their hunting camp. Most of the native people were out of the settlement hunting or trapping in the winter.

The more Andy and I discussed the case, the more normal procedures did not seem to be the proper road to social justice. I thought of my oath of allegiance to uphold the law, and of the motto of the RCMP -- Maintain the Right -- but was the strict enforcement of the law in this instance really maintaining the right? I was in charge of the police detachment, and I had to make a decision and have an alternative plan in mind before talking to Ben.

I talked to the widow Patoolik and she agreed that Sally could live with her for a while if I would provide some extra food. I then went over to the Hudson's Bay and talked to Ben. He readily admitted striking Sally because he didn't think she worked hard enough in the home and talked too much about wanting to go back to her people. I sensed, from talking with Ben, that although they had both attended the mission school in Aklavik, Sally thought herself too well educated to do all of the menial tasks expected of an Eskimo wife. I then told him that I thought his behaviour showed that he did not deserve to have a wife, and as Sally did not wish to live with him, we would help her to live with widow Patoolik, at least until Ben's parents came into the settlement at Easter time. To this, Ben smilingly agreed.

After a few days, widow Patoolik came to me and said she didn't want Sally living with her any more as she had stolen some of her sewing beads. I was now faced with a theft case. What to do? Widow Patoolik was not anxious to lay a charge against Sally but she didn't want the girl living in her home and was insistent that Sally be moved immediately.

The police special and his wife were the only other native family living in the settlement, so I asked David if Sally could live with them. David probably felt he had no choice in the matter and he agreed that Sally could live with them if I provided additional food and she did not steal. I then told Sally what arrangements had been made, but I must admit that I felt like I was telling her she was being made a prisoner. Over the next few weeks, Ben visited Sally at David's house and I was kept informed about their relationship.

Some five or six weeks later, at Easter time, Ben's parents returned to the settlement and found out what had taken place. I had a talk with Ben's father about the action we had taken and he was pleased with what we had done. Ben's parents were quite in agreement that Ben and Sally could now once again become husband and wife. I talked to Sally and she was quite happy to return to Ben, so the young couple was re-united. I reported my actions in detail to the sub-division office and the entire matter was concluded in one report.

A policeman today would not dare to take such action; he would be accused of setting himself up as judge, and aiding and abetting a wife to leave her husband. There is no doubt this criticism is justified and would have also have been justified then.

The question is, should I have taken such action or should I have carried out the letter of the law instead? The year after I left that settlement, I received a Christmas card from Sally and Ben, saying they now had a baby girl and they were both quite happy. This message to me was my answer that, in fact, I had maintained the right in enforcing what was commonly known as "Rural Justice."

Dick Mead

* * * * *

DON'T BE FOOLED BY APPEARANCES

On October 9, 1968, an elderly resident of Oak Lake, Manitoba, walked into the RCMP detachment at Virden and casually stated that someone had stolen $8,000 from him.

The statement made the general office noise come to an abrupt halt. Everyone looked up at the complainant and then at each other. I am sure that had it not been for the serious look on the old man's face, they would have had difficulty suppressing a snicker. The elderly gentleman looked as if he had never possessed a total of $8,000 in his entire life, let alone at one time.

The complainant, a man of 79, dressed in worn, old farm clothes, unshaven and dirty, certainly didn't appear to possess anything, which tended to cast some doubt on the validity of the complaint. This was, however, an understatement compared with what was found when his house was examined.

Situated south of Oak Lake on the corner of a quarter section, the house looked as if it was about to give up the ghost after one more hard prairie winter. Here the old man lived alone and kept about 50 head of cattle. The building was unpainted and consisted of three rooms, only one of which was in use. That was the kitchen where he slept, ate and supposedly kept $8,000 in a cardboard box under the sink.

Police questioned the old man extensively regarding visitors, relatives or anyone who had been near his house or had even talked about money. All they learned was that he was practically a hermit. The only thing outstanding about the theft was that the money was supposed to be made up of King George VI bills, issued before 1953. He was not sure of exactly how much there was, but stated that $8,000 would be the maximum.

All preliminary investigation was fruitless. There was no physical evidence and the only thing that could be established was that the money was probably taken between two and four p.m. on Sunday, October 8, while he was away. In the hope that the culprit might attempt to cash some of the old money, the theft was published in all division bulletins.

Even though the matter was being investigated, the police still had in the back of their minds that they might be looking for something that did not exist, and that probably after considerable work it would all go in the book as another unfounded complaint.

After three days of investigation, a list of possible suspects was compiled. Number four on this list was K....., an 18-year-old man from Oak Lake. K..... was relegated to fourth position, not only because he had no previous record, but because he was thought to have been out of town at the time of the theft.

On October 15, information was received from a local resident that K..... might have been in Oak Lake during the previous weekend and it was finally established that he had been seen around town at the time of the theft. His mother expected him home for his sister's wedding on October 17.

On the day of the wedding no one could be found at the K...... residence and it was not until October 30 that someone did return. It turned out that the wedding had been held out of town after a last-minute change of plans. K.....'s mother had mentioned to her son that the police would be looking for him, and on hearing this he told her he would not be home for a while. She had no idea where he was but thought he might have gone to Winnipeg. Suddenly K..... was not suspect number four!

The following day, October 31, was Halloween -- a night of trick or treat. For treats the following message was received from Nanaimo RCMP Detachment in B.C.:

"Subject K..... opened bank account this point with $500 King George VI money on October 22nd, 1968. Do you request further inquiries this point?"

Virden RCMP had a brief telephone conversation with the NCO in charge of Nanaimo Detachment, and two policemen were detailed to locate K..... and if necessary, obtain a search warrant for his hotel room. Constables P. Sabo and W. Ingenthron located him almost immediately and after returning to his hotel room he readily admitted the offence and turned over the money. Upon receiving it and before they had a chance to count it, police asked K..... how much money was left. He replied, "Oh, about 13."

"You sure must have a good time. We're looking for nearly $8,000," said police.

K..... looked up and replied, "Thirteen thousand, not 1,300."

Within an hour Virden RCMP received a telephone call advising that the investigation was completed and the exact amount recovered totalled $13,305. It was later learned that K..... had taken nearly $14,000 from the old man, who just didn't know how much he had. All that remained was to tell him of the recovery.

On December 11, 1968, K..... appeared in magistrate's court in Virden and pleaded guilty to theft over $50. He was sentenced to one year in the Brandon Correctional Institute.

The doubt in the beginning that the complainant had $8,000 was nothing compared to the shock police received when they returned his money on January 28, 1969. He had a bank account of over $10,000 and a great many more investments. A constable told him that he should take his money and go to Florida for the winter.

"You know, I once owned 20 acres of land in Florida, a place called Palm Beach," he said. "I let it go for taxes about 20 years ago because I didn't think it was worth anything."

J.D. Van Wart
RCMP Quarterly - Volume 35, Number 2

* * * * *

Chapter Three

Going to Court

A SUMMARY CONVICTION CASE ON
NEW BRUNSWICK'S NORTH SHORE

Many of our investigations on the north shore involved the apprehension of bootleggers. This case was in Newcastle in the 1950s. On summary conviction cases we prosecuted our own cases. It was not the normal procedure to send seized liquor that had originated in a liquor store to the lab for testing. Rather, the prosecutor took a sip from the seized bottle and advised the presiding magistrate of the nature of the liquor. This particular case was before Magistrate John Morrissey, a man of Irish descent with a good sense of humour. Apart from myself as prosecutor, the only other persons in the court room were the accused and his lawyer. Due to the passage of time the name of the defence lawyer escapes me, but I do recall that he was an excellent counsel for the defence, with many acquittals to his credit. The trial went something like this:

Prosecutor: "I would like to take the stand, Your Honour, to identify Exhibit Number 1 which I seized from the defendant present here in court."

Magistrate: "You may proceed."

Prosecutor: "I will open this pint of liquor which has Lamb's Navy Rum on the label and sample the contents." (Prosecutor opens bottle and takes a sip.) "In my opinion this bottle contains rum."

Magistrate: "Your testimony is duly recorded, sergeant. I think it is necessary for the presiding magistrate to sample the contents of Exhibit Number 1 to corroborate that the contents are indeed rum." (Takes bottle and takes a very healthy drink, leaving about half a pint remaining in the bottle.) "Yes, sergeant, I agree with you. This is indeed rum."

Defence Counsel: "I think that in the interests of defending the accused, defence counsel should also sample Exhibit Number 1."

Magistrate: "That is in order." (Hands bottle to defence counsel.)

Defence Counsel: (Opens bottle and completely drains the contents.) "Your Honour, I have in my hand a bottle identified as Exhibit Number 1 with a label on it which states Lamb's Rum. However the bottle appears to be empty. I would request the defendant be acquitted for lack of evidence."

Magistrate Morrissey thought this was very funny and laughed uproariously at the clever manoeuvre of defence counsel. Fortunately for me he denied the request and found the defendant guilty as charged.

Donovan Saul

* * * * *

RIGHT CASE -- WRONG COURT

The City of Lloydminster is located squarely on the 110th meridian which constitutes the boundary between Alberta and Saskatchewan. The actual "line" runs along the inside of the sidewalk on the west side of Main Street, so on the sidewalk, one is in Saskatchewan but inside a store, one is in Alberta.

The province of Saskatchewan provided the detachment from which the RCMP police that section of Saskatchewan and also a corresponding area on the Alberta side. Policing the two provinces was a constant problem and whatever situation arose, the first question was: "Where is it, Saskatchewan or Alberta?" The answer would then dictate the manner in which the investigation would be carried out, because each province, being governed by its own provincial statutes, required different policy and direction.

In the matter of court cases, we had a court room on each side of the street (border) -- one above the local post office in Saskatchewan and the other above the Bank of Nova Scotia in Alberta. Court would be conducted on one side, then the magistrate -- who was a magistrate on the Alberta side but only a justice of the peace on the Saskatchewan side -- would move across the street to hear Alberta cases. In those days the RCMP would act as prosecutor in many cases and this responsibility fell upon the senior constable or NCO.

On one occasion in the Saskatchewan court room, I had successfully prosecuted an individual on a charge of theft and His Worship passed sentence of "30 days in Fort Saskatchewan Gaol." (Fort Saskatchewan is a penal institute in Alberta, just outside Edmonton.) "Fort Saskatchewan Gaol?" I questioned myself. "How come not Prince Albert (the Saskatchewan counterpart)?" were my puzzled thoughts, but fortunately I did not say anything until the prisoner was led away.

All of a sudden I realized the mistake was mine -- that I had brought an Alberta criminal case before a Saskatchewan court! I immediately said to His Worship, "I just woke up to the fact that I brought this case to the wrong court."

He calmly said, "Yes, I know, but I didn't realize it either until I began to consider sentence and I had no alternative but to sentence him to the fort."

"What are we going to do about it now?" I asked, feeling a little better now that I could share the responsibility for this faux pas.

"Nothing," he said. "No one will know the difference."

"Yes, but if this guy appeals, we're in the soup," was my concern.

"Well, we'll cross that bridge if and when we get to it" was his final remark. There was no appeal and no one knew the difference.

P.M. Holmes

*   *   *   *   *

THE PENALTY HARDLY MATCHED THE CRIME

In Saskatchewan in the early 1940s many of the minor prosecutions in rural areas were dispensed by justices of the peace who were appointed from local residents such as municipal clerks, reeves, farmers, etc. The appointees rarely had any legal training. Until the 1950s, two justices of the peace acting together had the power of a magistrate and could handle criminal code summary conviction cases. The majority of these cases were prosecuted by a member of the Force.

This particular incident concerned a Swede whom we shall call Ole. When he was under the influence of alcohol, Ole had the bad habit of roughing up his wife. He had been brought before one particular J.P. many times with penalties increasing from admonitions to fines, and one short term of a few days incarceration. About the nth time, the prosecuting constable, in his submission regarding a suitable penalty for the crime, pointed out the failure of past penalties and suggested it was time for a more severe sentence.

The J.P. took this very seriously. The constable related afterwards that the J.P.'s face turned white as he ordered the accused to stand. "Ole," he said in a most foreboding voice, "I sentence you to death."

It was debatable who was more surprised, Ole or the constable. However, after a brief adjournment, the penalty was reduced to 30 days at hard labour in the Prince Albert gaol.

P.A. Anderson

*   *   *   *   *

LEGAL LESSONS

In the early 1950s Prince Rupert, B.C., was a busy, brawling settlement, popular as a destination of hard-working fishermen, loggers and millworkers, all in search of diversion. It was also a difficult area to police, and the courts were extremely busy.

Competition was strong amongst the local legal fraternity to participate in this lucrative court-room work and "grandstanding" was common. One barrister was particularly offensive in his disregard of the accused, the police and his fellow solicitors, while attempting to impress the spectators, all of whom he regarded as potential clients. This stalwart was prosecuting one busy Monday morning and in full flight, with arms waving and demands escalating, when the court liaison officer decided it was time he learned a lesson.

A new case was called and the barrister commenced a loud and ponderously impressive diatribe about the accused, a regular offender, while waving the thick prosecution file threateningly. He finally paused dramatically, then decided to open the folder and determine the facts of the case. With a grandiose flourish he pulled out a comic book and an assortment of "nudie" centrefolds tumbled forth. The laughter rolling through the court room was a humbling experience.

R.W. Morley[1]

[1]Author's Note: This was an ongoing method of chastening the inflated egos of some of the legal fraternity in the Prince Rupert of the 1950s.

*   *   *   *   *

QUIET IN COURT

In a crowded court room at Dalhousie, N.B., the magistrate was having difficulty communicating with the accused, a deaf-mute who could neither read nor write. As he struggled in vain to make himself understood, the magistrate was about to give up when a young RCMP constable, in court on another matter, stepped before the bench, and, without further ado, began conversing with the defendant in sign language.

The constable later explained to a grateful magistrate that he had learned the sign language from a deaf-mute prior to joining the RCMP.

Anonymous
RCMP Quarterly - Volume 30, Number 2

*   *   *   *   *

GOING TO COURT

The following story is based on notes relating to a Court of the King's Bench case heard many years ago. It is difficult to convey in a written transcript the tone and manner in which the questions were put and the answers given. Suffice it to say that the basic feeling between defence counsel and the witness, Corporal (later Deputy Commisioner) C.R. Eves was one of good-natured contention.

Question: Mr. M. (counsel for the defence): "How old are you, witness?"
Answer: Corporal Eves: "Twenty-eight years old, sir."
Mr.M.: "A mere boy! A mere boy!"
Corporal Eves: "Thank you, sir."
Question: "So you are a handwriting expert?"
Answer: "My evidence has been accepted as expert evidence on previous occasions."
Question: "But you are an expert, aren't you?"
Answer: "That isn't for me to decide, Mr. M. It is for the judge whether or not I may be qualified as an expert."
His Lordship, Chief Justice R.: "The witness is correct."

Mr. M. then proceeded to cross-examine the witness on handwriting features illustrated on the chart and explained during the examination-in-chief. Mr. M. pointed out difference upon difference.

The witness, in reply, explained them as natural variations of the same writer and gave his reasons for this opinion.

Two brothers had been charged separately with the forging and uttering of cheques. It was the Crown's contention that N.G. had forged some and uttered others, and that D.G., his brother, had done likewise. Consequently, in the hearing of each case, the handwriting of both N. and D.G. was entered as exhibits. The writings of the two brothers bore some resemblance to one another, but were readily distinguishable by the witness.

At one stage during the discussion of "differences" referred to, Mr. M. walked over to the desk of the clerk of the court and picked up what he apparently believed to be the writings of N.G. His surprise was obvious as he viewed these specimens; spreading out all the slips containing the specimen signatures in a fan-shaped fashion, he confronted the witness.

Question: "Look, witness. Look at these "R's" in these specimen signatures. There isn't one "R" which is similar to the one illustrated on your chart. How do you account for that, witness?"

Answer: "You are quite right, Mr. M. They were written by different persons."

The questions and answers then continued concerning additional differences. Finally a member of the jury, a young farm hand who, judging by his somewhat retiring appearance, would not be expected to speak on such an occasion, rose and addressed the Bench.

Juror: "My Lord. May I ask a question?"

His Lordship: "Well, I don't think I can give you permission to ask a question right now, but Mr. M. is conducting the cross-examination and I'm sure he will consider your request."

Mr.M.: "Sure, lad, sure. Go ahead. Ask your question."

Juror: "Mr. M, have you ever made a special study of handwriting?"

Mr.M.: "No, I haven't."

Juror: "Mr. M, do you claim to be a handwriting expert?"

Mr.M.: "No, I don't."

Juror: "Then why do you stand there and argue with Corporal Eves who has worked on handwriting for more than 2 1/2 years and you admit that you are not an expert?"

Mr.M.: "Have you finished asking me questions?"

Juror: "Yes."

Mr.M.: "May I ask you a question now?"

Juror: "Sure, go ahead."

Mr.M.: "Have you already made up your mind on this case?"

At this point the thought of a retrial based on the juror's premature decision prior to submission of all the evidence must have loomed large in the minds of members of the bar and the justice. The juror's response, however, came promptly and honestly.

Juror: "No, I haven't. But I'm sure trying hard to!"

Years ago the firearms and tool identification technician in the Ottawa Crime Detection Laboratory examined and compared tool marks on the lock fittings of a then recently burglarized Toronto pharmacy with the signature of a screw driver found in the possession of an arrested suspect. There was no doubt that the tool submitted was the one used to break into and enter the premises. In due course the case came to trial and the laboratory technician was subpoenaed.

En route to the railroad station -- in those days, in centre town, opposite the Chateau Laurier -- he dropped in at the National Research Council library and made certain he was up-to-date on the world population estimate. An unusual and certainly infrequent pre-trial quest. Why immediately prior to this particular trial? Extra-sensory perception? The law of probability is frequently considered in firearms and tool-mark identification cases in relation to the population figure.

Evidence for the Crown was brief and to the point and cross-examination by the defence was shorter than expected.

Question: Mr.K. (defence): "How many screwdrivers are there in the world?"

Answer: RCMP technician: "I have no idea."

Question: "Well! Then what is the world population?"

Answer: "Two billion, one hundred and sixty-nine million, eight hundred and seventy-three thousand, or thereabouts."

The defence attorney stood still for a moment, then he looked at the judge.

His Lordship: "Don't look at me, Mr.K.! You asked the question."

Defence Attorney: "No further questions!"

Expert testimony can often cause confusion and consternation in jurors and court officials alike. I recall a case many years ago that stunned a court with a sample of technical verbiage.

Counsel: "Doctor, in language as nearly popular as the subject will permit, will you please tell the jury just what was the cause of the man's death."

Witness: "Do you mean the proxima causa mortis?"

Counsel: "I don't know, doctor. I will have to leave that up to you."

Witness: "Well, in plain language, he died of an oedema of the brain that followed a cerebral thrombosis or possibly an embolism that followed, in turn, an arteriosclerosis combined with the effect of gangrenous cholecystitis."

A Juror: "Well, I'll be damned!"

Judge: "Ordinarily, I would fine a juror for saying anything like that in court. But I cannot in this instance justly impose a penalty upon you, sir, because the court was thinking exactly the same thing!"

J.A. Churchman
RCMP Quarterly - Volume 46, Number 4

*   *   *   *   *

SUMMARY CONVICTIONS

On one occasion during the 1930s on patrol, I came upon a farmer who was operating a vehicle which did not comply in several instances with the requirements of the Vehicle Act. I decided to charge him with the lesser of several possible offences. He indicated that as this was a busy time of the year for him he would like the case disposed of as expeditiously as possible. The local justice of the peace, a farmer, lived nearby but was not at home. We found him on a mower cutting hay. While he sat on the mower, I made out the information and complaint, swore to its truthfulness and opened court in the usual manner. Two horses were the only witnesses to the proceedings. The people involved were the J.P., myself and the accused.

He entered a plea of guilty and was fined two dollars and costs ($2.50 for the J.P.) and given 30 days to pay the fine and costs. While this procedure was pretty informal it saved a lot of time for all those involved and still justice was done.

I.C. Shank

*   *   *   *   *

RURAL JUSTICE

This incident happened in 1954 in a small town near McLennan, Alberta. The town policeman there was an amiable type, but not a young man. As he was walking down the main street one day, he observed a light truck that was stopped, double parked, while the driver was engaged in conversation with another man. The policeman walked over and asked the driver to move his truck as all traffic on the main street had to drive around him, creating something of a hazard. The trucker said he would, but seemed in no hurry.

About 20 minutes later the truck was still there when the policeman came back along the street. By this time his patience was being tried as vehicles were still detouring around the parked truck. He told the driver to move it at once. The trucker took exception to this, and jumping out of his cab he told the policeman he would move his truck when he was good and ready. Then, just as the policeman turned away, the trucker gave him a kick in his nether end.

With this turn of events, the policeman decided to get some help, so he returned to his small office and phoned the RCMP detachment at McLennan. Two members responded immediately, arrested the driver and formally charged him with assaulting a peace officer.

For want of a more suitable place, court was held in the McLennan Detachment office. The following day the magistrate from High Prairie came to hold court. The magistrate read the charge to the accused, and asked him how he pleaded. "Guilty," was the reply. The magistrate then chastised him, explaining that nobody had the right to assault a peace officer in the performance of his duty.

"Just cut the lecture," said the accused, pulling out his purse. "I pleaded guilty, so just tell me how much it is."

"Thirty days," said the magistrate. "See if you have that in your purse."

There was a complete silence as the six-foot-six member of the Force plucked the trucker up by the collar and gingerly escorted him into the cell in the office, clanging the door shut.

Anonymous

*   *   *   *   *

JUSTICE -- "G" DIVISION STYLE

Fort Smith is only one mile from the Northwest Territories -Alberta border. This detachment also policed Fort Fitzgerald, Alberta, which was 14 miles south in "K" Division. Fort Fitzgerald had no access to a legal liquor vendor and liquor was supplied courtesy of Jack Piche, a bootlegger who moonlighted by driving taxi for the Fort Smith Taxi Company.

One night in 1958 while on a routine night patrol to Fort Fitzgerald I encountered Piche in his taxi with an open case of beer. The box, of course, had NWT liquor-vendor markings. I charged Jack under a section of the Excise Act which prohibited transporting liquor across provincial boundaries.

Court was called to order by Sergeant R.R. Johnson, of the Fort Smith Detachment. There were only three other persons present: Inspector J.S. Craig, officer commanding the sub-division who was the local magistrate, Constable D.G. Hawker and the accused, Jack Piche. He entered a plea of guilty and was assessed the minimum fine of $400.

This might sound common place, as all of us experienced similar situations hundreds of times in our careers. The major difference about this particular case was that the trial was held in the Fort Smith Detachment police car, two miles south of the NWT - Alberta border on the Fort Smith - Fort Fitzgerald road: precisely the same spot Piche was picked up.

Dave Hawker

*   *   *   *   *

Chapter Four

Wives and Families

I, JOYCE, TAKE THEE, RCMP....

Generally a bride makes a vow to love, honour and (sometimes) obey her husband. But an RCMP bride does not realize that there is also an unspoken vow included: that is, to obey the RCMP, till death, pension or purchase do you part.

As an RCMP bride of five years, I feel I am well qualified to pass on to the newcomers -- and those who are thinking of joining the ranks -- a few tips I have acquired during the years. In the process of surviving such major calamities as surprise inspections, royal visits, Supreme Court appearances and weddings, I have discovered a few good rules of thumb.

Firstly, give your husband a place all to himself for his uniforms and equipment, and ensure that it is completely safeguarded from marauding cats, children and cleaning women. Nothing is more frustrating than to have him blame you because he can't find his braces, part of his Sam Browne belt or his dress spurs; especially when the only reason he can't locate them is that he needs them immediately and this automatically induces a state of semi-shock in which he is quite capable of tripping over what he is looking for without even seeing it.

Secondly, never offer to polish any of his equipment. If you do, the next thing you know it will be the eve of a royal visit, and instead of telling you what a beautiful bride you are, he will tell you what a beautiful polisher you are, and would you mind doing his stetson hatband after you finish the boots, because he could never get that good a shine. My rebuttal to this crude form of flattery is that if his poor standards of polishing managed to pass the probing eyes of inspecting officers during training, then with a little effort he should be able to get spruced up for a royal visit -- all by his lonesome.

Another sound idea is to come equipped with tailor's wax and heavy duty thread, the thickness of binder twine. Seldom-worn red serge uniforms always seem to require emergency treatment at the very last minute. For example, all the buttons must be changed for the plated non-polish variety, and here your prowess as a taker-off and sewer-on comes to the fore. I was on my umpteenth button before I saw the light and bought a needle with an eye big enough for the proverbial camel and also for eight strands of thread with which I sewed the button on in two rounds (buffalo right side up, too!).

Then comes the time for your first transfer. The practical side of you finally overcomes the sentimental as you regretfully dispose of all the menus, matchbook covers and paper napkins, brought home after romantic evenings out with your gallant spouse, and consign them to the trash can with all the other painfully acquired bric-a-brac which is just not worth packing and unpacking again in your new home. Nerves will fray and tears cloud the vision of any house-proud bride who watches moving men throwing the best crystal china dishes (a present from hubby's rich Aunt Jane) into a barrel, and bumping the piano from wall to wall in the stairway. There is only one way to cope with moving men and retain your sanity; that is -- leave. What the eye doesn't see, the heart doesn't grieve over, and this is an excellent time for that last cup of coffee with a favourite girl friend, and a silent prayer that your furniture will arrive at its destination in a condition to be used for something besides kindling.

Inevitably, at some time or other, you are going to be separated from your husband while he is on a course, away relieving somewhere, or detailed to some special duty. The last time mine went, I planned to be so brave. I drove him to the station and made the usual parting remarks: "It's only for six weeks -- no long-distance calls. We can't afford them," and "I'll meet you at the station when you get back." At this point, despite my good intentions, I was choked up and blinded with tears, so I pushed him out of the car and took off. I hadn't moved the car ten feet before it stalled. When it came to life again, I drove through a puddle and succeeded in splashing several innocent bystanders and nearly ran down another, until I finally made it home in one piece.

After two weeks of regular mealtimes and no late-night calls, I started to count and recount my monetary assets. Yes -- if mother would keep the baby and I took an upper berth and did not tip anyone, I could just make it to Montreal, where I could stay with friends and be within striking distance of Ottawa. So off I went, and after a glorious weekend returned home, savings all gone, but content with the knowledge that the remaining time would pass that much more quickly. It was hard to convince the landlord and creditors that the trip was a necessity, but I managed.

There are times when the Force to which you are wedded through your husband can be a most unreasonable bridegroom, and it is a bitter pill to swallow when you realize that you do not come first. Never will I forget the day when I came off duty at the local hospital. It was miserable, with freezing rain and high winds. The car wouldn't start, so I phoned my husband. An hour later he arrived. He tinkered for a few minutes and then announced that he couldn't get it going. He started to leave. I chased after him and asked for a drive home. "Sorry, but you aren't allowed in the police car." When I eventually staggered home, freezing and half drowned, I found him warm and dry, reading the paper and waiting for his supper. For days I was inconsolable but I think I have finally come up with the answer should the situation ever arise again. Next time I am going to pound him right there in the parking lot, and he will have to arrest me for assaulting a peace officer. That way I will be assured of a ride in the police car, and it will be well worth the cost of a fine, which he will have to pay anyway.

Every once in a while it pays to stop and take stock, and when you do, you have to admit that there are many advantages in your marriage to the Force. Among them are a nice home, a husband who loves his work, a chance to travel and make life-long friendships, and a membership in that widespread group of RCMP wives, who, like me, took on a second husband in the person of the RCMP when they made their marriage vows. A frustrating, illogical and selfish husband, yes, but one of which any girl can be proud, and with whom she can learn to live happily if she will just learn some of these basic rules.

Joyce Crosse

* * * * *

THE PLEASURE OF YOUR COMPANY

The year 1953 found us stationed at Morse, Saskatchewan, and as New Year's neared, we determined to make the holiday as memorable as possible. We would entertain at the detachment with a dinner party for six -- Gray, the young constable then stationed with us, Pat, his fiancee who was a nurse in Swift Current, Molly and Jock, an English couple we'd just recently met and, of course, ourselves.

This time, the inevitable phone call came in the afternoon. A woman had gone berserk in Hodgeville, a small town some 20 miles away. With the police car temporarily out of commission, Andy and Gray would have to take ours. Pat was asked to accompany them, doing double duty as police matron and nurse should the services of the latter prove necessary. That left Molly, Jock and me to smile our way bravely through what seemed like endless hours of three-handed cribbage.

It was a tremendous relief to finally hear the car door slam outside. Andy, when he joined us, was alone. Gray and Pat were at the hotel where it had seemed best to incarcerate the mental patient. She had proven to be violent, even kicking the rear window out of our car on the way into town.

Some time later, Gray phoned to say that he and Pat wanted to slip out for a bite to eat. Could someone go down to relieve them? He assured us the patient had become quite docile and would cause no trouble. It took a little persuasion, but since I was busy looking after the turkey, Molly reluctantly agreed to go with Andy.

When they arrived on the scene, the patient took one look at her new custodian and decided unreasonably that she wasn't going to let Molly come anywhere near her. She had used the receptacle under the bed and promptly threw it at Molly, narrowly missing her face but most thoroughly soiling the lovely black velvet dress which she had worn to grace our New Year's festivities.

The patient had by now become so violent that restraining her seemed to be the only way of handling her at all. Molly described the scene to us later. "There was Andy trying to hold the woman down while slipping and sliding in the mess on the floor, managing only to thoroughly tangle himself up in the sheets." Eventually, after most of the bedding had been destroyed and the towel bar had been pulled off the wall, the patient was wrestled into a strait jacket and lay on the bed cursing Molly roundly, saying anything to her which was foul and abusive.

In due course, Gray and Pat returned, thus relieving my dinner guest of her duties as the reluctant custodian. She made a flying entry into our house, face scarlet, shaking all over and very near to tears. Her first words were to her husband: "Pour me a drink, Jock, make it a double and don't spoil it with mix."

So much for my well-planned dinner party. Two guests had eaten at the Chinese restaurant downtown and were, even now, babysitting a mental case. One guest was too upset to eat and her beautiful dress had been most distastefully ruined. The fourth, with a near-hysterical wife on his hands was, quite understandably, more than a little annoyed. And Andy and I? Well, let's just say that no one, that year, enjoyed my New Year's dinner.

Angela Anderson

*   *   *   *   *

I THEE WED, RCMP

Over the years of being married to a Mountie, I feel the wedding service should have a phrase like this title along with the traditional vows. Then it might be easier to understand what a young bride is letting herself in for.

The circumstances vary greatly, depending upon whether you are stationed at a large or a small detachment, but it is not long after the glitter of a red serge wedding that the minor crises develop, like cooking all day for your first special dinner with friends only to hear on the radio or by phone -- if at all -- that He won't make it home in time, due to something that just came up. You survive this, of course, as the food is eaten and you play the part of the host and hostess, remaining outwardly calm although you are ready to resort to mayhem.

As in most occupations, the days off are something to look forward to in order to get away from the regular routine, and something is usually planned. However, these plans cannot go ahead until He makes a quick trip to the office to see if everything is all right, although He was just there 12 hours ago.

Then there are big plans to attend the annual ball or other social event, complete with a new dress and hairdo, a reliable baby sitter on order and all going smoothly, until rudely interrupted by a phone call. Away He goes, leaving you with the promise that "Next year we are definitely going to the ball."

There are times when you are called upon to act as matron -- usually the midnight-to-eight shift as they couldn't find anyone else. It doesn't matter if you have already been up for 16 hours. To work you go, battling to stay awake to watch over someone who is sleeping peacefully and couldn't care less if you were there. However, the extra money looks good in the form of a new dress or whatever.

Living in quarters has its compensations, but being awakened on Sunday morning early with the words "Eight extra for breakfast," followed by His departure on a call, is not one of them.

The time when you were awaiting the arrival of the stork, secure in the knowledge that hubby was handy even when the hospital was 30 miles away, only to find that He was also 30 miles away -- but in the opposite direction -- did little at panic time to convince you that motherhood was all it was cracked up to be. However, the neighbours came to the rescue and all was well.

If you are originally from a small town, the thought of being posted to another doesn't really throw you, but how small is small? Things like a bank, hospital, doctor or even a sidewalk that you always took for granted are just not there. Going into housing built when the railway went through, already occupied by spiders and other pests, with snakes in the crawl space, is not what you imagined as that "little white cottage with a picket fence." However, no one got bitten by a snake or even chewed a little bit, although it was comforting to know the serum was kept in the fridge should it happen.

When you marry into the Force you expect to see many parts of the country; then you find parts you never knew existed and sometimes wonder why they do. As time passes and you get to know the people, you find good friends you remember for years to come. Finally, just as you are getting settled in and know many in the community, in He comes with "Guess where we have been transferred to?" and here we go again. There'll be more dents in the furniture for which they sometimes reimburse you, but how can you keep food cold when the fridge door is out being repaired? You just know the drapes will not fit and wonder if one of the pairs downstairs in the trunk can be altered to fit the new windows. However, you can always look back and say, "Yes, we got that dent or that scratch on our second move."

These are just a few -- to say the least -- of the reasons that that one little extra vow, "I thee wed, RCMP" should be included in the marriage service. In most cases the good outweighs the bad and I can't help but wonder how many of us would change it if we had the chance to do it all over again.

This is not a criticism -- these are the facts!

Anne Stevens

* * * * *

MEMORIES OF THE 2/I/C

I always believed the term "one-man detachment" was a misnomer. In truth, neither the Force nor that one man would have survived had it not been for the presence of the detachment wife. My life on one-man detachments was not unlike that of my contemporaries.

I too married a Mountie who was going to take me out of the city with all its amenities into a world of new challenge and adventure. Like hell! Our house was one of the oldest and largest in that Saskatchewan town of 450 souls (Hanley). There was no real estate salesman to tell me that the kitchen and bathroom taps were missing because the house lacked running water. Nor was he there to show me that of the four upstairs bedrooms, two had closets but no electrical outlets while the converse was true in the other two. One had the choice of sleeping where clothes could be hung or in a room which had the luxury of a bedside lamp. I also did not know beforehand that the police office was in the sitting room. What a shock to see the freshly laundered diapers hanging in the dug-out basement after the oil furnace backfired. But what really bugged my husband was the fact that the Force leased these quarters for $50 per month and charged us $60.

Of course the "utilities" were thrown in. If I learned two or three basics, sanity could be retained. One -- always take a long drink of water as soon as it was delivered since the second day, removing the scum was distasteful. Two -- always check the slop pail before dumping the dish water. Even my husband got the hang of this after that first experience with wet feet. Three -- always take the "honey pail" out after dark to avoid embarrassment. Four -- during the winter, try not to leave dirty diapers in the pail overnight. Frozen diapers can be discouraging.

"What" you ask, "was the house cold?" In February of that first year the temperature hung in at -20 degrees Fahrenheit for a solid month. Our eldest was almost a year and the youngest two months. When the west wind blew our bed away from the wall I knew it was time to move downstairs into the fifth bedroom. An RCMP grey blanket (you know the kind) was tacked over the window, and while it was pretty dark, at least we survived the winter.

Oh yes, my husband was away on course that March. About the 15th of the month we were nearly out of oil. I called the dealer who informed me that our supply for the fiscal year was expended and he could not deliver without a requisition. What do I do now? A panic call to the Interior Economy Branch found a sympathetic clerk who took steps to ensure we three would not die of exposure.

By now, you know this complaining was done with tongue in cheek. I have many fond memories of detachment life. I joined all the other wives who were kept barefoot and pregnant. Four in rapid succession. I can easily burst out laughing when reflecting on bath night. There I am, sitting in the kitchen with buttocks in one laundry tub and feet in the twin.

I mustn't forget the two runaway girls whom I was detailed to "guard". That was late summer and I was seven months pregnant with the third. As I took the two to the outhouse my husband, in a very stern voice, cautioned the girls not to try anything funny since "she" (the guard) "had dealt with tougher ones than you." In my condition, it was difficult to catch our two-year old. Once again, I restrained laughter.

The next spring our spirits were lifted considerably for we were moving into a brand new Type Three police-owned building. How ironic that no sooner had we occupied the quarters than the water well ceased to function. Now, not only did we not have water in that lovely ceramic toilet, but we didn't have an outhouse either. As always, the neighbours "opened their door".

One day I turned around to find a man standing in the kitchen. He said the front door was locked. I suggested he go around and try it again. As he knocked on the office door, I answered, and asked if I could be of help. A somewhat bewildered man quickly said, "No, no -- I'm looking for the policeman." I offered to assist but he said he would come back.

It was about the same time when I locked myself out on a very cold day. The kids were sleeping and my husband was on patrol. I hastily sought help from a neighbouring bachelor. Well, word quickly spread throughout the town -- the policeman's wife was seen wearing the gentleman's sweater as he climbed through her basement window!

On one occasion, a very junior constable was sent to relieve while my husband was away (on course again). An excited call from across the lane took me to the back yard where the young constable was standing, revolver on hip, while a prisoner was washing the police car. I told him my husband did not do that.

In the absence of our husbands, we wives answered the door and the police radio. We filed gazette index cards, checked a farmer's brakes, cooked prisoners' meals, acted as matron and found time to raise a family. How foolish of a senior officer who implied one day that my place was in the living quarters, not the office!

Those six years on one-man detachments enriched my life and left memories I shall never forget. As I rub shoulders with the young wives of today, I sense they have really missed out on something unique. Through no fault of theirs, the majority know little of what police work is all about.

June Coutts

*   *   *   *   *

MAYO MEMORIES

Being engaged to marry a Mounted Policeman in 1939 was a waiting game. My future husband was in charge of Mayo Detachment and I was living in Dawson City. At that time the men had to serve for seven years before permission to marry could be obtained. If that criterion wasn't enough the intended wife's family was investigated, presumably to determine if they were fit to be the in-laws of a member. I thought this added block was most insensitive and short sighted. In retrospect, I firmly believe a man's wife was a definite asset. I was often left alone to answer the door and the phone when my husband was away on duty or patrol.

Permission finally came through two years later and we got married in 1941. The whole town turned out to make it a gala occasion and Bishop Geddes of the Anglican Church just happened to land by plane that day, so we were given the full treatment. I would have to say our honeymoon was rather exceptional, as not only did my husband have to make a census patrol of the outlying areas with me as his faithful wife of one day at his side, but the district dentist, who happened to be in town, went with us. So the three of us set off in the police truck, thence to various modes of transportation to reach these people.

I don't know what it's like today in remote areas, but in those days the men were on duty 24 hours a day, seven days a week. One never knew what a day would bring. Often I would be alone in my husband's absence to deal with situations. One day I was entertaining some ladies for tea when a knock, or rather a pounding, was heard at the door. Before I had a chance to answer, in came an old trapper complete with his dog team, hollering at the top of his lungs. When he didn't see my husband he pushed by me with his dogs into the room where the ladies were seated; then he proceeded to swear at them. It took all the feminine guile I could muster to get him to depart peacefully.

The war took away all of our good doctors. For a time we were without any. Then a doctor came to town who had personal problems, with alcohol and drugs. He was a good doctor when he was sober, so when an operation was pending my husband would lock him up and take him to the hospital when the patient was ready. He would then stand by. Once the doctor got away and the matron finished the operation! This sort of thing was too much for the board so they finally decided he would have to be sent outside. My husband was away one night and the doctor arrived at the detachment quite late in the evening with a gun. Both were loaded. He was gunning for one of the members of the hospital board. I was very frightened but self preservation is a potent weapon. I managed to get the gun away from him and talk him into waiting while I went for help.

When our first child (naturally a son) was about due we were without a doctor. The last plane for the winter season came in at the end of March and I was put on board in place of some freight which had to be removed. Weight was a major factor. I had to stay in Dawson until our son was born on April 30. There were quite a few members in Dawson while I was there so the young constables conducted a sweepstakes to guess the date the baby would arrive. The winner was gracious enough to pay for a day's hospitalization out of his winnings. This was most appreciated as medical expenses were paid only for the member, not his dependents.

Our first home at Mayo Detachment was somewhat primitive, as were most of the detachments in the north at that time. In the interests of privacy, a few alterations had to be made. The bathtub was in a tiny cubicle in the small office, which also contained the cell, so it had to be moved. We had it shifted to the unfinished upstairs where our bedroom was located. It was not too bad carrying the water up in a bucket, but we had to find some way to drain the tub. We drained it out the window when we could. In winter we would melt snow. Drinking water was purchased for 25 cents a bucket from Joe Longton who came by periodically with his cart and horse.

After some time at Mayo, my husband applied for Old Crow Detachment. The member in charge decided to remain another year, so it was arranged that my husband would be sent to Regina. We left by boat from Dawson City. One of the stipulations of our marriage was that my husband had to pay my way "outside". Fortunately, someone went to bat for us and it was agreed that I would be transported as far as Vancouver and pay my own way from there to Regina. It was quite a boat trip. I had to wash the baby's diapers, but there was no place to dry them until the crew were kind enough to let me hang them in the engine room. The trip from Skagway was even more difficult, as there were a number of mothers and their babies being evacuated from Alaska due to the Japanese subs in those waters. We were convoyed safely through Hecate Strait, and got safely to Vancouver.

I just want to say I am proud to be the widow of one of those fine men.

Antoinette Sutherland

* * * * *

A PRAIRIE STORM

Back in the late 1950s there was a small town called Vonda, about 12 miles off the highway between Prince Albert and Saskatoon. It was no longer on the main road and had lost a lot of its population. The railroad was still there as well as grain elevators and the RCMP.

The member in charge and his family lived in the designated detachment quarters which had an office at one end. It was, or had been, the beautiful home of a member of parliament. The outbuildings and fences were well painted; the lawns were large with several tea gardens giving the place a touch of elegance. The two other policemen lived in the hotel but worked out of the office at the house.

The second summer we lived there was hot and dry. By late October the trees and shrubs were still in their glorious colours, and it was an Indian summer. My husband had been transferred to Calgary which delighted us. As the wife and mother I was to remain in Vonda for the rest of my two older children's school term. My function was to organize packing and await the RCMP moving van. I was not keen on staying, but I did enjoy the weather, and knew we would be together in Calgary for Christmas.

One afternoon in late October it was quite warm, with the temperature well over 80 degrees Fahrenheit. There was no wind, so

I took my young son into a tea garden with my other two children and a neighbour boy who sat near my son's cot and we had a picnic. My son was recovering from jaundice and meningitis and had been indoors for several weeks. Just past mid-afternoon a breeze started to rustle the ten-foot lilac bushes, then a ground wind started. I looked around and could see dark clouds on the western horizon, so we moved indoors to watch TV. I thought a hail storm was imminent as it was that sort of chill wind coming from nowhere. We watched a program or two and then suddenly the TV went off. I looked out and was dumbfounded to see the fierce black clouds rolling rapidly towards us. The sky looked ominous. I had never seen it look so black.

My eldest daughter, an 11-year-old, helped me close the out buildings, take down the flag, and check the windows. We had just finished when our neighbour across the lane stopped to tell us about the weather report on the radio -- the warnings were for snow. I thought it was a joke; the afternoon had been so warm. The two-way radio in the office sounded agitated, but when I went in it was not decipherable. Our own radio, not a battery type, gave out nothing but static. What was going on?

I made two large pots of coffee before another neighbour arrived with bananas which were the diet recommended for the recovery from jaundice and meningitis. The entire town was banana conscious as about 300 persons out of a population of 650 had been laid low with the same illness. I was hoping the two constables would be in the office soon, as I didn't know what to do about the radio. They were, at that time, stuck in the snow on a side road west of Saskatoon with zero visibility, while as yet in Vonda it was not actually storming.

By dusk the snow began to fall. Then the wind hit. A tree came down very near the house. The noise was horrendous when the hail started. I was by then restless and nervous. I tried to sit still, as I didn't want to alarm my youngsters. The hail was so noisy that the two younger ones fell asleep, mesmerized by the noise. My daughter helped me get them to bed. Always the quiet one, she waited until we were downstairs to want me to hug her -- she too was scared.

We lit the furnace as the house was becoming very cool. Every hour we had to replenish it with wood. I planned on putting some coal, which was in very short supply, in the furnace about midnight. We kept busy in the kitchen and in making warm beds on the living-room furniture. We read, or tried to, but it was too difficult to concentrate. Since there was so much noise outside that I couldn't hear my two youngest, I brought them downstairs to the warmth of the lower rooms. We told scary stories until I thought I heard a noise outside. It was then I realized that the doors and windows were buried by snow. Another half hour passed and I heard a scratch at the window. We turned out the lights and I shone the big flashlight on each window. Mostly they were solid with snow; then I saw a man at the dining-room window. He looked wild, as he had burrowed through the snow. He wanted in.

About half an hour later, and after a lot of pushing on doors we finally made a tiny opening through the kitchen door. By the time the man got in we had several inches of snow indoors as well. By this time I was terrified, so I pushed him ahead of me into the office through a door from the kitchen. I couldn't understand him. I brought coffee to him and some hot soup. He removed his hat, scarf, jacket and mukluks. He kept crying and was agitated, but he finally told me in badly broken English that he'd walked nine miles, that he was sorry and that he had killed his wife (whom he called Meezes). I looked at him in horror. He stood up and said "I go -- I go." I told him, no, that he could go to bed in the cell. Then I closed and barricaded the door between the living quarters and the office. During this period I hadn't noticed the wind, but the house was cooling, and when I tried to see out there was only snow.

At six a.m., using the big flashlight, I went up to the attic and flashed an S.O.S. at the priest's window, which was next door in a narrow house which had originally been on the property. The house was only 25 feet from our place, but after a while I gave up, completely discouraged when I received no answering light.

About two hours later I heard shovels. It was a young priest and another neighbour. They were almost frozen. It had taken them two hours to dig their way out of their house and dig a path, which resembled a tunnel, to our door. They cleared two windows of snow and I could see that it was daylight. The snow had stopped. Various neighbours came over to the detachment on snowshoes offering their assistance. A few were concerned when they found out there was a prisoner in the cell and no police around. They felt relieved when I showed them the barricade I had pushed across the door.

By mid-afternoon several policemen from Saskatoon arrived behind snowplows, bringing two telephone linemen with them. It took me an hour, with assistance, to put everything in place in the house. Then I sat down and started to shake.

Later that afternoon, one of the police officers asked me to listen to the Ukrainian interpreter translate what had happened. It was an abysmal story. The man told of abuse to his wife and himself by two grown sons who arrived at their farm demanding money and homebrew. The mother fed the boys, but when they continued to drink they abused her more. She took a gun, pointed it at the young men and ordered them away. The old man said that he also was drunk. When he went into the house his wife gave him the gun as she was still angry. When a stone came through the window, the man said he turned and fired, but the booze made him see crooked. He hit his wife and she died soon after. A gruesome tale. Her body was still in the farmhouse.

A month later our family moved into our own home in Calgary and the episode faded somewhat. I still shivered thinking how that poor old fellow ploughed through the snow and wind in -38 degrees Fahrenheit weather. Months later, my husband brought me a copy of the results of the trial. The Ukrainian farmer, who was 63 years old, was found guilty of murder by reason of insanity. He was sent to the Battleford Mental Institute. I was gratified to know that the two sons had also received jail terms and tremendous fines for their treatment of their parents.

Even more than 30 years later I still remember that night. Yes, I was scared. I didn't expect to be in that situation. I wonder how the old fellow died. Then I shudder and think how different it might have been had he not been tired and docile while in the detachment.

M.I.Burke-Johnston

* * * * *

REMEMBER

From the genesis of the Force, housing and equipment for personnel have always been a problem. The vast majority of members who were constables or NCO's brought their brides and raised families in such surroundings! No plumbing (outhouses, or privies only), no running water.

My valiant young wife raised three children, pumped water in the summer and melted ice in the winter, on prairie detachments. A city girl by upbringing, the sight of her first Mounted Police residence with its wooden backhouse left her speechless, but she complained not! In the summer, I preceded her to this little edifice, stamping on the board walk to chase away the rats. In winter, I did the same to break trail in drifted snow.

Another common practice in the rigid economy of the dear old Force was to billet single men in the spare room of married quarters. Fortunately, most compassionate commanding officers frowned upon this stupid government economy. But Win, (my wife) and I did experience this situation in one outpost.

Other Force families, however, in many midwest posts, suffered the added inconvenience of having an iron cell or single gaol positioned in one room of their dwelling. Here on many a long weekend night, a drunken prisoner would howl and curse the night away, keeping the constable's wife and children in a state of fretful and sometimes fearful awareness. In spite of this, the policeman's wife often made breakfast or lunch for the sobered inmate who would be shamed into tearful gratitude, and because he enjoyed her cooking so much, would soon endeavour to get arrested again!

That was the way it was, right up until the middle and late 1940s and later, in some parts. But if we thought that was bad, let me quote from an ancient report by North West Mounted Police Commissioner L.W. Herchmer, addressed to the government in Ottawa, December 1888:

"I regret extremely to have to again call your attention to the wretched barracks furniture now in possession of the Force. This, the finest body of men in the country, still sleep on boards and trestles, while the prisoners in the gaols have neat iron cots."

Fortunately there is such a thing called progress and as a result, the conditions described no longer exist in the Force.

Frank Spalding
from *100 Years in the RCMP Saddle or, Stop the Musical Ride, I Want Off!*

*   *   *   *   *

MOVING HOUSEHOLD EFFECTS

In the late 1940s, and I believe also in the 1950s, moving household effects in at least two divisions was accomplished by police truck. Names like "Waddy", "Dusty" Miller, Albert Taylor and "Greaseball" Brown come to mind. There was no packing or slings for the proper securing of furniture, and the truck drivers had to be quite ingenious to pack the effects without causing damage. As a matter of fact, they were not always successful, due to road conditions prevalent at the time. The drivers were generally pleasant, being acutely aware that this method of transferring their prized possessions was not generally approved of by the members. In Saskatchewan married members on transfer had their effects moved by the RCMP stake body truck. They had no assistants but "Dusty" Miller, the driver, was forever cheerful and could always get all the goods into the van, regardless of the condition in which they were unloaded at the other end of the trek. One member hurt his back attempting to lift a stove onto the back of the big International truck as there were no self-lifting devices to assist.

In another instance at Prince Albert, the officer commanding had received a large refrigerator, shipped from Regina through the RCMP canteen. The express company simply dropped it off in his backyard and several junior men were detailed to go over and put it into his kitchen for him. As one member described the incident, "I used to deliver large goods in Winnipeg when I worked for Eaton's before joining the Force, but we always had a sling attachment for handling awkward, bulky objects. In this instance we had nothing. We were junior constables, this was the inspector's house, so we were stuck. However, on arrival at the house, I noted it was to go in the back door on to a little landing, and then a sharp right turn up a few stairs into the kitchen. This would have been easy with the proper equipment. As we had nothing, I asked the inspector's wife if she had a tape measure. She provided it and I made elaborate measurements of the fridge and of the doorways, etc., shaking my head and muttering all the time. She asked me if there was a problem and I assured her we could get it in. It would be a very tight fit, and we didn't have the right equipment which a proper moving company would, and it might get scratched up a bit. When the word SCRATCHED entered the conversation we were put on hold until she phoned the inspector about this problem. A few minutes later she told us to leave as the inspector would arrange for a moving company to put her pride and joy into the kitchen in a professional manner. I guess there is more than one way to skin a cat!"

To put it as gently as possible, one must say that the Force was penurious. The furniture movers were not given an assistant and it was the lot of single junior members to assist in loading and unloading the furniture at each end. This was an unpopular assignment, particularly when such items as stoves, refrigerators and pianos had to be lifted on and off.

The poor married member whose goods were being moved felt quite guilty about the imposition on the single members, who were inclined to voice their discontent quite audibly. There was no way he could reward these men, but I recall that he usually purchased a case of beer to at least assuage their thirst.

There was one instance in which a member was being moved to the third floor of division quarters. The second floor contained the single men's barracks and this floor had formerly been used as cell accommodation for errant members. Packing all the furniture up three flights of stairs was a real chore. The married member bought the traditional case of beer. Not wishing the men to drink alone, he assisted them in disposing of the beer. Suddenly the sergeant-major burst into the room and threatened to charge the two single men with drinking in barracks. He told the married member that he was not included as it was his private quarters. Fortunately he thought better of his threat and nothing came of it.

Anonymous ex-members

*   *   *   *   *

A "MOVING" EXPERIENCE

I was happily stationed in Hamilton, Ontario, when in May 1955, I received a memorandum instructing me to proceed on transfer ahead of my family to North Battleford, Saskatchewan. Despite the rather callous tone of the memorandum, there was some reason for it. I was married and had three children aged eight, five and two. Because of the distance to and the nature of the place to which I was being transferred, there was a question as to what suitable accommodation would be available, so the powers-that-be, in their wisdom -- or lack of it -- decreed that I should proceed alone. The family could follow -- sometime!

Being the proud owners of a 1946 Chevrolet (the cost of which in 1946 had been $1,400 and which we had agreed to accept at time of delivery sans tires due to wartime restrictions still in effect), I elected to travel west by car rather than by rail and applied for travelling expenses in lieu of rail fare. It was mentioned in my application to travel by this means that there would be a monetary savings to the government as my wife and children could travel with me at no extra expense. It was also pointed out that my family would not be an encumbrance as arrangements would be made for them to stay with an aunt in Saskatoon until I had been definitely posted and had obtained accommodation. Since I had put forth such a convincing argument, the Force now agreed I could take my wife and family.

A date was set by Ottawa for me to report to the NCO i/c North Battleford Detachment. That meant that I must get estimates from three moving firms to move our household effects west with all possible dispatch. Finally the date of our departure arrived, but unfortunately we still had no decision from headquarters as to which moving firm won the contract and consequently no way of knowing how or when our furniture would be shipped. We packed into the car all those items essential to travelling with three children (including a turtle, which at this particular time in Lynda's life had acquired a very high social status in our family circle and received top priority) and walked out of the house as though we were just going out for the evening. We gave the keys to our neighbour and asked if he would be good enough to let the movers in -- whenever or if ever they came -- and to check the house after they had left. We said good-bye to all our friends and neighbours who had been watching this performance with interest and consternation, and with that a pretty sad and dejected Holmes family pulled out of the driveway and headed west.

The trip west was uneventful but fraught with many emotions and certainly some misgivings. How would I measure up doing criminal work when, despite 15 years service, I had not served in a contract division? My service to this point had been in Intelligence throughout the war, and after the war it was in Customs and Excise, Opium and Narcotic Drug Act, Preventive Service, Foreign Exchange Control Board Regulations, Immigration, Atomic Energy of Canada screening, National Research Council screening, etc. All this type of work necessitated being in mufti and the thought of going back into uniform, which I hadn't worn since I was a recruit, was not particularly to my liking. The immediate future did not look terribly rosy to me!

We arrived in Saskatoon where Marian, the three children and our dog, Boots, disembarked to stay with Aunt Janet and Uncle Alan until they got the signal from me to proceed further. Up to now I hadn't done too badly. I had left all my furniture behind in Hamilton for an unknown fate and now I was leaving my wife and kids and dog in Saskatoon -- for God alone knew how long.

I blew into North Battleford about 11 a.m. to be greeted by the massive, six-foot-six, 200-plus pounds "Butch" Welliver, the NCO i/c the detachment. He sized me up with what I felt were very critical eyes in which I thought I could read "What am I going to do with a senior constable who has no criminal investigation experience?" He instructed me to change into uniform (breeches and boots) and report forthwith to the O C North Battleford Sub-Division whose office was located in the post office building.

The O C instructed me not to go house hunting. He had a "plan" for me. "My God!" I thought. "My world is sure crashing in around me now. What the hell next?" He sent me back to the detachment where I was detailed to do foot patrol, on shift, on the streets of North Battleford. "Some plan," I thought. I felt I had really hit bottom now. Being in uniform was bad enough -- now I had to patrol those damn streets at three a.m.

After two weeks of that performance, I was again paraded before Inspector McComb, the officer commanding. He told me his "plan" had materialized; he was sending me to a choice detachment, Glaslyn, 45 miles north of North Battleford. I found that the only good thing he could say about the place was that a brand new police car had just been issued to that point. He went on to say that Constable Bradley, the member now at that detachment, was being transferred to Cumberland House, and while I was to proceed immediately to Glaslyn I would have to live in the single men's quarters until he left. Bradley was waiting for a moving firm and it was not known when the movers would arrive. I felt like saying "I've heard that story before," but decided it would be more politic if I held my tongue. The OC further instructed that I was to leave my private car in North Battleford because I was to pick up the new car here and take it with me to Glaslyn. I was really doing well now: my home and furniture in Hamilton, my family and dog in Saskatoon, and now my only remaining prized possession, my 1946 Chevrolet, to be abandoned in North Battleford. What next!

I got to Glaslyn. Bradley was a bit annoyed about his transfer to that Godforsaken spot up north of nowhere, and appeared to be purposely dragging his feet. He was making a good showing by having all his furniture stacked up in a pile in the living room, ready for the movers. His wife and two daughters were just about as distraught and upset as he was.

Glaslyn, being a one-man detachment, was nevertheless de-signed to accommodate one or two single men as well as the married constable in charge. My new home was in the single men's quarters adjacent to the office and immediately above the cells in the basement. This meant that I was frequently subjected to all-night "entertain-ment". I lived there for two weeks, during which time I put every available moment into learning how to handle fatal accidents, inquests, safeblowings, breaking and enterings, Highway Traffic Act, Liquor Act, etc. etc.

Then the big word came; my furniture was on its way and would be arriving in the next day or two. Simultaneously, Bradley got word that his mover was coming and would also be arriving in the next day or two. I couldn't wait to get on the horn to my wife to give her the green light to head out. She already knew that our car was "somewhere" in North Battleford. By one means or another she and the kids and the dog got to North Battleford. We were soon re-united and had our possessions all in one place -- Glaslyn.

There was still a fly in the ointment. Bradley and his family were still occupying the detachment quarters. There wasn't room for all of us in the building so authority was given for us to live in the local hotel until Bradley moved out and our furniture arrived. That wasn't too bad, except for one big problem; the constant fear of the kids falling down the toilet. Marian kept a perpetual watch to ensure the kids did not go in unattended. There was good reason for this concern. There was no running water or sewer in this town with a population of about 350. The toilet facilities in the hotel consisted of a seat under which was a vertical pipe about 20 inches in diameter down to a tank below the ground floor. There was a clear passage from top to bottom and the possibility of one of the kids falling down that pipe was always a terrible thought.

After a week or so our furniture finally arrived, but Bradley's movers had not been heard from. So in went our furniture stacked and stored all around Bradley's possessions in the living room. In due course his movers came and the whole mess got straightened out.

Paul M.Holmes

*   *   *   *   *

A MYSTERIOUS ILLNESS

There are many stories told about C.L. "Spike" Donaldson, a legend in his time. My first contact with Donaldson was classic, not that it gives credit to Donaldson, but rather as it indicates his ingenuity and imagination.

I was stationed at Regina Town Station when I got two-hours notice of a transfer to Broadview Detachment as the incumbent was evidently seriously ill and might not return to duty for some time. The fact of the matter was that Spike had been taken on a stretcher to Regina and tests were being given to determine a mysterious illness that he had suddenly developed. As it turned out, they were unable to find the cause of his ailment; he appeared to have made a remarkable recovery so he was discharged from hospital, declared fit and returned to resume his duties as constable in charge of Broadview Detachment.

Some time later Spike told me the facts and circumstances of the case. Spike's girl friend (she later became his wife) was a nurse at the Grey Nuns' Hospital in Regina. She decided to pay a visit to Broadview one weekend, but as times were tough they decided she would take a chance by staying at the detachment. It was considered a very serious offence to have a female in the detachment, unless it was strictly on police business. The detachment was located on the main street of Broadview between the hotel and the garage. It consisted of three small rooms: an office with a pot-bellied stove for heating; a small room with two issue beds and a wash basin, and a room for storage which contained one portable prison cell. Under these circumstances it would be difficult to conceal a female in the place for any length of time. However, Spike, who was well regarded in the community, decided it was worth taking a chance.

Later in the day, after his girl friend's arrival, a long-distance telephone call came from Regina, advising Spike that a complaint had been received that he was harbouring a female in the detachment and an investigation would have to be done to determine the validity of the complaint. Spike could see that he was confronted with a serious situation and would most likely lose his command, and quite possibly be discharged from the Force. In those days jobs were hard to come by.

Spike consulted his friend, the local doctor, who advised him (after a dozen beer) that he was a sick man and needed immediate hospitalization. As no adequate hospital facilities were available locally he would have to be sent to a hospital in Regina. To make sure his condition did not worsen he would have to be placed on the train on a stretcher. His girl friend, a nurse, would have to accompany him so nothing could go seriously wrong.

As I have indicated, Spike made a remarkable recovery but there was one loophole in the story to be covered: namely the presence of his girl friend in the detachment. Spike maintained that in view of his illness he had phoned his girl friend in Regina, advising her of his condition. She insisted on coming to Broadview to see what she could do to help, and that explained her presence in the detachment. The subsequent investigation cleared Spike of any wrong-doing, but not without some suspicions remaining, and a grudging admiration for his inventiveness.

I .C. Shank

*   *   *   *   *

MEMORIES OF A WIFE

In one of the first postings after our marriage there was a Red Cross Outpost Hospital in the village, with two doctors who were very good friends of ours. One day, one of the doctors called from the hospital saying that a patient, a young man who was being treated for epilepsy, had left the hospital and was running up the road in his johnny-shirt. The doctor wanted Earl to go out and cut him off, while he, the doctor, followed him. Earl took his young recruit along. When they saw the patient coming towards them, Earl said, "You get out and grab him and I'll turn the car around and pick you up." Young Harry, the recruit, jumped out and grabbed a very sedate little old man in a dark suit, shirt and tie with a walking stick, while the patient in his johnny-shirt sailed blissfully down the road.

Earl yelled, "Not him, you fool." Harry let his frightened old man go and started running. He was wearing britches and boots with low rubbers. The rubbers flew off, slowing him up somewhat and Earl headed the man off with the car, got out and stopped him. The doctor then came along and left for the hospital with the patient.

Another story that comes to mind was when we were stationed in the seaside town of Bathurst, N.B., for several years in the 1950s. We enjoyed it very much in spite of the cold winters and deep snow. One summer day the Crown prosecutor, later a judge, reported thefts from cars parked in the yard at his cottage at the beach. He had a pretty good idea who was doing it, but needed to catch them in the act. He and Earl concocted a plan whereby Earl and Al, a constable stationed with us, would take their wives and our two little boys down to the beach near his cottage for a picnic. The men and another constable would stay in the cottage and watch. We were all very pleased with the idea of a picnic, as of course we were not told the reason for it until we were nearly there. We did not have a car at the time and did not get to go on many picnics. The boys did not hear the explanation, as they were only seven and five years old.

We arrived at the cottage and left an old purse of mine containing one five-dollar bill on the seat with the window vent open. The men took our baskets, etc. and got us established on the beach. The boys were quite excited and Al's wife, Marge, was still game until we discovered the beach was littered with dead herring. This didn't go over too well as she was eight months pregnant. However, Al built us a smudge to keep the flies away and the men went back to sit and wait in their nice, cool cottage.

It seemed like forever, and the boys were doing a lot of complaining about being hungry, until Al came running down the beach, shouting that they had taken the money and gone into the woods. He kept on running, followed by me, Marge and the two little boys who had no idea what was going on. (The boys said later that they thought someone had dropped a bomb.) As we ran through the woods, although you could hardly say that Marge was running, we saw the other constable pedalling a bike for all he was worth down the road, pointing ahead of him. Al and Earl were still running. Marge and I decided we'd had enough. They finally caught a man and his nephew who lived nearby and took them in to the cottage.

We thought, "Great -- now we can eat." We were wrong. The five-dollar bill had been thrown away in the woods, and we could not eat until the evidence was recovered. The whole picnic party combed the patch of woods until someone finally found it.

The thieves, as I said, were neighbours. They were quite nonchalant about the whole thing, saying, "See you tomorrow, Al." He replied, "You sure as hell will. I'll be prosecuting."

By the time all the excitement was over it was too cold for the beach and everyone was too tired and hungry to care, so we quickly ate our supper in the cottage and headed home.

Ruth Evans

*   *   *   *   *

CHILDREN OF THE FORCE

The children of members of the Force residing in the training depot in Regina lived a life which was unique in many respects, not the least of which was the opportunity of getting into mischief.

(1) The five-year-old son of an officer discovered the ease with which he could cadge an extra quarter or two from soft-hearted recruits, especially when they knew who he was. Kids living on the "Square" were able to get their hair cut at the post barber shop and they would be given 25 cents to pay the barber. This enterprising young fellow, with a long face, would approach a recruit and give him a heart-rending story about losing his haircut money and the certain punishment he would face at home from his stern martinet of a father. This the recruits could readily relate to. The recruits were a soft touch until the scam was broken; the boy was informed upon after treating his pals to candy bars and pop on a spending spree at the canteen.

(2) For many years, a fire engine hauled by manpower was located at Depot. The reasons for this are somewhat obscure, possibly due to the distance from Regina or the desire to have the training depot completely self contained. For years, fire drill was conducted with recruits acting as the horses . The engine was finally retired and was stored outside awaiting disposal by Crown Assets. The seven-year-old son of an NCO was the leader of a "gang" of barracks kids who found out what a wonderful plaything the "retired" fire engine made. In no time at all, they just about demolished it. Investigation unearthed the culprits and identified the leader of this gang of young vandals. There is no doubt they did some sweating over the dire consequences they felt surely awaited them. Crown Assets advertised the fire engine and a few interested bidders came to the barracks to view this piece of equipment. No bids ever came forward, except one to haul the fire engine away for its value as scrap. That bid was accepted and the vandals were let off the hook. Fortunately, no Board of Enquiry was ever held!

(3) There was always construction work of one kind or another going on at Depot. In this instance, a huge Caterpillar tractor belonging to a construction firm doing work at the barracks was parked on the edge of the sports field adjacent to the officers' residences. Was there ever a better toy for a group of young boys to play with than a D-7 Caterpillar tractor? Well, they got it started, and

in motion. It moved ahead ten or 12 feet until the blade ploughed into a pile of dirt and it stalled. Fortunately, there were no casualties, although one boy, running alongside, lost his shoe when it got caught in some moving part of the tractor. Obviously a close call. The only time the parents ever got to hear about it was when the boy had to explain his "chewed-up" shoe.

A. Pennock

*   *   *   *   *

AN ISLAND DETACHMENT

A few years ago I revisited Grand Manan Island, situated off the Atlantic coast, where we were stationed on our first detachment in the early 1930s. Nothing seemed changed -- the towering cliffs, the small fishing boats, and the pungent Atlantic breeze sweeping over the small island.

I was interested to note that the one-man detachment of our time was now a three-man detachment, and that most complaints were first relayed to the mainland. No more hammering on the detachment door, or irate midnight calls regarding a rowdy party, or a disgruntled inhabitant. Our former detachment house was now renovated with all the modern conveniences, and occupied by the owner's family. It was a large house with three bedrooms and an enormous kitchen dominated by the shiny black "monster" -- the STOVE -- which had to be fed regularly with fuel from the wood pile. The latter was kept well supplied through the wood-chopping efforts of my husband. Somehow or other I managed to come to terms with the stove and between us we produced some very good meals.

The living room was pleasant, and after a while I even became accustomed to sharing it with the gaol cell, complete with steel grills, adjoining the office. The French doors softened the bleak scene, and after a short time we completely ignored the whole situation. During our three years, the gaol was occupied overnight only a few times, and that usually for some minor transgression. It was always an amiable arrangement, perhaps due to the fact that I felt compelled to make it easier for the "prisoner" by producing endless cups of coffee, sandwiches and cookies, even supplying our small radio to while away his visit, and to ensure his incarceration was not too stressful. We would discreetly retire to the kitchen while my offerings of "goodies" were consumed.

"Inspection" with the arrival of the inspector was an occasion to really shape up. It seemed reasonable to have the inspector use one of our three bedrooms. Since we had only enough bedroom furniture for one bedroom, the poor man was to occupy a guest room which was furnished with the classic regimental iron cot, complete with the equally rigid mattress, topped off with the famous iron-grey, prickly, regimental blankets with RCMP resolutely stamped thereon. It must have certainly taken him back in time to his barrack days.

During the visit the inspector would always gamely accept our invitation to dine with us, giving me a chance to show off my newly acquired culinary skills. Perhaps the freshly caught island lobsters helped a bit. I remember always leaving the kitchen when the "*coup-de-grace*" took place, with the inspector and my husband dropping the unfortunate crustaceans into the boiling pot. It was well known, and evidently verified on the island that lobsters invariably squeal when they meet their fate, and to this day I believe they *do* -- at least those island lobsters did.

All this was a very long time ago, but my return visit certainly revived many memories, and I think perhaps we had a more interesting tour of duty -- even more fun -- than any young constable could hope to encounter these days.

Patricia Mabee

*   *   *   *   *

LIFE'S EMBARRASSING MOMENTS

A memory I shall never forget is the time the O C had lunch with us while we were stationed in an oil town, living above the post office on Main Street. Our son, who was very observant but not known for his diplomacy, sat placidly through the first course of the meal, then remarked to the officer, "You sure don't have much hair!"

I thought the embarrassment he had caused should satisfy him for the rest of the day but no! His next comment was to say to the visitor in a most injured voice, "You got the pudding with all the nice crispy topping."

Ruby Hodgson

*   *   *   *   *

TELL IT TO MY WIFE

During the earlier days of the Force, and especially in the prairie provinces, there were occasions when wives of detachment men were required to perform a variety of police duties during the absence of their husbands. This unusual situation existed at Telegraph Creek Detachment, about 257 miles north of Prince Rupert, B.C. This was a one-man detachment under the charge of Constable R.D. Nelson who resided there with his wife.

After they were posted to Telegraph Creek, Constable Nelson's wife accepted appointments as government sub-agent, sub-mining recorder, deputy registrar of births, deaths and marriages and marriage commissioner.

During May 1968, the magistrate serving the area resigned. As a result it was necessary for Constable Nelson to travel a return distance of 320 miles in order to obtain a summons or search warrant. This also applied to complainants who wished to prefer charges, and a large number of them had no transportation.

This situation was resolved when, on June 17, 1968, an order-in-council was passed appointing Constable Nelson's wife, Gail Marilyn Nelson, a justice of the peace in and for the province of British Columbia. It was approved the following day by the lieutenant-governor.

Afterwards, Constable Nelson had to apply to his wife to obtain a search warrant, summons or to prefer charges. One could visualize the following conversation: "Uh...dear...uh, your worship...may I please have a search warrant for..."

Anonymous
RCMP Quarterly - Volume 34, Number 3

* * * * *

TOAST TO THE LADIES
by Tom Crawshaw -- with apologies to Rudyard Kipling.

When the young detachment rookie started working on his own,
Enforcing law and order as a constable, full blown,
In addition to constabulary duty to be done
He had to clothe and feed himself, and do it on the run.

He'd wash his socks and underwear, and drape them on the cells
Which were in the middle bedroom, so he could hear the yells
Of drunks, of vags, of ne'er do wells, and other types of guests,
Who would oft disturb his mealtime, and prone to spoil his rest.

He'd eat down at the greasy spoon, or if he was in clover
He'd drop in to the teacherage, or the nurse would ask him over.
And many a romance blossomed with a plate of pork and beans,
And many a start with coffee ended up with wedding scenes.

Our hero would grow weary with this hard and spartan life,
He'd scratch his head, and work his charms, to get himself a wife.
He'd have to have TWO HUNDRED BUCKS, and a girl who'd pass
        inspection,
A clean crime sheet, appearance neat, or he'd face a quick rejection.

He'd write "I have the Honour, Sir, to ask to take a wife,
And, if you give permission, I'll keep her all my life.
She's a lady without blemish, a girl of common sense,
With respect I beg approval, at your convenience."

The constable would chew his nails, but still maintained his diary,
While the Sub-Division NCO would start a stern enquiry,
To find out if this paragon was fit to live in Quarters,
And run the show when left alone -- and that was just for starters.

At last would come permission -- "You may hereby wed this beauty,
If your reports are up to date, and it doesn't clash with duty.
You must also marry in a Church of Christian persuasion,
And you may wear your red coat, just for this one occasion."

The die was cast, the wedding held, and the honeymoon, if any,
Would be spent with distant relatives, so it wouldn't cost a penny.
Then it was back to detachment life, and a future bleak and iffy,
In the town's worst house for this new Force spouse -- and at forty
        below -- A BIFFY!

Now all you men who did this thing should be deep in bitter tears,
To think of all the misery you handed these old dears.

So stand up straight and raise your glass, -- and do it without fail,
For the female of the species is more deadly than the male.

THE REPLY
by Louise Crawshaw -- with no apologies.

It's nice to state you appreciate
The skill of the Force's ladies,
As we worked and obeyed, but were never paid,
Though we suffered the heat of Hades.
The detachment wife was "in" for life,
And nothing seemed to daunt her,
As she matroned the naughty girls
Who swore they'd return and haunt her.

We'd follow escaping prisoner guys,
Till our man arrived and got 'em.
And cook him steak and kidney pies
After a tough post mortem.
We'd press the suits of the new recruits
Who thought it was part of the plan,
But we drew the line at cleaning boots --
Or, cleaning out the barn.

We did all this for the married bliss
Of being a policeman's spouse.
Our sole reward was a hasty kiss --
And the village's oldest house.
We made the best of an unpaid life,
And we loved it, I must confess,
It was worth it, being a Mountie's wife.
We'd do it again ....I GUESS.

*   *   *   *   *

The Musical Ride, 1887, drawn by Frederic Remington.
(*Courtesy* RCMP QUARTERLY)

The RCMP Show Band, entertaining a large crowd. (*Courtesy* RCMP QUARTERLY)

Corporal Clare Dent presenting the Coronation Medal to
Kingualik, 1954. (*Courtesy* RCMP QUARTERLY)

Constable Alan Foster at the dynamite cache, *ca* 1939. (*Courtesy*
RCMP QUARTERLY)

Left: Constables Cardinal and Brown, undercover in 1967.
(*Courtesy* RCMP QUARTERLY)
Right: Constable A. W. "Buns" King, shot by "The Mad
Trapper", 1931. (*Courtesy* RCMP QUARTERLY)

Mayo Detachment, *ca* 1942. (*Courtesy Mrs. Antoinette Sutherland*)

One of the originals, Staff Sergeant John A. Martin, *ca* 1875. (*Courtesy* RCMP QUARTERLY)

Dale of Cawsalta, the first dog in the Force. (*Courtesy* RCMP QUARTERLY)

Klia with his doghandler. (*Courtesy* RCMP QUARTERLY)

Constable R. A. Taggart, 1928, before the legendary dog-team patrol with Inspector Joy. (*Courtesy R. A. Taggart*)

Fort Carlton, Saskatchewan, 1884. (*Courtesy* RCMP QUARTERLY)

The crest on Lieutenant Commander R. A. S. MacNeil's corvette, *Dauphin*, in World War Two.

Chapter Five

Moonshine and Rum-Runners

TRANSPORTING MOONSHINE EFFECTIVELY

In the summer of 1951 there was an influx of home brew coming into Winnipeg. It was being produced in quantity and hundreds of gallons were arriving in the city to supply the numerous bootleggers. The Winnipeg Liquor Squad was very conscious of this influx, and had every reason to believe it was coming in from the north. Suspicion was centred in the Stonewall or Teulon districts.

There was only one highway from that area so Constable Hooper and I were detailed to check vehicles coming from that direction. Day after day we checked cars. If there was some reason to arouse our suspicions we searched the trunk and looked through the inside generally. The results were negative.

After several weeks of this duty it didn't appear we were going to be successful, particularly as there was still moonshine getting into the city. Finally it was decided that we would do some spot checks of the country near Komarno to see if we could locate a still. With the amount of booze being manufactured, it had to be a large one. We decided on the bush country west of Teulon and north of Komarno. Constable Whitbread, a member of the Liquor Squad, was with us. He was known to have an uncanny knack of locating stills. I had heard this many times, but must admit I was a non-believer, primarily because such a knack, to my mind, was an impossibility.

We hadn't gone too far before I changed my opinion completely. The three of us were walking down a municipal road and there were numerous trails into the trees. We had passed quite a few of these trails when suddenly Constable Whitbread stopped at a gate. It was the entrance to a trail which had very large trees. "Let's go into this one," he said. To this day I wonder how he selected this particular road, as we had passed many others that didn't look any different. About a mile into the bush, there it was. It was a very large still, and going at full strength. We surrounded the still. The operator, who hadn't noticed us, was caught red handed and didn't get a chance to run. After we handcuffed him we checked the still very carefully. Its capacity was astounding. It was obvious we would need several semitrailer trucks for the seizure. We noticed that there were quite a few gallons put to one side, obviously in preparation for immediate pick up and transportation to Winnipeg.

I was assigned to intercept the person or persons involved in the conveyance of the brew. I hid the police car back in the bush and went down the trail to the entrance of the road leading in to the still. I crouched down in the heavy grass behind a bush and was well hidden. I was in a good spot to observe any vehicle being used, if and when it drove up to the gate.

It all worked out perfectly. After about an hour a large car drove up to the gate and came to a stop. The driver got out of the car and opened the gate. I ran out of my hiding place and immediately grabbed him from behind. To my surprise it was not a him but a her. Not only was it a her, but a very pretty girl to boot. Despite this, I was pleased to have found the person responsible for transporting all that brew. There were some empty jugs in the trunk and it was obvious this vehicle was the one used for transporting the brew into Winnipeg. Now the mystery had been solved, but I was highly embarrassed in that the young lady was quite well dressed, as if she were on the way to a wedding or reception of some kind. To make the subterfuge complete, there was a child, also well dressed, standing on the seat next to the driver. The child was old enough to stand on the seat and watch out the windshield.

Thinking back, I recalled that this vehicle with the young lady and the child standing on the front seat had passed us many times when we were checking vehicles. How could we have been so stupid as to not have stopped her and at least ask where she was going? A check of her car would have yielded a trunk full of brew en route to Winnipeg, or many empty jugs going to the Komarno district. On second thought, what policeman would have thought to stop a pretty girl driving down the highway with a child standing beside her as a suspected bootlegger?

It turned out she was the wife of the still operator and the child was theirs. Thinking of the old saw "The RCMP always get their man," we can add that they also get their woman too.

Ronald S.Brown

*   *   *   *   *

THE DEMON RUM

Members of the Force transferred to the maritime provinces in the 1930s were for the most part rather surprised, and in some cases somewhat dismayed, to find that the main thrust of their duties consisted of enforcing the Customs and Excise Act and Provincial Liquor Act. The provincial police forces of Prince Edward Island, Nova Scotia and New Brunswick were taken over by the RCMP in the early 1930s and the Force wasn't used to the ways of the maritimers. The policy of the Force at that time was to transfer recruits born in the western provinces east and vice versa. Thus, the majority of the members who were originally Mounted Policemen came from the west.

The importation of illicit spirits into the maritime provinces from the West Indies or via the French islands of St. Pierre and Miquelon had been an active industry for a number of years. It was considered to be a worthwhile investment by many prominent business and professional maritimers. It wasn't considered a disgrace to be associated with rum-runners and many young maritimers supplemented their income working with them. At least two subsequently joined the RCMP. One young fellow from Lunenburg worked in the trade as a young man and later became the chief of police for Lunenburg. He has passed away but before his death he wrote a book describing his experiences entitled *Both Sides of the Law*. With the repeal of the United States Prohibition Act in 1933, east-coast smuggling activities were greatly reduced and largely confined to the maritime provinces and the St. Lawrence area in Quebec.

The RCMP acquired full responsibility for the enforcement of the Customs and Excise Act in 1932 when the Department of National Revenue was absorbed. Involved in this acquisition was a Marine Section, consisting of approximately 200 personnel and 38 vessels of various shapes and sizes with headquarters at HMC Dockyard, Halifax, N.S.

The enforcement of the Liquor Control Acts in the various provinces extended to all communities, and called for the presence of Liquor Squads in the larger centres. These squads were kept continuously busy raiding "kitchen bootleggers" and harassing persons engaged in the delivery of "milkers" of rum to residences. A milker was a quart milk bottle, painted white, filled with rum, and selling for two dollars at that time. The most popular import was 40-overproof Demerara rum in five-gallon kegs, known as "Black and Dirty", with Belgian alcohol in 2 1/2-gallon cans being favoured in the St. Lawrence area.

My own participation in efforts to protect government revenues included a six-month stint as a wireless operator aboard the RCMP cruiser *Bayhound* in 1933 when I was 19 years old. Later I flew on aircraft patrols out of Sydney in 1934, and the Eastern Passage in 1935-36. This was followed by shore patrols along the coast of Cape Breton in the years 1937-38. I'll provide a few amusing and unusual incidents I encountered during the struggle.

In 1933, I was approached by one of the more successful rum-runners in the Halifax area and asked if I was interested in being a wireless operator aboard one of his vessels at $200 per month and a percentage cut on any successful landings of rum. I was then receiving a constable's pay of $60 per month. The offer was tempting and it occurred to me that it would be an excellent opportunity to provide information on the movements of rum-runners. I reported this overture to Inspector L.H. Nicholson, then "H" Division Criminal Investigation Branch officer, later commissioner. He indicated some surprise at my naivety and said, "Bryan, I'm afraid if we undertook such an operation your body might be found floating off the beach one morning."

I was once aboard a cruiser that was pursuing a vessel we believed to be loaded with rum. A warning shot was fired in front of the vessel. To our embarrassment it killed a cow on the shores of Prince Edward Island.

An attempt was made to seize a liquor-laden schooner *Kromhout* off Scatarie Island in December 1933 by the patrol vessel *Number Four*. Four police members boarded her and were kidnapped by the crew of the schooner; they were later released on St. Pierre Island.

In 1938 information was received that the *Henry Joe*, owned by the Moraze brothers of St. Pierre Island and reputed to be one of the fastest rum-runners on the east coast, would attempt a landing of rum at Point Edward in the upper reaches of Sydney Harbour. Members of the preventive squad, including yours truly, hid in the woods around the landing site. Unloading operations proceeded without a hitch until one of the shore-based smugglers answered a call of nature over a pile of spruce boughs under which one of our members was hidden. The offended constable could not avoid a yell of protest and chaos ensued. The *Henry Joe* departed with a roar of powerful engines, leaving a dory with three kegs of rum floating in the harbour. It wasn't a complete disaster as two members of the shore gang were arrested and 60 kegs of fine rum were placed under seizure.

I clearly recollect the horrified look on the face of a Cape Breton rum-runner when a shot from a .45 was fired into the engine hood of his prized La Salle sedan. He had been trying to shove a police vehicle off an icy road.

Information received from a Catholic priest resulted in the seizure of two vehicles and 75 kegs of rum. The priest was reluctant to accept an informer's award of several hundred dollars until I suggested it might be used to redecorate his church. It was later noted that the exterior of the church had received a fresh coat of white paint. In appreciation the priest gave me a rosary and a missal which are still among my souvenirs.

During a chase in Mahone Bay, Jack Kelly, skipper of the RCMP vessel, fired a warning shot. The bullet ricocheted off a rum keg on the deck resulting in the death of one of the crew. He was known thenceforth as "Machine Gun Kelly". To my knowledge this was the only fatality during the smuggling wars. Weapons were used by the police only for efforts to stop escaping vessels and vehicles in the form of warning shots. Each side had a great deal of respect for the tactics of the other and the struggle became more of a game than a battle.

Despite increased land, sea and air patrols it was obvious we were not preventing continued landings of illicit spirits. It was clear that if any charges were laid the smugglers had the general sympathy of the judiciary, and the best defence lawyers were always available. However, the tide of battle turned in 1938 when Inspector Zaneth arrived, armed with warrants and writs under various acts, permitting the seizure of bank, telegraph and telephone records. This resulted in successful charges of conspiracy against the principal rum-runners. As a result of this, and the emergence of informers wishing to avoid prosecution, the smuggling fraternity found itself in disarray. The charges were not all successful, but the action put an end to large-scale smuggling operations.

I had rather a grudging admiration for most of the rum-running fraternity that I encountered, and their ingenious tricks to avoid capture. Rum-running was a way of life and they were not the type to become involved in crimes such as the drug trade.

I couldn't resist the opportunity of a meeting in June 1991 with one of the more successful rum-runners in Nova Scotia, now 94 years of age. It was an afternoon of reminiscing with much laughter -- and no rum.

W.C."Bill" Bryan

* * * * *

CUSTOMS SEARCH

I recall a Customs search in the city of Prince Albert which had a unique twist. The subject of the search was a well-known bootlegger, so we had a member of the Prince Albert City Police with us. We thought we had searched the house thoroughly but we found nothing, although the information we had received was supposed to be pretty good.

The sergeant in charge of the detachment came along on the search. He was a very good carpenter and was somewhat taken by the kitchen wash stand which had a large bowl of dirty water on top. The stand was built out from the wall and was enclosed. He looked inside and found nothing. He indicated to me that the stand was built farther out from the wall than the inside space showed. I took the bowl off the top of the stand and the sergeant lifted off one of the top crosspieces which looked nailed down, but wasn't. There, in a secret cache, were a number of "mickeys" of rye, all wrapped in cloth to prevent clinking. The Prince Albert city policeman was elated, as he had been trying to get this bootlegger for some time.

The bootlegger was incensed and wanted to know who had spilled the beans to us on his hiding place. There was no way we were going to tell him it was the sergeant's observations that made the discovery, so we let on that people are bound to talk about such things. This upset the bootlegger and he told us that the carpenter who had done the work for him had also done one for a "madam" elsewhere in town. He told us it was in her basement, cunningly concealed in the top of a bench. We went to her place and just "happened to find her cache". She was furious and wanted to know how we had found it. We just told her that people talked.

Doug Roberts

* * * * *

MEMORIES OF MY SERVICE IN NOVA SCOTIA

During my tenure at one detachment in Nova Scotia I worked almost exclusively on liquor work which consisted mainly of raiding bootleggers, blacklisting suspected bootleggers, and searching for stills where illicit liquor was suspected of being made. I recall how another constable and I repeatedly raided the bungalow of a little old lady who was known to be bootlegging, but search after search did not turn up any liquor on her premises. One day I took out a junior constable to raid with me and he apparently had a stomach stronger than I had. This young fellow entered the old girl's bedroom and as usual, just under the bed, was a chamber pot "floating full". He removed this odorous item from under the bed, dislodged two loose boards, and there was the cache that put an end to the old lady's bootlegging days.

Although a good portion of my work was on the Liquor Squad, I had relatively little to do with the local winos as they were the responsibility of the town police. In those days, most small-town police forces didn't have a police cruiser so they would save up two or three winos, put them in the local lockup, and wait until we had a prisoner to drive the 15 miles to the county gaol. We would then take their prisoners to the gaol for them. I remember one morning while taking one of the habitual "alkies" to the county gaol, I asked him what he had been drinking to be picked up. He told me he had been drinking shoe polish. As a joke I asked him if the shoe polish had been black or brown. He said he always drank black shoe polish as he found that the brown upset his stomach.

R.D. Wallace

*   *   *   *   *

A RUM STORY

At an eastern Canadian seaport during World War II, information was received that a 45-gallon cask of "uncut" rum destined for the Liquor Control Board had been "diverted" by longshoremen during unloading operations. An immediate investigation was launched by the local detachment.

Naturally, the longshoremen involved knew nothing and our investigation was at an impasse until a hot tip was received later in the day from the local underworld. With a ring of credibility, our informant told us that the heist had been engineered by the local kingpin of the bootlegging fraternity and that the cask had been concealed in an open grave at the local cemetery.

This graveyard covered an area of about a city block and when darkness fell a detail of six or seven sleuths descended on the scene. Each member approached it from a different entry point, clad in nondescript attire so as not to arouse undue interest. The cemetery was something of a thoroughfare for pedestrians so it was felt our presence strolling around would not arouse any suspicion.

Well, our investigation over the next several hours deteriorated into nothing short of hilarious, although this didn't become evident until our debriefing session afterwards. At midnight, all but one of our party withdrew for a conference at a nearby marshalling point, and only then, when we were telling of the suspicious characters and goings-on we had observed, did it become clear that the suspicious characters were none other than ourselves during our surreptitious surveillance.

A "graveyard" detail of one man was left for the balance of the night and at dawn, a thorough reconnaissance was made of the entire area. No gravesites containing a 45-gallon cask of rum could be found.

We never discovered what happened to that precious cargo the longshoremen allegedly spirited away from the dock that fine day. We couldn't help but admire the professional planning and execution involved. Whether the police were diverted on a wild-goose chase to facilitate the covert movement of the cask will never be known. But I'll wager present-day stevedores are still being regaled about the saga of the missing cask of rum.

A.Pennock

* * * * *

A POTENT BREW

I was stationed in a small village in northwestern Saskatchewan in the 1940s. The detachment office was located in a house that also doubled as single and married quarters. My penthouse apartment was a single room on the second floor and my bathroom consisted of a toilet in the basement. It was only accessible through the kitchen of the married quarters.

The village was notorious for the quantity and quality of the "home brew" manufactured in the surrounding district. One cold winter day, the corporal and I, ably assisted by the Liquor Squad, seized seven gallons of brew at a local farm. To tell the truth, Police Dog Tel found the cache in a snow drift. In any event it was a red-letter day for us as we had been frustrated by a number of unsuccessful searches.

Subsequent to the conclusion of the court case, we received instructions to destroy the exhibit. The corporal concluded that the only logical method of doing so was to pour all seven gallons, one gallon at a time, down the single man's toilet. We proceeded down to the basement with a civilian friend in tow as an independent witness to the act of destruction. He thought we were out of our minds to pour what he considered nectar of the gods down a toilet. Nevertheless we were resolute in carrying out our duty and in due course all seven gallons disappeared.

The village did not have a sewer system and all the waste from the detachment building ended up in the septic tank in the back yard. For weeks afterwards the entire basement was permeated with the odour of home brew each time the toilet was flushed. I wondered afterwards what that home brew must have done to the bacteria that are supposed to function in a septic tank. One blessing was that the line to the tank never froze over that winter as it had on occasions in the past.

Ed Willes

* * * * *

MEMORIES OF A MOONSHINER

It was a fine summer morning for running off our "wash", which after five days in the woods had tested well yesterday. With the stealth of Indians, John and I walked quietly deep into the woods over that path we knew so well which led to the brook where our 90 gallons were waiting.

With experienced eyes, we watched for freshly broken twigs, disturbed branches or footprints in the soft earth which might indicate an intruder or, more important -- the Mounties. Much to our relief, all was well.

Arriving at our concealed still site, John and I started right to work utilizing the sack of gallon jugs and the propane gas burner we had carried in from town. Retrieving our boiler, cooler, worm and other paraphernalia which was carefully hidden nearby, we assembled our still, only to find that the gas burner was not functioning properly.

As daylight was breaking, I thought it best to return to town and obtain another burner: it was evident we would produce no shine without a replacement. Leaving John to guard the site and try to get the malfunctioning burner operating, I began my hurried trip. Within the hour, I was on my way back with another burner.

The sun was just now breaking over the horizon and it looked as if we would have a good day in the woods with the only problem being the pesky mosquitoes. The Mounties would never walk in on us now in broad daylight without being detected, as there was only one path to our still and it was surrounded by heavy, noisy woods.

As I neared the site, I saw John up ahead still working feverishly in an attempt to get that burner operating, apparently without luck. He looked somewhat different from the back, but I guessed he was getting tired and would be welcoming my return with open arms. I remarked to him that I had a better burner now.

He turned around and to my surprise, a person I did not know identified himself as a member of the RCMP and told me I was under arrest. In shock and horror at what I saw and heard, I dropped my burner and fled into the woods, as do all good Cape Breton moonshiners in such a situation. I would have got away too, if it hadn't been for that darn dog -- I think his name was Sultan -- and the five or six other redcoats who seemed to come out of nowhere.

Now that John and I have served our six months and paid our fines, I look back on this episode with a smile. Arresting John at the still while I was away getting another burner and replacing him with a Mountie wearing his clothes was pretty slick. Slicker still though, was how those guys with that dog got near our impregnable still without detection.

I guess it just goes to show you, the early bird gets the "worm" and they sure did in this case.

A true story as told to E.W. Hamilton
RCMP Quarterly - Volume 34, Number 2

*   *   *   *   *

TAMPERING WITH EXHIBITS

This story was told to me by the late Charlie Sweeney. In the 1940s Sweeney was the junior constable at Campbellton Detachment. The corporal in charge, whom we shall call Hughie, had a brother, Nat, stationed at the dockyards in Halifax.

One fall day Nat appeared at Campbellton Detachment and told Hughie that he had a few days off and thought he would come to visit. The two brothers were not at all close, but blood being thicker than water Hughie decided to let him in. That evening Nat produced 26 ounces of rum. This gesture made Nat a lot more popular with Hughie. The three of them (Nat, Charlie and Hughie) spent the evening imbibing from the bottle Nat had provided. They consumed the contents and went to bed.

The following day Nat visited friends in Campbellton during the day and that night appeared at the detachment with another bottle of rum. The same procedure followed as on the previous evening and Hughie went to bed quite content with the way the visit was turning out. When the same thing happened on the third day, Hughie was mystified, but not wanting to look a gift horse in the teeth drank his share of the bottle. When it was finished, Nat got up and said, "Well, I'm on duty tomorrow afternoon in Halifax. I enjoyed the visit, but all good things must come to an end." With that he shook hands all around and left.

After he had gone, Hughie sat at the table deep in thought. Finally he said to Charlie, "You know, Nat and I have never been close. For the life of me I can't understand why he was so generous on this occasion." Then he jumped to his feet, "My God, the exhibits!"

He ran to the exhibit room, unlocked the door and discovered to his dismay that three quarts of rum were missing. Nat must have spotted the keys to the exhibit room on Hughie's desk and helped himself to three bottles of rum. To say Hughie was upset was most certainly an understatement, and it was lucky for Nat that he got away before the purloined liquor was discovered. Fortunately, the three bottles had been before the courts and were awaiting destruction by the Officer Commanding Moncton Sub-Division on his next inspection. Hughie had to go to the liquor store the following morning and purchase three bottles of rum matching the three bottles Nat had taken and return them to the exhibit room for eventual destruction.

Donovan Saul

*   *   *   *   *

UNDERCOVER

It was the fall of 1940. I was a very junior member at Moncton Detachment. Early one Saturday evening I was instructed to proceed to Shediac Detachment in civilian clothes; not just ordinary civilian clothes, but rather attire that would make me look like a seaman. I was to wear nothing that could possibly identify me as a member of the RCMP. Completely mystified, I put on an old pair of pants and a turtle-neck sweater that had seen better days. No further instructions were provided and I was driven to Shediac. When I went into the office, Fred, the member in charge of the detachment, was there with Constable Barry Valois, who had come in from Buctouche Detachment.

We then received our instructions from Fred. They were very basic and provided adequate leeway for an imaginative approach to the job at hand. He informed us there were a number of bootleggers in his area and he instructed us to purchase beer or liquor from them and bring the purchases back to the detachment, identified with our initials. He told us there was a Danish ship in port and we were to represent Danish seamen on shore leave. I was told that I couldn't speak English at all and Valois could speak a limited amount with a Danish accent. Fred gave us the location of about five bootleggers. He said there were actually six locations but we were not to bother with the last as he was too cute and would probably warn off the others if we tried a purchase there. He did provide us with his address. He then gave Valois funds to make the necessary purchases.

About ten o'clock at night we sallied forth. I practised talking mumbo jumbo to Valois in what was supposed to resemble Danish and we entered the first bootlegging establishment. The purchase went off without a hitch. Valois had been given expense money for the liquor purchases, but we were not told we couldn't drink some of the beer, providing we retained sufficient for identification, suitably marked with both our initials so we could identify the purchases in court. So at each place we went, we imbibed a little. After each successful buy we returned by a round-about route to the detachment and left a sample of our purchase, suitably initialled. By the time we had been to about four bootleggers we were feeling pretty good and enjoying our duties. About one a.m. I suggested to Valois that we attempt a purchase at the establishment where Fred had told us we wouldn't be able to buy any beer. We sat at a table and ordered a beer each. I clearly recall that we bought Moosehead beer because I pointed at the moose head on the label and asked Barry in our manufactured Danish what kind of an animal it was. Valois told the bootlegger that I had never seen an animal like that and asked what it was. The bootlegger told him it was a moose, which information he relayed to me in our version of the Danish language. The bootlegger was quite amused as we departed with the balance of the case of beer.

When we told Fred where we had made our latest purchase he seemed quite disturbed. The following morning we obtained arrest warrants for all the bootleggers where we had made purchases, but when we got to the last place, we found the bootlegger had flown the coop. As this was a provincial statute it was only enforceable in the province of New Brunswick, so it became an unexecuted warrant. From then on, the detachment had to submit a monthly report detailing the reason the warrant could not be executed.

Shortly afterward I was given leave of absence from the Force and joined my comrades in Number 1 Provost Company (RCMP) in England and the undercover operation completely left my mind. I returned to Moncton Detachment in 1946. I had been banged up a bit in Holland, had spent quite a long period in hospital and was unable to walk very well. I was relegated to work in the sub-division headquarters records office where my duties were to put reports in the appropriate file and give them to the sub-division crime report reader.

I had only been doing this duty for a short while when a crime report came in from Shediac Detachment. It was a brief request for an unexecuted warrant to be cancelled. This was not too unusual but the wording immediately caught my attention. Memory dims with the passage of time, but as near as I can recall this was the gist of the report: "This warrant has been outstanding for many years. The only two witnesses for the prosecution are Constable Valois and Constable Saul. Constable Valois has left the Force and his present whereabouts are not known. Constable Saul went overseas and is now believed to be dead. In view of this it is requested the warrant now be cancelled."

I retained a copy of the crime report and sent it back to the detachment with the following note attached. "Far be it from me to interfere with your objective. I just want to let you know that I don't know the present whereabouts of Barry Valois but that the death of Don Saul is highly exaggerated as I am very much alive."

I signed my name and sent the copy of the report back to Shediac. Thus ended my only undercover operation.

Donovan Saul

* * * * *

MISFORTUNE COMPOUNDED

The enforcement of unfair and discriminatory laws is invariably viewed as an onerous task by most policemen. Many officers operate on the theory that if an unreasonable statute is zealously enforced, an aroused public will demand a change. Some provisions of various provincial liquor laws once permitted people in the larger cities to buy alcohol 24 hours a day, but citizens of rural areas were restricted to daylight hours of sale. This situation obviously encouraged bootlegging in smaller centres.

On a singularly unsuccessful safari to a small town near Prince Rupert, B.C., in the mid-1950s, two of us on the RCMP Liquor and Gambling Squad were returning in plain clothes to our motel early one Sunday morning when we met a taxi that had just struck a deer. The animal was dead and a damaged radiator had immobilized the vehicle. In our casual dress we stopped and offered to assist, but the driver said it wasn't necessary as he had radioed for a tow truck.

He then surveyed us critically, appeared satisfied, and said, "I've got a whole trunkful of booze that I can't sell now. There's usually cops around the garage where they'll be towing my car. Do you guys want to buy some or all of this stuff?"

Some days you should never get out of bed...

R.W. Morley

* * * * *

Chapter Six

The North

MAN HUNT IN THE ARCTIC

On the "mystery roll" of the man-hunt scroll is written the
    trapper's name,
But no-one knows just who he was, from whence or why he
    came.

                      J. Robert Barrett

In 1931 a routine police investigation developed into a hunt for
a desperate killer in Canada's frost-bound northland. The tense
drama involving "The Mad Trapper of Rat River" has been the theme
of countless stories, but here are the facts of the case from RCMP files.

A stranger arrived at Ross River Post, Yukon Territory, on
August 21, 1927, and after a cursory look around, made his way to
the Taylor and Drury trading store. Although not too much
information was volunteered, trader Roy Buttle learned that the
newcomer's name was Arthur Nelson, that he was a trapper, and that
he intended to stay just long enough to build a boat.

The store-keeper said he would lend a hand and Nelson,
although not too enthusiastic at first, finally accepted the offer. Buttle
sized the newcomer up fairly well and in view of the fact he did not
outwardly show too much curiosity or ask too many questions, the
reticent Nelson did confide a few things to Buttle over the nine days
it took them to put the boat together.

Buttle found Nelson intelligent and highly rational in all conversa-
tions, but there was something odd in the man's make-up. For one thing,
Buttle was the only person around the post the trapper would have
anything to do with. He camped about half a mile from the settlement and
openly showed that he welcomed no guests. Also, the Indians living around
the post were visibly afraid of the stranger and would have absolutely
nothing to do with him. This was not because Nelson was a towering giant
of a man. Of average height, his well-proportioned frame packed about
170 pounds. His speech carried the trace of a Scandinavian accent and he
seemed to walk with an habitual stoop as if he had been used to carrying
an extremely heavy shoulder pack.

Nelson told Buttle he was an American and had been raised on a small farm in North Dakota. He appeared to be in his early 30s. He said he had reached Ross River via the headwaters of the Big and Little Salmon rivers, having come from Teslin Lake. The previous winter he had been trapping in northern British Columbia in the area between Teslin and Dease lakes. Buttle learned that Nelson had reached the Dease Lake area by way of the Stikine River and prior to that had worked at the mines at Anyox, B.C.

When the boat was finished, Nelson left the post on August 30, travelling up river. The RCMP officer at Ross River, Corporal Claude Tidd, himself a newcomer to the district, was on patrol up the Pelly River at the time of Nelson's arrival. Although he returned a day or two before Nelson left, he did not meet the trapper; he heard about him from Roy Buttle.

Arthur Nelson returned to Ross River Post on June 16, 1928, and stayed around for a month until the trading store's annual supply boat arrived. He told Buttle he had been trapping at Ross Lakes during the winter. After the supplies came in, Nelson purchased a few provisions, a Savage .30-30 carbine and some .22 shells. He left suddenly in mid-July.

About a month later, three trappers, Ole Johnson, Norman Niddery and Oscar Erickson, were travelling up the south fork of the Stewart River. One morning as they were eating breakfast at Twin Falls, they noticed a stranger walking toward them. They invited him to join them, but he refused, saying he had camped overnight upstream a piece and had already eaten. He told them his name was Arthur Nelson and asked the way to Keno.

Nelson said he had come from Ross River Post where he had built a boat and that he had hit the Stewart River above the Rogue River (a branch of the south fork of the Stewart). The three men did not see Nelson's boat, as he was on foot when he approached their camp, and after learning the way to Keno, he hiked off in that direction.

Robert Levac, who operated a trading store at Fraser Falls, was the next man to come into contact with Nelson. The latter asked if he could stop over a day or two and Levac put him up in a spare cabin. Nelson wanted to get rid of some marten skins he had trapped, but Levac wouldn't buy them. He said he would bid on them, but suggested that Nelson take them to Mayo to sell.

Nelson kept pretty much to himself for the two days he stayed at Fraser Falls, doing nothing but lie on his bunk. Occasionally he went into the store to buy something to eat, but he seemed moody and answered either a curt "yes" or "no" to any questions Levac asked. Before leaving, however, he did tell the trader that he had come from Ross River Post where he had built a boat the previous summer, but that it had been wrecked up the Ross River. When Nelson departed, he did so without saying a word to Levac.

A few days later, Arthur Nelson appeared in Mayo. One of the first things he did was to peddle his marten skins at the Taylor and Drury store for $680. This transaction was completed between Nelson and W.H. Jeffrey of the firm on August 30, 1928. Nelson received this amount in cash through an arrangement between Taylor and Drury and the Bank of Montreal in Mayo, as the store did not have that much cash on hand.

Before the summer was out, Arthur Nelson joined James Mervyn who was ferrying his supplies up the Stewart River to his store at Lansing Creek. Mervyn put Nelson and his outfit off at the mouth of the south fork of the Stewart where the trapper spent the winter of 1928-29, and when Mervyn was returning to Mayo on his boat the following summer, he passed Nelson on a raft. The trader offered Nelson a ride, but he refused.

Prior to this, in March 1929, trapper Jack Alverson, who had first met Nelson in Mayo in 1928, stayed one night at Nelson's cabin at the mouth of the south fork of the Stewart, but once again, Nelson was in one of his reticent moods; other than some talk about trapping, the only thing Alverson learned from Nelson was that he was Danish.

The next two winters Arthur Nelson spent trapping in the Macmillan River district between Ross River Post and Mayo. On two occasions he visited the trading store at Russell Creek run by Mr. Zimmerlee. Although Zimmerlee did not see Nelson carrying firearms at any time, the trapper asked for some shotgun shells on one occasion when he purchased supplies at the store.

In the spring of 1931, trapper P. Fredrickson of the Russell Post area sold a canoe to Nelson who paddled off up the Macmillan River; later, some Indians in the district found the canoe abandoned on the upper waters of that river. Nelson returned to Mayo shortly after leaving the Macmillan River area, stopping off long enough to pick up a few provisions, including an abundant quantity of kidney pills. Clerk Archie Currie of Binet's store was rather startled when Nelson bought six boxes of pills but Nelson was so uncommunicative that Currie thought twice about engaging the man in any conversation.

In May 1931, Nelson headed north to Keno. He stopped there briefly, making a small purchase in the store then managed by Joe Clifton, and began walking north again. Frank Gillespie was having a cup of tea at the mouth of Crystal Creek one morning when Nelson happened upon his camp fire. Gillespie offered the traveller a cup, but Nelson refused, asking where the bridge on the McQuesten River was located as he was going to Haggart Creek. At the time, Nelson was labouring under the weight of a heavy shoulder pack.

"Snoose" Erickson and his partner, Sullivan, had a cabin on the McQuesten River in May 1931 when Nelson passed that way at noon one day carrying the heavy pack and a small rifle. Erickson asked the stranger to have lunch with them but he curtly refused the offer and kept walking in the direction of the eight-mile cabin near the head of the Beaver River.

From the head of the Beaver River, Yukon Territory, in May 1931, trapper Arthur Nelson seemingly vanished just as strangely and suddenly as he had first appeared at Ross River Post nearly four years earlier.

On July 9, 1931, a stranger arrived at Fort McPherson, Northwest Territories, under unusual circumstances. This man drifted down the Peel River from the direction of the Yukon Territory on a raft consisting of three large logs, to a spot about three miles above Fort McPherson. There he abandoned his crude craft and apparently with either little or no outfit, walked the remainder of the way into the fort where he purchased supplies. He was said to be well stocked with cash.

This information was passed along to Inspector Alexander Neville Eames, who commanded the Western Arctic Sub-Division of the RCMP (with headquarters at Aklavik, NWT) by Bishop Geddes. Constable Edgar Millen, in charge of the Force's detachment at Arctic Red River, was sent instructions to interview the stranger.

Constable Millen located the newcomer in Fort McPherson on July 21 where he was purchasing more supplies. He told the policeman his name was Albert Johnson, that he had come into the country via the Mackenzie River and that he had spent the previous year on the prairies. Asked about his plans, he said he was undecided but had considered going over the Rat River portage. He told Constable Millen he would not live in the settlement as he did not want to be bothered with anyone and wished to live entirely alone. The policeman realized that Johnson did not wish to divulge much in the way of information about himself.

Constable Millen later learned from Northern Traders Limited and the Hudson's Bay Company that Johnson was definitely getting an outfit together for a trip over the Rat portage. On the next patrol to Fort McPherson in August, Constable Ronald Melville found that Albert Johnson had left the settlement on July 28, paddling down river in a canoe he had purchased from an Indian. The policeman learned from Arthur N. Blake, who lived at the mouth of the Husky River, that Johnson passed his place looking for the Rat River, but had apparently missed it, because a few days later he returned and stopped at Blake's home.

Johnson then paddled up a creek behind Blake's which leads to the Rat River by a chain of lakes and portages, even though the settler told him he didn't think it was possible to reach the Rat that way with a large canoe. Johnson told Blake that he was going into the Yukon Territory and not returning and after he left via the nearby creek, Blake did not see him again.

Johnson was not heard of again until December when some Indians trapping in the Rat River district reported to Constable Millen at Arctic Red River that a strange white man had been interfering with their trap-lines. They said the man lived alone in a cabin about 15 miles up the Rat and believed his name to be Albert Johnson.

At seven a.m. on Boxing Day, Constable Alfred W. "Buns" King and Special Constable Joseph Bernard left Arctic Red River by dog team in bitterly cold weather to investigate the complaint and also to see if Johnson had a licence to trap. The previous summer in Fort McPherson Constable Millen had told Johnson he would have to obtain a trapper's licence either at Arctic Red River or Aklavik if he intended working that area, but there was no record of his having done so.

Constables King and Bernard stopped overnight at Fort McPherson and by evening the next day, reached the mouth of the Rat River, where they set up camp. They left early on December 28 to cover the remaining 15 miles to Johnson's cabin.

"I spent nearly an hour at the cabin, knocking on the door and calling to Johnson and informed him who I was and that I wished to speak to him, but he refused to open the door or answer," Constable King noted in a subsequent report to his officer commanding. "I saw him peeping at me through a small window near the door, which he immediately covered when he saw me looking at him."

King decided to mush on to Aklavik and obtain a search warrant. This was issued by Inspector Eames. In view of Johnson's peculiar attitude, the O C strengthened the patrol by adding Constable Robert McDowell and Special Constable Lazarus Sittichiulis. The four men left Aklavik at seven a.m. on December 30 and arrived at Johnson's cabin at 10:30 a.m. on New Year's Eve.

Johnson's cabin was only a few miles above the junction of the Rat River and Driftwood Creek, a place which a third of a century earlier had been dolefully tagged Destruction City. It was here, in the bitter winter of 1898, that four men died of scurvy while waiting for a break in the weather before continuing their trek to the Klondike in search of a fortune. The Rat River at this junction is marked by a series of rapids so severe that at gold-rush time, the banks were lined with the wreckage of equipment -- hence the name Destruction City.

Buns King walked up to the door of Johnson's cabin, knocked, and asked, "Are you there, Mr. Johnson?" He had hardly uttered the words when a shot rang out and he slumped to the ground. Struggling to his feet he staggered toward some brush nearby, while Constable McDowell poured rifle shots through the wall of the cabin to try and draw the fire away from his wounded comrade. The shooting from inside the shack continued and two bullets narrowly missed the other policeman.

Seeing that King's condition was serious, Constable McDowell abandoned the idea of attacking Johnson's cabin and thought only of rushing the wounded man to medical aid. The two dog teams left Johnson's cabin about 11 a.m. and, travelling all night, covered the 80 miles to Aklavik in 20 hours. King was placed in the All Saints Mission under the care of Assistant Surgeon J.A. Urquhart.

In view of the seriousness of criminal charges now facing the man known as Albert Johnson, Inspector Eames decided to lead a larger party to the lonely cabin on the Rat River. Others making the trip were Constables McDowell, Millen, Specials Sittichiulis and Bernard, trappers Ernest Sutherland, Karl Gardlund and Knud Lang and 42 dogs. The inspector also obtained 20 pounds of dynamite with caps and fuse, figuring he might have to blast away the walls of the cabin if Johnson still refused to answer the summons.

The party reached the mouth of the Rat on January 5, 1932, and replenished the stock of dog food at Arthur Blake's store on the Husky River prior to leaving for Johnson's cabin. An Indian guide, Charlie Rat, was asked to return from Fort McPherson where he had been spending New Year's to lead the party along an Indian trap-line south of the Rat as it was felt that travel along the river itself afforded

Johnson too many opportunities for ambush. The lower reaches of the Rat run through a large canyon over 1,000 yards wide in most places with the banks varying in height from 200 to 600 feet. The river itself is narrow and the valley is well timbered and covered with brush.

Due to the insistence of the guide, the party camped late that afternoon at a spot he said was only four miles from Johnson's cabin. Next day, however, it was found the Indian had made a mistake because when they reached the river, they found that they were six miles above the shack, and so spent the remainder of the day -- January 8 -- returning to the camp of the previous night. Travel was slow and tortuous due to the fact that temperatures since New Year's Day had been hovering around -45 degrees Fahrenheit and the footing through loose snow and willows was extremely hazardous.

A check of the dog food at the camp showed there was less than a two-night supply left and no chance of securing more within 80 miles, so Inspector Eames decided to storm Johnson's cabin the following morning. They arrived half a mile from the shack at noon on January 9, about an hour and a half after day-break at that time of the year. Securing the dogs in the timber, they moved forward and partially surrounded the cabin. As they approached from the river bank, the men could hear Johnson moving about so the inspector called to him to surrender. Johnson ignored the order.

The officer decided they would attempt first to break the cabin door down by smashing it with rifle butts, and the three policemen and three trappers started to rush the cabin. The wily Johnson was a step ahead of the party and commenced firing as soon as they clambered over the top of the bank. It was then noticed that he had cleverly fashioned out shooting holes above the bottom logs of the cabin in eight different locations.

Despite the hail of lead, two of the party were successful in bashing in the door as they raced around the cabin, but this only led to Johnson pouring out a steady fire through the opening. When the six returned to the cover of the river bank, Knud Lang told the inspector he had seen Johnson crouching on the floor of the cabin -- which incidentally appeared to be four or five feet below ground level -- with two automatic pistols.

The party was compelled to build a fire in order to thaw out as the temperature was still 45 below. They kept up the siege until after three a.m. the following morning -- 15 hours in all -- as it seemed Johnson had an unending supply of ammunition. About nine p.m., small charges of dynamite were thawed out and thrown at the walls of the shack in the hopes that some of the logs would be dislodged, but as far as could be seen, they had no effect and most did not even explode. One of the group succeeded in rushing through Johnson's fire to throw a larger charge on the roof, but all it did was blow a small hole in the roof and not stun Johnson as had been hoped.

The last of the dynamite -- four pounds -- was lobbed against the front of the cabin at three a.m. on January 10, where it exploded successfully. Karl Gardlund and Inspector Eames ran forward with a spotlight intending to blind Johnson, but he heard them coming and commenced firing. Gardlund switched on the lamp anyway, but Johnson's accurate fire blasted the light out of his hand within seconds. The police party then retired to catch an hour's sleep before returning to Aklavik through necessity -- food for the dogs. They arrived there on January 12.

Two days later Constable Millen was sent back to the Rat River with orders to camp two miles from Johnson's shack and see if the fugitive was still in the cabin. Millen took along Karl Gardlund. On January 16, a party consisting of Inspector Eames, ex-Constable John Parsons, Quartermaster Sergeant R.F. Riddell and Staff Sergeant H.F. Hersey of the Royal Canadian Corps of Signals, Noel Verville, Ernest Sutherland, Frank Carmichael and Special Sittichiulis left Aklavik in another attempt to apprehend Albert Johnson.

Upon reaching the mouth of the Rat, the officer was handed a note from Constable Millen, sent by an Indian, which reported that Johnson had taken his outfit and left the cabin. Inspector Eames recruited a party of 11 Loucheux Indians camped at the mouth of the Rat to join the posse. The party set up camp on the river nine miles above the cabin. A severe windstorm on January 15, 16 and 17 had obliterated all tracks, so for the next four days, the party fanned out along the whole of the Rat River canyon to the Bear River, visiting old cabins and Johnson's trap-line, but no evidence could be found of his having been there recently.

Inspector Eames now found that it was impossible to keep so large a party supplied with dog food and provisions, so the Loucheux Indians were dismissed. The supplies on hand were enough to keep four men going for nine days, so Constable Millen, Army Sergeant Riddell, Noel Verville and Karl Gardlund were chosen to remain and travel as far as the Yukon divide if necessary. Sergeant Riddell was equipped with a portable short-wave transmitter and receiver, with which he was able to receive messages from Aklavik and occasionally transmit back. The inspector and the remainder of the party left for Aklavik once more, arriving on January 23. He planned to keep hauling provisions to the mouth of the Rat and replace the four searchers after their nine-day stint.

Constable Millen's party scouted a portage from near Johnson's cabin to where the Bear River joins the Rat, and from there into the higher hills that had not previously been searched. On January 28, an Indian who had been with the large party the previous week, overtook the four men and told Constable Millen that two shots had been heard the previous day from the region around the mouth of the Bear. The party returned and picked up Johnson's track, which led to a thick patch of timber five miles from the mouth of a creek which empties into the Rat a mile north of the Barrier River.

On January 30, the four-man party split up, Constable Millen and Verville electing to rush down the hill into a creek where Johnson had holed up and Sergeant Riddell and Gardlund taking the opposite direction. They could hear Johnson coughing. Johnson apparently heard Millen and Verville coming down the incline and when Millen went past an opening in the timber, the trapper snapped off a shot at him. All four men fired a volley blindly into the timber where they figured Johnson was hiding and when there was no return fire, they believed he had been hit.

Millen and Riddell entered the patch of timber and a shot rang out at extremely short range. Riddell scrambled back over the bank for cover, but Millen remained and fired two shots into the thicket. Three rang out in answer. When Sergeant Riddell scrambled over the bank farther away, he saw Constable Millen lying in the snow.

Riddell and Gardlund sought the cover of large spruce trees and began pouring fire into Johnson's thicket. Gardlund watched his chances and while Riddell kept firing, he crawled forward and reached the feet of the inert Millen. He undid the policeman's boot laces and tying them together to form a handle, pulled the body over the bank. An examination showed that Edgar Millen was beyond help. Johnson's aim had been deadly.

Two days before this, Army Staff Sergeant Hersey and Special Constable Sittichiulis had left Aklavik to bolster Constable Millen's party, but en route met Sergeant Riddell who was returning to report the policeman's death. Sittichiulis returned with Riddell, and Hersey continued on to assist Gardlund and Verville who were keeping watch on Johnson's activities. Riddell brought the sad news that Millen had been killed on Sunday afternoon, January 31.

Shortly after this, Special Constable Hatting, Reverend Thomas Murray and Ernest Sutherland left Aklavik to relieve Gardlund and Verville and two days later, after Eames made an appeal over the local amateur broadcasting station, he left for the site with Sergeant Riddell, Special Constable Sittichiulis, ex-Constable Ethier, Peter Strandberg and E. Maring. En route they were further bolstered by Knud Lang and Frank Carmichael, and later at Rat River by ex-Constable Arthur N. Blake, August Tardiff and John Greenland. Near the Rat they were overtaken by a messenger with news that an airplane was leaving Edmonton, Alberta, to lend assistance.

On February 5, the large group reached the spot where Constable Millen had been shot, and discovered that Johnson had taken to the high ground. They spent the day searching the nine- mile ravine. They were now in the larger foothills which contained numerous creeks, deep ravines and canyons running from the watershed. Between these creeks was frozen tundra covered with snow, hard packed by the ceaseless strong winds. Fresh tracks made by Johnson were located February 6, 7 and 8 in three different creeks four to six miles apart showing that he had been crossing the tundra from creek to creek and circling eight to ten miles back over his own tracks.

The well-known bush pilot, Captain W.R. "Wop" May flew over the area February 7 and seeing the scouting party on the Barrier River, landed two miles from them on the tundra. Constable William S. Carter from Edmonton bolstered the searchers and Captain May returned to Aklavik to start ferrying in provisions and dog food. Prior to landing he scouted the area ahead of the party and saw where tracks, undoubtedly Johnson's, ended at the Barrier River, apparently a camping spot.

Another patrol, headed by Constable Sidney W. May from Old Crow Detachment in the Yukon with Special Constable John Moses, two trappers and two Indians, joined the party on February 8. They came via La Pierre House, the Bell River, Loon Lake and the Rat. Next day a patrol led by Constable May went as far as the last timber on the Barrier River and found a recent track made by Johnson heading for the Yukon divide. Earlier, Indians in the party had told Inspector Eames that it was not possible for anyone to cross the divide alone, so it appeared that Johnson was becoming desperate.

With the exception of Constable May, Special Constable Moses and Frank Jackson, the posse returned to the Rat River where it was decided supplies could be landed more easily. These three stayed at the Barrier River camp and on February 12, Constable May and Indian Peter Alexis rode into the camp on the Rat with a note from a trapper at La Pierre House, Harry Anthony, stating that a band of Indians had spotted a strange snowshoe track near La Pierre House. The description of the track was that of Albert Johnson.

In view of this, a change of plans was necessary, and the following men formed a party headed for La Pierre House: Constable May, Specials Moses and Sittichiulis, Staff Sergeant Hersey, Joseph Verville, Constant Ethier, Frank Jackson and Peter Alexis.

Inspector Eames, Sergeant Riddell and Karl Gardlund flew with Wop May back to Aklavik to obtain larger snowshoes for the party and on February 13 they crossed the divide to La Pierre House, landing on the Bell River in deep, soft snow. A sudden storm prevented further flying that day, but on Valentine's Day, Captain May scouted the Bell River for 25 miles and found Johnson's track which he followed as far as the mouth of the Eagle River in the Yukon where he lost it in a maze of caribou tracks.

Searchers scoured the Bell and Eagle rivers February 16, finally camping about 15 miles from the mouth of the latter; they were able to follow Johnson's trail quite easily as the snow was softer and there was little wind. He had, however, managed to take advantage of the caribou tracks and had hiked in them without snowshoes for about ten miles.

As the searchers believed they were narrowing the gap on the fugitive, they broke camp early on February 17. Also, another danger threatened. Johnson was headed toward the cabin of a trapper named Barnstrum and although no one in the party seemed to know the exact whereabouts of the cabin, it was felt the man should be warned of Johnson's treachery. To further complicate matters, it had been planned to have Wop May search for the cabin from the air the previous day, but dense fog had prevented him from taking off from La Pierre House.

Before noon, the patrol, which consisted of eight men with dog teams and three on foot, was approaching a sharp bend in the river when Staff Sergeant Hersey, driving the lead team at the time, spotted Johnson coming down river only 250 yards away. Johnson saw the posse at the same instant and quickly laced on his snowshoes. Then he made a dash for the river bank, rifle in hand.

Hersey and Joseph Verville, driving the next team, drew their rifles and started firing at Johnson from the centre of the river. They were quickly joined by Karl Gardlund and Frank Jackson, and in a short time, the whole party began moving up stream, some on the river and others on either bank. All this time, Johnson was firing rapidly at the pursuers, but suddenly his fire ceased and he started to run back up river. Before he stopped shooting, however, his deadly rifle had taken a further toll; Staff Sergeant Hersey had fallen in the snow, shot through the lungs.

Johnson was running back in his own tracks, stopping occasionally to turn and fire, and was actually drawing away from the party. He was making for the opposite river bank which was not steep. Called upon once again to surrender, Johnson ignored the command and kept running for the bank, whereupon the posse threw a concentrated volley at him. Reaching the bank, Johnson threw himself in the deep, soft snow and began to dig in, using his heavy pack as a cover. He then resumed firing.

But this time, the effect of numbers began to tell, and with men completely surrounding Johnson and a few on higher ground firing down on him, he was no longer shooting back.

"At 12:10 p.m., February 17, it was found that Johnson was dead, having desperately resisted to the last," Inspector Eames noted later in his report. And so the 48-day "Arctic Circle war", which started out as nothing more than a routine investigation, ended in the deaths of two men and the serious wounding of two others.

All of Albert Johnson's effects were gathered up and checked. A total of $2,410 in cash was found on his corpse in denominations of $20, $50 and $100 as well as two American five-dollar bills and one ten-dollar bill. There were also two small glass jars containing five pearls (later evaluated at $15) and five pieces of gold dental work.

Firearms found in his possession included a model 99 Savage .30-30 rifle, an Ivor Johnson sawed-off shotgun and a .22 Winchester rifle, model 58 with cut-down stock. His supply of ammunition included 39 .30-30 shells, 84 .22 shells and four 16-gauge shotgun shells. There were other miscellaneous items including packages containing a total of 32 pills.[1]

Significantly, there was no trace of any written matter found either on Johnson's body, at his cabin or at any of the caches and camps he had made in the area of the Rat River. The two automatic pistols seen in Johnson's hand on January 9 by Knud Lang were never found. An old canoe was at the cabin, and about 300 yards away, a carefully concealed stage cache containing a quantity of provisions.

Johnson's cabin was constructed of logs about a foot in diameter. The inside dimensions were roughly eight by 12 feet. The door stood four feet high, of which three feet were above ground level, and the roof was made of heavy poles covered with frozen sod two feet thick. The floor of the cabin was not as far below ground level as first appeared, perhaps because of the depth of the hard snow outside. It was 38 inches below ground level, providing Johnson with plenty of protection when the siege was taking place.

A physical description of Johnson, after death, by Assistant Surgeon Urquhart listed his height as five foot nine, estimated weight 145 to 150 pounds. He had light brown hair which was receding, pale blue eyes, snubbed upturned nose, moderately prominent cheek bones, lobed ears, low set and close to the head. The only mark on the body was a small wart or mole, two inches to the left of the spine in the mid-lumbar region. The surgeon set his age between 35 and 40 years, the size of his feet as 9 1/4 inches, and said his teeth had been well cared for but contained numerous fillings.

The task of identifying the man known as Albert Johnson was one that has never been successfully concluded. All the Force had to go on was that he had told the late Constable Millen in Fort McPherson that his name was Albert Johnson; the Indians complaining about trap-line interference said they too believed this was his name. Fingerprints taken from his corpse were sent to both Ottawa and Washington but they were not linked to anyone with a criminal record in either country.

The first reports of the other stranger in the lower Yukon who called himself Arthur Nelson came to the RCMP in August 1933. From the physical descriptions and "lone wolf" attitudes of the two men, it seemed likely that they were one and the same, but this has never been proven conclusively.

There are, however, some facts that make it seem likely Nelson and Johnson were identical. Sergeant James R. Purdie of the Dawson Criminal Investigation Branch made inquiries at the banks there to see if he could trace any of the currency found on Johnson's body. The Bank of Montreal traced two bills. One $50 bill had been received at the bank as one of a shipment of 100 such bills on September 7, 1926, and the other, also a $50 bill, was one of 100 bills sent to the branch at Mayo on March 22, 1928.

There is no actual record of either Johnson or Nelson having been in Dawson, although Corporal Arthur Thornthwaite of Old Crow Detachment, in a report dated the same day Johnson was shot, said that a local Indian gave a description of a man he had worked with on the 12-mile dredge out of Dawson in 1930, and except for this man having brown hair (Johnson's was light brown) they seemed identical. The Indian said the man called himself Al Johnson and left the district in the fall of 1930 after telling the Indian he was going to the Peel River district to trap alone.

It is reasonable to assume that Nelson received the second $50 bill from Mayo, as on August 30, 1928, less than six months after the bill was sent to Mayo, Nelson received $680 in cash there from the Bank of Montreal after selling marten skins to the firm of Taylor and Drury.

The firearms found in Johnson's possession were not successfully traced, due to the company records having been destroyed, but it is significant to note that Arthur Nelson had purchased a .30-30 Savage rifle and a Winchester .22. W.W. Douglas, who worked for Northern Traders Limited in Fort McPherson, recalled selling Johnson a 16-gauge, single-barrel shotgun and a box of 25 shells on July 12, 1931, three days after he arrived at that post.

All the persons who had seen or talked to Arthur Nelson between Ross River Post, where he was first seen, and McQuesten River, where he was last seen, were eventually shown facial photos taken of Albert Johnson after death, and most thought it could be the same man, although none could be sure. Johnson was in such an emaciated condition at the time of his death (145 to 150 pounds) that it is likely that his gaunt features would look somewhat different from the sturdy Nelson (170 pounds).

There was one other question that arose when attempts were made to link Johnson and Nelson and that was whether or not a man could travel from the McQuesten River near Keno where Nelson was last seen in May 1931, to Fort McPherson, a distance of some 250 miles, in just over two months on foot -- Johnson had appeared there on July 9, 1931. To do so, he would have had to cross over the Ogilvie Range. This was answered by Superintendent Thomas B. Caulkin who commanded the RCMP at Dawson. He said he knew a man who left

Mayo on June 28, 1934, went to Fort McPherson and returned to Mayo in the latter part of August 1934, thus doing double the trip in a two-month period.

Over the years since this bizarre affair, the Force has answered numerous inquiries from persons all over the world claiming to be relatives of "The Mad Trapper of Rat River" as he had been described in numerous articles, but in each case the RCMP has patiently checked photos and descriptions, and in all, has had to write back, "We find that ... is not identical with the man known as Albert Johnson".

T.E.G. Shaw

RCMP Quarterly - Volume 26, Number 2

[1]Editor's Note: In retrospect, it would have been interesting to know whether these pills were kidney pills. If so, it would confirm that Nelson and Johnson were one and the same person.

*   *   *   *   *

YUKON PATROLS

Despite all the writings about "The Mad Trapper", Albert Johnson case, the participants were simple ordinary men, who chose to serve in the Force, and they, like all men of strong character, wished to be known and considered as such. They chose to serve in the north and considered themselves fortunate when chosen to do so. I had a small part in the Albert Johnson encounters and our persistent patrols to bring him down in the Yukon in 1932.

The "Dirty Thirties" were now creeping upon us and a noticeable change was taking place. Many strangers were coming in, especially in the Mayo-Keno and the Dawson area. They were closely watched and we were almost playing super-sleuth in poring over the Wanted posters. However, some disappeared from the scene and many went "down river" or "inland" and established trap-lines, which meant that patrols had to be enlarged and stepped up to keep the "cheechakos" from starving to death.

Communication was spotty and unreliable, but we became aware of something going on over east of the Mackenzie Mountains in the adjoining Western Arctic Sub-Division in "G" Division, but were not sure what it entailed. "Buns" King had been shot and was in hospital in Aklavik, so we learned. He wrote me from there and gave me a sketchy outline of what had happened. We thought little of it, as we expected that "G" Division would have it under control. However, by various communications we began noting the chase, as it was then called, as closely as we could from a great distance. It didn't become "The Mad Trapper of Rat River" until the imaginative news writers got into the act. We surmised that "G" Division had holed him up and had him suitably contained and the rest would be routine. How wrong we were.

Our own "B" Division (Yukon) was fully occupied in keeping its own house in order and patrols were very intense. Then about the middle of January 1932, we learned that Johnson had slipped away and was on the loose, probably heading for our bailiwick. We were spread thinly. There were only two detachments, Fortymile and Old Crow, within the periphery, and there was a strong possibility that Old Crow would become involved as the Western Arctic had picked up trails which indicated that Johnson might try to use that far northern outlet to Alaska.

The chase dragged on. Now our patrols were out and far reaching. Peter Paton Lee, who was at Fortymile, had his area well in hand, but there was a distinct possibility that an experienced traveller could evade him and get into the Miller and Glacier creek areas which were not patrolled. Therefore these had to be kept under surveillance.

There were quite a few trappers on the many small creeks running into the Yukon River and we constantly patrolled them between Fortymile and Fort Yukon, which is the first post on the Alaskan side and is just on the Arctic Circle. It is approximately 225 miles northwest of Dawson. The route was not difficult and good time could always be made if weather permitted.

On January 31, news came through that "Newt" Millen had been bushwhacked and was dead. This indicated that Johnson was headed into our "B" Division territory, and contact became more likely. We continued the dogged patrols, searching every outlet. The country was unfamiliar to us and we were at a disadvantage; we had to rely on any scrap of information we could, and unreliable as it turned out to be, we had to check it out. But we stuck with it.

On February 1 the Officer Commanding, Dawson, sent out a message that Johnson was believed heading for the vicinity of the Porcupine River. (It leads down into Alaska.) Romeo May, then at Old Crow, took it in hand and started working the Bell River area. He established contact with Eames (from "G" Division to the east), scoured the Loon Lake area and kept a close watch on McDougall Pass. He also worked the country around La Pierre House and had assistance from a police guide, Moses. Inspector Eames carried on the erratic chase, and wisely left the western reaches to Romeo.

As stated, we had been patrolling constantly and were working farther north each sweep. On the afternoon of February 8 the O C again sent out a message giving sketchy details, and urging extreme caution for all patrols. We got his message on the 10th. A further message came through for our patrol to proceed to O ld Crow to assist if necessary. We re-supplied and proceeded forthwith.

We were unfamiliar with the country. However, by making inquiries and picking the right trail and cut-offs we made out alright. Travelling was tolerable, although it was extremely cold. We arrived in the vicinity of Old Crow on the afternoon of the 15th. All was confusion and excitement. Everybody was trying to be the star of the show. But we did learn, with some accuracy, that Romeo was in the vicinity of La Pierre House, and with some guidance from a young Indian boy we pushed off in that direction, cross patrolling. We bedded down at La Pierre, and in the morning we heard the news that tracks of a strange snowshoe had been found and apparently had been made during the night. We went to the spot, about two miles away, and verified this. Amazingly, Johnson had approached, then had doubled back.

It is sheer conjecture on my part, but it would appear that Johnson realized that patrols were approaching from the west and that he was bottled up. It is also conjecture that he may have realized that, with patrols fanning out, he would have a better chance to slip through the eastern patrol, regain familiar ground and make his get-away.

In any event we were approaching very cautiously, keeping to the open spaces. He was now pinched between patrols. We kept on following, and the trail he left was fresh. About that time there was a plane circling and we felt there was contact with the Eames patrol. We came to the bank of the Eagle River, and could see a man on the ice. Then the firing commenced and it was concentrated and heavy. We were quite a distance away from the object and looking down. A strange thing happened. Sammy Glenross looked over and said, "One for our side", knelt and fired a shot. I don't think at that distance it had any effect. Then there was a bit of a lull, and we could see the other patrol cautiously descending to the river. About noon or thereabouts, February 17, 1932, Albert Johnson lay dead on the ice of the Eagle River.

We went down and reported to the other patrol on the ice, but other things were more important at that time, and this is understandable. The part we had been called upon to play was over, and we started home. We returned to Dawson and strange as it may seem, learned more about the chase from those who had listened than we knew ourselves.

In all writings of the north, I have never come across any mention of our dogs. To the patrolling policeman, a good leader is as essential as a white cane to the blind. Here, I pay tribute to them. My leader was Spotze, meaning smart, and I am proud to say that his picture "Ready for Patrol" is contained within the walls of Fort Calgary. Time is getting on, and it is only natural that I will be called on to perform "the last patrol." I am ready. I hope when I reach wherever old patrollers go, and have a chance to sit around and chew the fat with Millen, King, Cronkhite, and all those I knew, I will feel a little nudge and look around and see old Spotze wagging his tail. I hope he turns and licks my hand.

Fred Burt-Johns

*   *   *   *   *

ARCTIC PATROLS

In the late 1940s life in the Eastern Arctic was still rather primitive. This was particularly so with respect to the Eskimos. They were a very kind and generous people who always made room in their igloos for hungry, cold and tired policemen who arrived at their camps on winter patrol. They were eager and willing to help out -- the men of the camp assisted with unloading the sled and feeding the dogs while the women dried our deer-skin clothing and repaired it if necessary.

Their small igloos made of snow blocks consisted of one room, heated and lighted by seal-oil lamps. Approximately one third of their dwelling was reserved for a sleeping bench where all the family and visitors slept. We were always made comfortable and given the best spot on the sleeping bench for the night.

Following the evening meal and several hours of chatting and tea drinking, during which the special constable brought the inhabitants up to date on all the news throughout the area, the family and guests retired for the night. Needless to say, there were no indoor toilets in the igloo and the bitter cold was not conducive to answering the call of nature outside. So the last thing at night, before retiring, a bucket was passed into which everyone, with as much modesty as possible, urinated. Whether due to embarrassment or modesty, or both, I always declined the opportunity and passed it on.

On one particular night when the steaming cauldron finally made the rounds it was placed to one side, just under the skylight which was made of seal intestines. As I lay in my sleeping bag and the igloo cooled, I noticed the steam from the bucket rising and freezing to the skylight. I woke the following morning to the sound of the host's wife scraping the frost from the skylight into a large teapot to which was added a quantity of tea for the breakfast brew. To have refused a cup of this nectar would have been bad manners, but when the wife squirted a quantity of breast milk into her husband's tea and gestured towards my cup with her breast -- I declined.

"No thanks," I said. "I like mine black."

Bud Johnson

*   *   *   *   *

LOST IN THE BARRENS

When I was taking my recruit training at Depot Division (now called the Academy) I was particularly interested in the lectures on the history of the Force. One of the most dramatic tales was the tragic account of the McPherson-Dawson Lost Patrol in 1910 - 11, an RCMP patrol in the frozen Yukon that had lost their way and gradually perished one by one from starvation and exposure. Little did I know that one day I would also face a situation similar to that encountered by the earlier patrol, fortunately without the tragic results.

In 1949 I was stationed at the Reliance Detachment at the eastern end of Great Slave Lake in the Northwest Territories. The complement was an NCO, a constable and a native special constable. George, the special, had lived all of his life in the north and his main duty was to act as guide on our frequent patrols. Jim Wegren was the constable and I was the NCO.

The rationale for the detachment was two-fold. First, it served as a base to check on the trappers, to make sure they were in good health and surviving, and second, to ensure that no one was entering the Thelon Game Sanctuary. This sanctuary was believed to contain endangered species such as the musk-ox and therefore it was sealed off to all persons. Even planes were not allowed to fly over it.

On February 19, 1949, George and I started out on patrol to the Thelon area, leaving Jim Wegren behind to look after the detachment. As I had recently moved to Reliance, I had not been on this patrol before and was unfamiliar with the route. However, George had been on this patrol several times.

To carry our supplies we each took a carryall, a toboggan-type sleigh with canvas sides and a raised back with handles for the driver to grasp. Pulling each carryall was a team of six dogs. Besides rifles, sleeping bags and food, we took a tent with a small drum heater and stove pipes leading to a hole in the top of the tent. This would provide heat for our cooking.

Trailing along behind each carryall was a length of rope called a "lifeline". This served a very useful purpose. If the driver was running along behind to get warm or to help the dogs over a difficult area and he fell, by the time he picked himself up, the sleigh would be beyond his grasp and sleigh dogs do not always obey the commands of their driver. The driver would be in dire straits indeed if he were travelling alone and his team took off and left him stranded with no food, rifle, sleeping bag or tent. By grasping the lifeline, however, the driver could hang on until the dogs got tired of pulling him and stopped.

At the end of the first day we left the tree line and entered the barrens. Before leaving, however, we gathered a good supply of wood in case we were unable to find any in the barrens.

The patrol proceeded in a routine manner for the next three days and we reached Whitefish Lake on February 23. At the northern edge of the lake there was an abandoned cabin. Here we stopped for two days, hunting, gathering wood, establishing a cache and resting the dogs. The cabin had not been used for a number of years and hoar frost covered the inside of the building. When we started a fire the frost melted and we got a veritable rain storm. However, we covered everything we wanted to keep dry and weathered the storm. After all, it was -40 degrees Fahrenheit outside and we thought that we would rather drown than freeze to death.

The second day there, George went hunting game and I walked quite a long way from the cabin looking for wood. Suddenly I felt the hairs on the back of my neck stand on end. I turned and saw a very large wolf standing about 30 feet behind me, and between me and our camp. I remembered all the stories I had read to the effect that a wolf would not attack a human. I sincerely hoped the wolf had also heard these stories.

When the wolf saw me looking at him he began to jump in circles and gambol around like a puppy. Then he started to run away and come back. It appeared that he wanted me to follow him. Knowing that wolves travelled in packs, there was no way that I was going to let him lure me into an ambush. As I had no rifle, I threw snowballs at him and finally he slunk off.

We started out again on February 27. The weather looked a little unsettled but we thought it would blow over. At nine a.m., a raging gale hit. The snow was as fine as flour, and knocked the visibility down to zero. It was so bad that neither of us could see our lead dogs. To avoid getting separated, we tied my lead dog to the rear of George's carryall. If we could have found some trees we would have "holed-up" and waited for the storm to blow itself out. However, erecting a tent would have been impossible, so we kept on going, using the direction of the wind to keep us on course.

Just before dark we came across some scrub pine trees. Fortunately, the wind had died down a bit and we set up camp. We tied the tent to the trees to keep it from blowing away and it was fortunate that we did for the wind came up again and persisted on and off for the next five days. In between squalls we hunted, managed to shoot several deer and established a cache.

When we broke camp we started in a southerly direction because George considered that we had drifted north. As we found out later, the wind had changed direction and had put us off course. We travelled south, even though George was unable to recognize any landmarks.

Later, we came across an abandoned shack. On the premises were traps, a canoe, an outboard motor, dishes and cutlery and a number of magazines dated 1935. We also came across a diary. Upon reading it we found that apparently two men had been using the cabin as a base for their trap-lines. The man who owned the diary expressed fears about his partner's sanity. He wrote that his partner had refused to speak to him for several days and just stared at him all day long. The cabin had been deserted for 14 years and we wondered if we had stumbled on a 14-year-old murder-suicide. I decided to investigate the matter when I got back.

On March 5 the storms abated and we again started out, hoping to come across some caribou. Unfortunately, they seemed to have vanished from the earth. Our supplies were very low, so men and dogs were strictly rationed. We found to our dismay that somehow one of the dogs had managed to reach one of the snowshoes and had ripped it up, so our progress was slow. We had no more food for the dogs.

On March 8 we came across the remains of a caribou. It had apparently been the victim of wolves. We chopped it up and fed it to the dogs but there wasn't much nourishment in it. However, it revived them somewhat. George and I were subsisting on two small canned meat-balls a day. As there were four meat-balls in a small eight-ounce tin, it will indicate how small they were. We had a discussion as to when we should eat our lonely meat-ball and decided it was to be in the morning and not at night. We put up the tent at five p.m. We had no food for the dogs and they were weakening fast.

The next day a storm arrived as we were eating our frugal breakfast. We sat it out all day. On March 10 we went southwest all day hoping to hit Whitefish Lake but the terrain was different and we were no nearer to our cache line. Eventually, we came to an old cabin with no roof so we pitched our tent outside. George put the dogs inside the cabin to give them some shelter from the weather.

That night we heard the dogs howling. We ran in and found that Pepper had died and the other dogs were tearing him to pieces. This was strange as when Pepper first collapsed, the dogs nuzzled him for encouragement. Now, however, with starvation looming, it became survival of the fittest. We chopped Pepper's body up and fed it to the rest of the dogs.

For the next five days we were pinned down by one storm after another. In the lull of one storm George went out and shot an Arctic hare. We made it last two days. When that was consumed I found a bacon tin in the carryall. It was empty except for an inch of bacon grease in the bottom. George and I shared that and it tasted wonderful. Apparently our bodies were craving fat and that is why it tasted so good. I'm sure if I tried to eat it now it would make me sick.

During our forced inactivity I studied the map. It was badly out of date and had large areas marked "NOT MAPPED". However, I came to the conclusion that we were south of where we thought we were and that we should go north to hit our caches. George at first demurred.

"There is nothing up there but the Arctic Ocean," he said. I was willing to play my hunch by splitting up if necessary. Finally George shrugged his shoulders and agreed to go north when the weather calmed. His next remark, however, made me wonder when he said "I always wanted to see Edmonton before I died". I jollied him along and told him we had lots of life in us yet and he seemed to snap out of it. From then on I watched him closely.

In between storms George wandered around the area looking for game while I went collecting wood. On one occasion I entered the shack to see how the dogs were getting along. I suddenly realized that they had surrounded me and were snarling at me with their heads down. Obviously they were preparing to attack. I grabbed a piece of wood and beat my way through them to the door.

During our enforced stay our dogs gradually died one by one. After Pepper, Steve went next, then Blackie, Jumbo, Tip and Blaze. As each dog died, we chopped it up and fed it to the rest of the dogs.

On March 17 the storm finally diminished in the early morning and we got ready to go. We combined the essential equipment into one carryall and abandoned the other. We put the five best surviving dogs into the harness and left the others to follow if they could.

We both knew that although we might be on the right track, it was possible that we would not have sufficient strength left to travel the 40 miles or so to our cache. We did not tell each other at the time, but when we got up that morning we both suffered from dizzy spells and cold sweats breaking out on our heads. After hanging onto something for a few minutes we found our strength seemed to return, at least enough of it to keep us from falling down.

We started out with George pulling and me pushing. The five dogs pulled as long as they could and then two collapsed in the harness. We released them and continued. They followed us for a short time and then disappeared. After about two hours of travel we came to a large lake and our morale, and apparently our strength, improved, as we were sure that we were on Whitefish Lake.

At noon we stopped to rest and to have a drink of tea. We had been existing on tea and a small jar of honey for the past week. Once again we started out and continued till dark. We were utterly exhausted and found making camp almost beyond our ability. We walked back a short distance after we had made camp to see if we could see the dogs that we had left behind but we did not.

As soon as it was light we saw the big bluff with the single tree on it and we knew we were on the right track, as that was our marker. We arrived at the cabin at noon and found our cache intact. After feeding the dogs we got into the flour and made a big batch of pancakes. Much to our surprise, after eating one small pancake we were stuffed. Our stomachs had shrunk but it wasn't long before we were able to eat larger portions.

We stayed there for nine days, getting our strength back, chopping meat for hamburgers and rendering caribou fat as well as playing cards with a deck we found in the cabin. The three surviving dogs soon got their strength back as well.

We considered that it would take us five days to walk back to Reliance. We took off on March 29 and made it to our cache at Sandy Lake. Our muscles had stiffened up because of our recent inactivity at Whitefish Lake so we decided to stay over one day. As it turned out, that was a good decision because during the afternoon we heard a plane and we were sure they were looking for us.

I had saved a piece of shiny tin to use as a reflector and, when the plane approached, I tried to reflect a beam at it but it went over without seeing us. We thought they would go out to our original destination and work their way back, so we got some brush together to make a smoke and also made an arrow on the ice with trees. We watched the dogs and when they pricked up their ears and looked in the direction the plane had gone, we lit the fire. Although we had lots of smoke, the wind blew it along the ground and again the plane passed over without seeing us. However, when they got over the lake they saw the arrow and then saw us and landed on the lake.

There wasn't enough room for us and the dogs so I went with the plane back to Reliance and George stayed behind with the dogs and remaining equipment. He was picked up by the plane the next day. So ended the lost patrol of 1949. I was surprised to note that my weight had dropped from 180 to 130 pounds and George had a similar decrease in weight.

Checking on the abandoned shack with personal effects and trapping equipment that we had encountered, we found that a plane had come by and been flagged down by the partners. As they had no further interest in trapping, they abandoned their equipment and flew "outside". Thus no further investigation was warranted.

Ivan Rolstone

* * * * *

USAF CRASH AT CAPE DUNSTERVILLE

The east coast of Ellesmere Island did not have many inhabitants in the early 1950s. The most northerly RCMP detachment at the time was located at Craig Harbour on the southernmost tip of Ellesmere. RCMP staff consisted of two regular members and a native special constable. The native settlement had around eight to ten families.

In 1953 the government decided to open an RCMP detachment about 350 miles north of Craig Harbour. A suitable location was found about half-way up the coast of Ellesmere at Alexandra Fiord. This would be roughly 620 miles from the North Pole. Personnel consisted of two regular members of the Force and two native special constables who came from around the Pond Inlet area of Baffin Island. The purpose of the detachment would be to study game conditions, and living in such extremes as prolonged total darkness and continuous sunlight. The intent was to rehabilitate Inuit families from Port Harrison and Baffin Island to an environment more suited to their hunting and trapping skills.

Long and short dog-team patrols would be made from Alexandra Fiord, the longest to the southern detachment at Craig Harbour and on to Resolute Bay on Cornwallis Island. There the mail would be waiting for pick up and return to Alexandra Fiord, a round trip of approximately 1,200 miles. It was on this return trip by dog team that Fred Stiles, one of the Alexandra Fiord Detachment members, and two native special constables came across an unusual event.

Thule Air Base in Greenland was approximately straight across Smith Sound from Craig Harbour. The United States Air Force had a fighter/interceptor squadron there as well as a reconnaissance patrol that roamed over the ice fields of Smith Sound and Kane Basin. During the latter part of April 1954, a four- engine aircraft similar to a World War II Liberator bomber took off from Thule with a crew of nine on the ice-reconnaissance patrol that would be their last. As they approached the coast of Ellesmere Island, visibility deteriorated due to ice crystals and some fog creeping in.

Flying at about 3,000 feet above the sea ice the pilot found himself in a complete white-out, a condition where the horizon and the sky meet and cannot be distinguished from one another. The pilot did not realize that he was above a glacier and not the sea ice. The glacier rose sharply and blended with snow-capped Cape Dunsterville. As the pilot realized what had happened he attempted to raise the aircraft above the summit. His discovery was too late and the plane struck barely 50 feet from the top. The aircraft was completely destroyed and took the lives of all crew members.

It was hours before the alarm was raised at Thule Air Base, but once it was, a search-and-rescue aircraft with paramedics aboard began combing the known area of the missing aircraft. Late the next morning the Albatross search-and-rescue aircraft discovered the wreckage on top of Cape Dunsterville. The rescuers had a choice of landing on the sea ice below the summit and climbing up the mountain to the crash site, or allowing the paramedics to jump from the aircraft and parachute to the site without delay. They chose to jump.

In the meantime, the RCMP Alexandra Fiord patrol had kept the Cape Dunsterville landmark in sight for two days. Travel was slow and they could only make 25 to 35 miles per day depending on the ice conditions. They had been sleeping in snow houses for the past week and upon emerging into the cold crisp air that morning found that the sun was high and super bright but had little warmth. Fred and the two native special constables prepared to break camp for they were now only two sleeps from home. The only sounds were from the dogs which were now awake and eager to get into harness. After the initial burst of energy the dogs slowed to their travel gait, half fast walk and half run. The sled runners had been re-iced that morning and the sleds were swift because most of the dog food they had started out with had been consumed. It was cold, with a north wind blowing steadily. Fred and the two special constables were dressed alike, caribou-fur parka, polar bear-skin trousers, sealskin and polar bear-skin boots. Fred had over a week's growth of beard that made him look as dark as his Inuit guides.

In the crisp air the only sound was the squeaking of the sled runners moving across the hard-packed snow. The droning sound was hardly noticeable at first but it was the unmistakable sound of an aircraft and the three men searched the sky. They spotted it flying above Cape Dunsterville which was just ahead of them on the left. The natives were perplexed because they had just seen something fall from the aircraft. Fred knew that two parachutists had just come out and he suspected that a search-and-rescue mission was taking place on top of Cape Dunsterville. The search-and-rescue people did not see the two dog sleds far down on the sea ice, and although they were American service personnel on Canadian soil, they felt that no one would ever be aware of it. Back on the sea ice Fred told the specials to secure the dogs because they were about to climb the glacier to the top of Cape Dunsterville and find out exactly what was going on.

When the two paramedics landed near the crash site it soon became obvious that no one had survived the plane crash. The Albatross set course for Thule Air Base to be replaced by helicopters to complete the rescue mission. The paramedics were now organizing the removal of the bodies and were awestruck by the silence once the aircraft had departed. As far as they were concerned, they were the only human beings on the east coast of Ellesmere Island, being unaware of the RCMP detachment locations.

One can therefore understand their total astonishment when they saw three figures appear on the crest of the summit and come towards them. All three were dressed alike and appeared to be some of the nomadic Eskimo hunters of the high Arctic. They were dumbfounded when the tallest one spoke in perfect English and introduced himself quite casually as if he were out for an afternoon stroll.

"Hello, I'm Constable Fred Stiles of the Royal Canadian Mounted Police. We seem to have a problem here."

A. Blake McIntosh

*   *   *   *   *

A BUSH PILOT'S LIFE IN THE RCMP

From 1930 to 1954 the RCMP utilized three rugged bush planes: the Norseman in 1930, the Beaver in 1950 and the Otter in 1954. These airplanes were all built in Canada. The Norseman was built by the Nordine Company of Montreal; the Beaver and the Otter were built by the De Haviland Company of Toronto. The Norseman and the Beaver were equipped with skis and floats while the Otter had skis, floats and wheels.

All three aircraft were excellent bush planes, ideally suited to the north. As time passed, advancing technology contributed to increased efficiency, thus making the Otter the best of the three. It was roomier and had the added advantage of being a short take-off and landing aircraft (STOL), making it even more suitable, as adequate landing areas were at a premium in those days.

One of the drawbacks of the Norseman was very limited cabin space. There is a story that must be told, as it makes this deficiency very apparent indeed. I was pilot of a Norseman based at Fort Smith in the mid-1940s. The weather had been miserable for about a month, precluding use of the aircraft. Finally the weather cleared, and though the temperature was -30 degrees Fahrenheit, the skies were clear, permitting us to make some delayed patrols. The Officer Commanding Fort Smith Sub-Division instructed us to go to Fort Reliance, pick up the corporal in charge and take him to Yellowknife for temporary duty pending his formal appointment as NCO i/c Yellowknife Detachment. This was a town-policing assignment, most unpopular with the majority of northern men.

When we arrived at Fort Reliance, the second member informed us that the corporal was on patrol in the barrens with the dog team. When advised of his intended route the crew tracked him by his sled marks, eventually locating him on the barren lands. A landing was made close by and the corporal was advised of the OC's instructions. There we were, a sight to behold -- the Norseman on skis, the crew in winter gear, and a very upset NCO, with a full beard, dressed in caribou skins (pants and parka) with ten husky dogs and sled on the windswept barren lands in the dead of winter.

The corporal refused to believe the directive of the OC; the instructions were not in writing, and no matter how much persuasion we employed, he emphatically refused to discontinue his patrol unless a formal letter was produced from the inspector. We were forced to return empty to Yellowknife and get the transfer notice, -- not a simple matter.

Two days later we again tracked the corporal, landed alongside and produced the letter he had demanded. The angry, distraught corporal with his sled and dogs, complete with gear, finally boarded the Norseman and returned to Fort Reliance without incident. Picture if you can ten huskies, sled and gear with an angry, bearded corporal in caribou skins jammed into the small cabin of the Norseman. It wasn't a pleasant trip.

After two days at Fort Reliance the corporal was flown from his detachment -- a district that he loved -- to Yellowknife, and town policing which he despised. The story has a sad ending. Six months later he actually took his 20-year pension and left the Force.

Summer Inspections

In the 1950s it was customary for the Commanding Officer "G" Division to inspect the detachments in the division. These patrols lasted up to three months. Due to lack of alternative accommodation, the party was mainly housed at the detachments, the CO getting the master bedroom, with the aircrew and other passengers spread out in sleeping bags on the floor. Most of the detachments were on government rations. For some reason, officers were allowed double rations and others single, all of which the NCO i/c the detachment deducted from his allotment. The choicest ration issued was tinned ham. Naturally, every member offered the best he could, and that was the ham. Believe me, after visiting 20 or 30 detachments we all became quite sick of the sight of ham.

Fort Reliance Detachment was on the east shore of Great Slave Lake. It has long been closed, its main reason for existence having been to patrol the Thelon Game Sanctuary which extended from Fort Reliance almost to Baker Lake. The detachment had a beautiful setting. It was quite isolated, had good fishing and clean water, and above all a comfortable outhouse -- a rare commodity. Usually the CO would request a two or three day stopover there and all aboard would do their laundry, bathe, do a little fishing, and just relax.

Due to the proximity of the game sanctuary, caribou were in abundance at Fort Reliance. I don't know where the meat came from but dinner at Fort Reliance was usually fresh meat rather than the familiar tinned ham, possibly some animal that strayed away from the sanctuary. I never inquired. The CO would comment to the corporal in charge that it was a "Lovely tender roast beef" and the corporal would smile appreciatively.

Cheese and tinned biscuits, "Mother's Own" were invariably the fare for dessert. Again the CO would comment "Lovely cheese, corporal."

The corporal would invariably reply, "It should be sir, you've been eating off the same round for at least two years."

J. "Wing" Reid

*   *   *   *   *

INDOOR FACILITIES AND BREAD BAKING

I was the senior member of Coppermine Detachment in early 1950 and there is no doubt the first members stationed there years before would have found it extremely modern and comfortable compared to their time. Headquarters must have felt we were treated quite lavishly, as not only were we privileged to possess an oil stove, but the toilet facilities were comparable to others at this Eskimo settlement.

This luxury consisted of an enclosed room at the far end of the outside porch. The toilet itself, which was naturally portable (due to permafrost), consisted of an empty, five-gallon grease can which was lowered into a larger galvanized container and adorned with the usual wooden toilet seat and cover.

Summer months posed no problem. However, during the long cold winter months, the contents of the toilet can would often freeze solid, due to the unheated toilet area, and as a result prevent the normal dumping of the contents on the sea ice. Therefore, we had no alternative but to place the toilet can on top of the kitchen oil stove (covered, mind you) for a period of time, to thaw and permit outside dumping.

It is fortunate one is not always aware of the bizarre road to a good finished product. Through circumstances beyond our control the defrosting process took place while bread was being baked in the oven of the same stove. I swear it had absolutely no effect on the taste of the fine bread we baked.

Victor Cormier

*   *   *   *   *

RUM RATIONS -- NORTHERN DETACHMENTS

Members of "G" Division stationed in isolated locations were well looked after, food-wise. Rations were shipped in once each year in accordance with the annual requisition the detachment had forwarded to "G" Division Headquarters the year before.

One could not complain about the quantity and variety of the food supplied, given that refrigeration (except the natural element) did not exist and food supplies had to be tinned, dried or dehydrated. The food requisition even permitted one bottle of rum and one bottle of brandy per detachment per year "for medicinal purposes".

Guidelines as to what illness constituted authority for the administration of brandy or rum did not exist and that made any audit during inspections too difficult. The authority for the decision to consume these liquids rested with the NCO in charge and the timing of medical treatment was left to his discretion and judgement. Some detachments were known to require "treatment" almost immediately the supply ship departed -- the rationale being that the ship's crew could have carried some virus, and it made good sense that preventive treatment be administered immediately.

Other detachments seemed to regularly require treatment during the Christmas season, and at those settlements where there was a missionary or Hudson's Bay clerk it was only "neighbourly" that they too shared in the treatment.

At one detachment where there were no white people other than the detachment personnel and only two Indians -- I was stationed there -- the NCO followed a philosophy that small doses were completely ineffective and he therefore threw the bottle cap in the garbage immediately a bottle was opened. His reasoning was quite sound because that method of providing medical treatment always allowed for some letting down of hair, disclosing of secrets, lots of laughs and things to talk about and reflect upon until the next treatment, which would be a long time off.

All in all, one has to think that those in Ottawa deserve credit for their concern with "the health" of its members in the far north.

Ed Lysyk

*　*　*　*　*

DENTISTRY AT ARCTIC RED RIVER DETACHMENT

Members of the Force stationed at remote Arctic detachments were usually expected to dispense medical, dental and a host of other services along with their police duties which alone were broad, to say the least. This routine continued up to and during the late 1940s to the best of my knowledge. In any event, Arctic Red River Detachment was no exception when I was there from 1948 through 1950.

We were provided with adequate quantities of substances normally used for treating diseases, healing, relieving pain or improving health. This ranged from cough medicines to ointments, liniments, antibiotics, sedatives and pain killers. Unfortunately, we had no medical training other than numerous first-aid courses over our years in the Force. We were provided with literature covering the medicines but we had to use our own good judgement to diagnose medical problems. As a bare minimum, we were expected to utilize a great deal of common sense. For example, the arrival of a new constable at one of these detachments often saw the outbreak of a rash of aches and pains, usually called rheumatism, caused by net fishing in the spring and fall when the water was cold. Without exception, the only remedy patients would accept was rubbing alcohol, dispensed in sufficient quantities to last until they returned to the settlement. It sometimes took an inexperienced young constable two or three prescriptions before he got wise and ran out of rubbing alcohol, substituting liniment. The native patients knew before the constable that the skull and cross bones on the issue one-gallon bottles of alcohol did not really mean that the stuff could not be taken internally. When liniment was given instead, the epidemic of rheumatism rapidly ceased.

But this story is about the practice of dentistry. Arctic Red River had a box of assorted dental tools such as picks, forceps, needles, hammers and syringes. Yes, there was even a box containing a number of vials of Novocaine (oral anesthetic). Alas, there were no instructions, and as I had spent many agonizing hours in a dentist's chair, this scared the hell out of me, particularly as there was no doctor or dentist for miles or days away. We never had a visit by a dentist and only once a year by a doctor, and that was primarily to pay the Indians their treaty money. The good doctor did not care too much about the art of dentistry. I heard of him extracting a bad tooth for a native without using any anesthetic. This was done while they were both standing beside the treaty table after which the forceps were wiped off on the grass and returned to the doctor's back pocket. He then continued to pay treaty. No one else complained of a toothache that day.

My first experience along these lines came when a woman brought her daughter to the police office to have a troublesome baby tooth removed. It was then that I first learned an anesthetic cannot be effectively injected around the gum or at the root of the tooth -- it just squirts back in your face and does the patient no good whatsoever. My state of nervousness increased to alarm when I could not extract the tooth, even though it appeared loose enough to almost fall out by itself. Finally, the tooth came away, but at the same moment I demolished it by squeezing too hard on the forceps in my anxiety. I thought of the consequences if the tooth had crumbled sooner. Mother and daughter thanked me profusely and left in a happy frame of mind. I still had over two years to serve on my tour of duty at Arctic Red River so I wasn't quite so happy.

My immediate reaction was to write a long letter explaining my problem to a friend who was a dentist in Charlottetown, P.E.I. He promptly sent me two medical text-books on oral anesthesia together with a bundle of notes and plenty of encouragement. My dentist friend then sent my letter to the manufacturers of Novocaine who, in turn, sent me their latest publications on oral anesthesia and the art of extracting teeth in general. This information was largely in lay language, complete with a number of large diagrams which greatly helped me in learning the overall process. Last but not least, the Novocaine people sent my letter to the dean of dentistry at the University of Toronto who also took a personal interest in my problem, and more probably in the plight of the people of Arctic Red River. He also sent me volumes of notes and diagrams which were very helpful and we corresponded for the balance of my term at Arctic Red River.

Within an amazingly short period of time I became the "Painless Parker" of that part of the north and the word spread to the point where people who had nursed toothaches for years were coming in large numbers to get rid of teeth that were rotted to the gum line due to long-term neglect. One Easter holiday when more trappers and their families than usual were in the settlement, I was called upon to remove 60-odd teeth from just about as many different people.

Through continued study and experience I gained confidence in what I was doing. However, at the same time I learned more and more of the dangers such as infection, a broken jaw or a bad reaction to Novocaine, none of which I was equipped to handle. In addition, there was no doctor available to take over in the event of a problem. This was also becoming very time-consuming and got to the point where I had to set up one day a week for dentistry, except for emergencies which took up even more time. I felt maybe I was getting a little carried away when one Saturday as I was escorting the last patient from my office (the kitchen) he said, "I didn't come to have a tooth out. I came for a hunting licence."

On another occasion, and this was one of my last patients, Margaret, a young mother of four, came in. All her teeth were decayed beyond repair and her body was noticeably emaciated. As she told me she had no other health problems, we concluded her very bad teeth were probably poisoning her system and that she would be better off without them. By this time I felt ready to provide her with a full set of dentures with the help of a dental mechanic I knew in Edmonton. I removed all her teeth and in a very short time she regained her health and her lost weight. The problem was that before her gums had healed well enough to take an impression, I was transferred out of the north and my replacement had no dental knowledge.

Over the years we kept track of Margaret, our toothless friend, through mutual friends and acquaintances. Would you believe she was toothless for the next 17 years -- things being the way they were in the Arctic in those days. The next time we met her was 20 years later at the celebration of the Northwest Territories Centennial in 1970. We could not help but notice she was sporting a brand new set of store teeth and had the nicest smile you could find in a day's travel.

John Morrison

* * * * *

STRANDED

Editor's Note: The following story appeared originally in *The Northern Times*, February 12, 1979. It has been supplemented with excerpts from the notes of Corporal R.R. Tait, NCO i/c Carcross Detachment, who was assigned the investigation.

"I killed time for a while, but then time started to kill me and I had to do something." With those words, 28-year-old Mike Macy ended the story of his harrowing trip from Skagway to Atlin, B.C., on cross-country skis. The Fairbanks resident set out from Skagway on January 23, 1979. His destination was either Atlin or Carcross.

"That was my first mistake," said Macy, who added that he should have chosen only one destination. An experienced skier, Macy had already completed a 500-mile cross-country trek that took him from Lake Clark to Mount McKinley and lasted 2 1/2 months.

This trip was designed to try out a new toboggan he had purchased as well as give him a chance to see Atlin and the surrounding country. Macy figured the 80-mile trip would take him 14 days. After 18 days, he was still miles from Atlin.

In the beginning, he was averaging three miles a day and the going was tough. Macy had to leave his toboggan behind, ski ahead a couple of hundred yards to break a trail and pack down the powdery snow, ski back along the side of the trail to create a wider one, then harness himself to the toboggan and pull it over the path he had just made. With a 60-pound load on the toboggan he was sinking approximately 11 inches into the snow. "Nothing horrendous," he said. There remained only one section of trail and the rest was lake travel. Macy said he thought the going would be a lot easier and that he would make better time once he got down the pass and onto the flat surface of the ice.

"You always figure it's easier going on flat stretches." The map he carried with him had 500-foot contour lines, which hid 490-foot cliffs. "I'm not used to contours and it was a hard adjustment to make. What I didn't know was that there was an unduly steep cliff at the bottom of the hill." A back-country ranger for ten years, Macy admitted to making a lot of mistakes that either he had made before or people he had known had made.

Trying to get down the cliff, Macy was skiing down ten to 15 foot drops. "I'd stop but the toboggan would keep right on going. Finally I reached a place where I couldn't go down any farther and I had to climb out of a small canyon. I was scaling 60-foot cliffs in my ski boots and pulling a toboggan."

At the end of the first week, Macy had covered only 15 miles. He faced another canyon, and only 200 yards from where he would have been able to see to plot his course, he tore the metal plate from one boot. "I was totally unprepared for that and I had no way of fastening my boot to my ski." As if that wasn't enough, the yoke with which he attached the toboggan to his body splintered. It took him two hours to go 200 yards.

"I couldn't go back so the best thing to do was to keep going to get to a lake where people could see me." It took Macy seven hours to cover one mile.

Two days later, he was faced with the prospect of more of what he had just come through or waiting for someone to find him. At this point, he'd been out for about eight days and had only enough food to last him another six days. He thought about making bindings for his ski but figured he wouldn't be able to do a good job. He also considered walking, but it would take him a week or longer to go five miles. In the end he waited there five days. The first three days, the weather was nice and Macy said he knew he had blown it because he hadn't told any officials where he was going. The next two days were stormy and he worried that his tracks would be covered by the snowfall.

"I had no idea when people would come to look for me. I figured about February 4," he said. On the afternoon of February 5, Macy was trying to make an igloo using his tent when the poles broke from the snow load.

"Then it became quite clear. If people were going to come looking for me, they would have come by then. I had two days worth of food left and I figured I'd better move." Early the next morning, he made bindings for his ski and took off for Tagish Lake. The going wasn't too bad because there was a trail and Macy covered three miles in four hours, setting up camp that night on a ridge. The temperature went down to -30 degrees Fahrenheit and it took him six hours to break camp the next day.

"I left everything I didn't need to survive," he said. "My toboggan, my watercolours, and paint brushes." The next day he made it to Kirtland where he found an abandoned cabin. All that remained of his food supply was a pound of cheese and a pound of figs. This he supplemented with some baby food he found in the cabin.

*

Corporal Tait's notes:
February 8 - 8:15 p.m. Corporal Wilson, Whitehorse Detachment, called to say he had been contacted by Mrs. Anne Harrison, of the University of Alaska in Fairbanks. She received a post card from Macy which said he would be leaving from Fraser, B.C., by himself, to Carcross via Tutshi and Tagish lakes. If the going was good he would try for Atlin, via Fantail Lake and Graham Inlet. He had ten to 14 days worth of food.

8:30 p.m. I advised Inspector Pettit of the call and he replied that CIB (Criminal Investigation Branch) would look into it in the morning. Until now, he said, it had been too cold to fly.

February 9 - 11:35 a.m. I spoke to June Kline at White Pass, who had found out that Larry Roth of Skagway, Alaska, was the conductor of the train which apparently had let Macy off.

11:45 a.m. I spoke to Mr. Roth and he confirmed that Macy had been on the train. He had last been seen travelling north on Fraser Lake, pulling a black skimmer. Macy had not confirmed his route but appeared to have been well equipped.

1:20 p.m. I called Max Hyde at "M" Division HQ. CIB readers to apprise him of the situation.

2:45 p.m. Max called back to say we should get Atlin to check if Macy made it to Jim Brook's cabin via Graham Inlet. Apparently George Shawl of Atlin had daily contact with Brook. Max also stated that if nothing comes from Brook we will fly the area tomorrow.

3:15 p.m. I spoke to Atlin Detachment and passed on the information.

4:30 p.m. I called Mrs. Harrison back. She had heard nothing further from Macy. The card had been mailed in Skagway. She did say, though, that Macy is 28 years old and is experienced in this kind of adventure.

9:40 p.m. I called Rick Lawton at Atlin Detachment. He has not heard back from Shawl. Radio reception is poor.

9:50 p.m. I spoke to Max Hyde and told him of developments. If the weather permits, the area will be flown tomorrow, but if not, as soon as possible.

*

For three days Macy stayed in the cabin, getting his strength back. With an old needle, some dental floss, and pieces of material cut from an old sleeping bag he found in the cabin, he made himself some mukluks.

*

February 10 - 9:00 a.m. Rick Lawton called to say that Brook had not seen or heard of Macy.

10:00 a.m. Jim Kelly called from Whitehorse. The Twin Otter will leave at 11:50 for a fly over.

11:45 a.m. We left Carcross in the Twin Otter, flew down Bennett Lake, along Fantail Lake to Tagish Lake.

*

At 10:00 a.m. on the 18th day of his trip, Macy set out for Atlin once more. His face was protected with a piece of nylon he had cut from his tent. He intended to use it to signal any planes he might see. Half a mile from the Golden Gate he heard a plane and looked up to see a Twin Otter bearing RCMP officers.

Macy stamped out the word "frost" in the snow and pointed to his feet. Then he stamped out a big heart. "That's the way I felt when I saw them. I was so happy."

*

12:45 p.m. We spotted Macy on Tagish Lake and contacted Atlin Detachment to come with the helicopter. He was picked up at 1:15 p.m. at the Golden Gate and taken to Atlin. There he was transferred to the Twin Otter and taken to Whitehorse to see a doctor.

*

"There was a period when I thought I might never see anyone again," Macy said. "I came close to panicking. If I didn't love the out-of-doors, I would have gone nuts. Sometimes just the waiting can get to you."

The last part of his journey was a forced march. "If I wanted to live, I knew I had to get out of that cabin. I had no choice in the matter and that sometimes makes things easier."

Macy wants people to know about the mistakes he made in hopes that they won't make the same ones. He admits he won't go into strange country again and will probably be better equipped next time.

*

February 11 - 2:20 p.m. Macy advised us that he was headed to Fairbanks by air. He was very happy with our action.

RCMP Quarterly - Volume 45, Number 4

* * * * *

FROM DUNDAS HARBOUR TO BACHE PENINSULA

The history of the Force, from 1873 to the present day, contains many stories of sheer courage, endurance and resourcefulness. At the top of the list must be the superhuman efforts of some of the northern patrols, especially those before the days of practical flying, Bombardiers and skidoos. Yet, sadly, these stories, mostly from dry, laconic, matter-of-fact diaries, are buried in the archives in Headquarters, Ottawa, perhaps never to be seen again except by librarians. Older people, veterans and civilians alike may remember the story of the March West and perhaps the Mad Trapper of Rat River, but the younger people know nothing of these things. What a pity! For this was a part of our nation's history.

One of the hardest patrols ever was made by Inspector Joy, Constable Taggart and Eskimo Nookapeeungwak. It began on March 12, 1929, and ended on June 1, a total of 81 days. It was described in the commissioner's report of that year as "the most noteworthy event of the year in the north."

Both Inspector Joy and Constable Taggart kept diaries. The following much-shortened account contains excerpts from both. Truly an inspiration and challenge to all who followed.

Constable Taggart -- Inspector Joy and Eskimo with lead sled 13 feet x two feet with 13 dogs. Myself with 11 dogs and sled 11 feet x 2 1/2 feet. We had a ton of supplies and a ten-gallon drum of coal oil for the Primus stove. Constable Hamilton and an Eskimo are to accompany us part way to haul supplies for us.

Inspector Joy -- Start at nine a.m. March 12, 1929. Between the post and Croker Bay the snow was soft and unusually deep, the result of frequent and heavy snowfalls during the last month, and for several hours we made scarcely more than a mile an hour. On reaching the more exposed part of Croker Bay, however, the snow became harder and less deep. Our speed increased to a marked extent. We reached the west side of the bay and camped. Later in the afternoon we killed a small bear which was fed directly to the dogs. The weather was clear and cold, with a sharp breeze from the north.

Next day fair progress was made until we reached Cape Home. From here onward for several miles rough ice on the sound compelled us to travel almost constantly on the ice foot where deep soft snow was met with. Late in the afternoon we came abreast of drifting ice and open water extending to the ice foot. Here, repeated pressure from the sound had built up a wall of ice, varying from 20 to 100 feet high all along the shore line. Huge cakes of ice had been forced over the wall and lay thick and loose in the narrow passage between the ice wall and the vertical cliffs forming the coast line where we had to travel. Our progress then became more difficult and demanded the utmost exertion of both men and dogs, although one or more of the party was kept constantly in advance of the teams chopping a trail.

Taggart: March 13 -- We got into rough ice and had a bad time. In places the pressure ice was pressed up against the cliffs. Then we had to climb over the top, all the men pushing one komatik (sled), the dogs climbing over the ice and around. Sometimes two or three dogs would be away on top of a block of ice ten feet high, while others would be scattered about amongst other blocks. They have a rough time. If anyone from outside could hear the noise of dogs yelping and the language of the men they would wonder what it was all about. Nothing exciting today.

Joy: March 14 -- Just before dark we found our path obstructed by pressure ice a full hundred feet high lying hard against the cliffs for about three miles. We therefore had to retrace our steps and seek a place whereby we could reach the lowest shelf of the mountains. This done we built an igloo and camped for the night.... The following day the three of us packed all the loads up to the first shelf of the mountain, about 150 feet above the shore line, and advanced the heaviest pieces beyond the roughest part of the talus, whilst the remainder of the party strengthened the weak komatik.

Taggart: March 15 -- After breakfast we had a good look at the ice and found it was quite impossible to proceed along the shore. The Eskimos repaired my komatik. Inspector Joy, Hamilton and I portaged our loads up a steep snowbank. We had to cut steps all the way up -- guess the drift was about 150 feet high. The land is very rocky and rough. During the afternoon Joy and I walked to a deep inlet about a mile away and I was lucky enough to shoot three ptarmigan.

Joy: March 17 -- I had intended Constable Hamilton and Eskimo Kamanuk to start on their return journey to the detachment this morning, but as we failed to arrive at the glacier a short distance west of Graham Harbour where very rough ice was reported to be, I determined to retain them until we reached there.

Joy: March 19 -- The following morning the provisions and equipment carried on the assisting komatik were taken over by us and Constable Hamilton and Kamanuk started on the return journey to Dundas Harbour.... The exceptionally bad travelling and heavy loads since leaving the post had greatly affected the condition of our dogs; it was astonishing how much they had failed in so short a time.

Joy: March 21 -- On arriving at Beechey Island late in the evening we found our cache of dog food, pemmican and coal intact left by *S.S.Beothic* although a 50-pound tin of pemmican was afterwards found unfit to eat.

Taggart: March 22 -- ....also a tablet erected to Franklin and his men by Captain McClintock, 1858, one to the memory of Lieutenant Bellot and another to Doctor Kane and his companions.

Taggart: March 23 -- Cold and foggy. Stayed in our bags till noon .... The dogs having a wonderful rest.

Taggart: March 25 -- Cold heavy fog over Wellington Channel which we have to cross.... Joy decided not to risk crossing in such weather. Anyway, another day's rest won't do the dogs any harm where they are. We have lots of meat to give them. I went for a walk to the north end of the island and discovered six graves. Three of the graves were made by men of the *Erebus* and one by men of the *Terror*, two of Sir John Franklin's ships. The other graves were marked by plain pieces of rock without any inscription on them. The first four graves were dated 1846.

Joy: March 27 -- At three p.m. we came abreast of a cairn surmounted by a pole standing on a hill about 800 feet high, a full half mile from the beach, and about 15 miles north of Cape Hotham. We opened the cairn and took from it a record dated August 8th, 1850, by Commander William Penny of *H.M.S. Lady Franklin* and *Sofia.*

Taggart: March 27 -- Shortly after starting we saw a cairn on top of a high hill about 15 miles north of Cape Hotham. Stopped the teams and left the Eskimo to look after the dogs. Joy and I climbed up to see what was in it and found a message from Captain Ommaney to Franklin and his men containing directions to find three caches, one at Mary Point, North Devon Island, one on Leopold Island and one at Cape Hotham. The finder of the message was requested to forward same to Admiralty Office, London, England, and we brought it along.

Joy: March 31 -- During the night a bear came to our camp. He was quite unafraid in the darkness and was shot where he stood, beside the komatik, only a few feet from our igloo.

The following morning a few more bears were seen entering the rough ice about two miles south of our camp. Our dogs being well fed with fresh meat, I decided to rest them here for one day. A blizzard broke over our camp that afternoon however, and continued until the afternoon of April 3.

Early in the morning of April 2 another bear came to our igloo and was shot while standing beside one of the komatiks by Constable Taggart.

The following night still another bear came. On being aroused by the barking of the dogs, I told Constable Taggart and the Eskimo not to shoot the bear as we had then all the meat we could conveniently carry. I soon considered it expedient to withdraw my instructions, however, for instantly the brute was seen tearing our clothing and provisions from one of our komatiks. On making an attempt to get outside we found that the door of our igloo was buried by a deep drift of hard snow, making a quick exit by that way impossible.

The bear's attention now being diverted from the komatik by the noise we were making to drive him away, turned swiftly to our igloo, and by the time a hole was made through the ice-lined wall large enough for a man to crawl through, was waiting opposite on the outside. He instantly made a desperate plunge to get inside the igloo but was beaten back. As he retreated a pace or two Constable Taggart simultaneously seized a rifle standing outside near the hole[1]. The bear, quick as a flash, struck the rifle from Taggart's hands. Then, as if to frustrate any attempt to recover it, stood on it with both forepaws, snarling angrily at us all the while through the hole. A few seconds later he made another desperate charge to get at us and was met by some vigorous blows with a stick and a butcher knife. Following this he retreated a pace or two, giving Taggart an opportunity to recover the rifle and put an end to the bear's sinister purpose an instant later. He was a large animal, wretchedly poor, and almost mad no doubt from prolonged starvation.

Taggart: April 4 -- We shot three caribou and Nookapeeungwak loaded them up and hauled them in. We had tongues, briskets and tenderloin for supper.

Joy: April 6 -- On the 6th we continued to travel northwest following the most practicable route on the outskirts of the rough ice. During the afternoon the left runner of Constable Taggart's komatik split and caused us to halt for the day. We dismantled the komatik, ripped the runners, and rebuilt it, which took us until 2:30 a.m. the following day.

We left camp at four a.m. on the 11th, and in less than an hour a runner of Taggart's komatik broke. The old ice was found to be very ridgy and covered with several inches of unpacked granulated snow which kept the dogs' feet continually bleeding. Towards the west side of the channel, however, we met with new ice and excellent travelling for about two hours, then old and rough ice alternatively until we reached Melville Island a few miles north. During this march Constable Taggart's dogs showed unmistakable signs of weariness ... At this time one of his dogs was found unable to get onto its feet; it was frozen stiff and was destroyed.

Taggart: April 11 -- We had to work our way through more rough ice to the land. Arrived 9:30 p.m., the dogs nearly all in. Travelled a few miles south until we reached Richardson Point where we built our igloo and camped. Weather is very hazy -- guess we are going to have another storm. While we were eating our supper Joy said that if he had even dreamed that the ice was in such condition he would never have thought of the trip.

We are going to try and reach Winter Harbour on Melville and pick up supplies from the government cache there, cross over Melville to Sabine Bay from Bridgeport Inlet, travel to Borden Island, then turn east and make for Bache Peninsula on Ellesmere Island. We have two weeks dog food to carry out that program; if our luck fails and we get no more bears we are going to be up against it.

Joy: April 17 -- Leaving camp at ten p.m. the same day we followed the shore until within four miles of Dealey Island. When about half a mile from the island a large bear approached us in the rough ice. Our dogs saw it first whilst we were working at the komatik and instantly started after it, dragging the komatik with them. We did our utmost to stop them, but we might as well have tried to stop an avalanche. Finally, to save the komatik, they had to be cut loose. A few minutes after we arrived at the Kellett-McClintock cache on the south side of Dealey Island, a second large bear came along and was captured after a long chase through the rough ice. Later in the day another bear was killed. We now had a good supply of fresh meat; also wood and coal in the cache to enable us to conserve our fuel. I therefore decided to leave Constable Taggart here to feed and rest up his dogs while the Eskimo and I proceeded to Winter Harbour.

We found the door of the government shack open and the floor at the north end of the building covered by a full two feet of soft snow. The shack is a good structure and is in good repair. The contents of the shack were as follows: seven tins of flour, each about 50 pounds; 25 pounds of tea, sealed; 12 ten-pound tins of Bovril (tins are corroded and contents spoiled); one double-barrelled hammerless shotgun; a few rounds of shotgun ammunition, (spoiled by moisture); one .303 calibre rifle; one case .303 rifle ammunition unopened; three large oars for rowboat; one wooden komatik (manufactured); miscellaneous articles of cast-off clothing. An 18-foot clinker-built rowboat, apparently in good repair, was lying bottom up at the back of the shack. Inside the shack I picked up a note dated July 8, 1917, left by Vilhjalmur Stefansson, commander of the Arctic expedition 1913 to 1918 which I replaced with a note of our visit .... We reached our camp on Dealey Island early on the 22nd.

The cache on Dealey Island was deposited during the winter of 1852-53 by Commanders Kellett and McClintock, then in search of Sir John Franklin.

Taggart: April 22 -- Overcast and snowing. Joy and Nookapeeungwak returned from Winter Harbour about three a.m. They made a fast trip as the ice was fairly good. They brought back some flour, compressed tea and Bovril.[2] Nothing else in the cache as Stefansson had cleaned it out when he was there. Inspector Joy and I had an argument about dates today. He maintained that it was the 21st and I was convinced it was the 22nd.

Joy: April 28 -- At two p.m. on the 28th we reached the head of Hecla and Griper Bay. We passed six caribou shortly before reaching the coastline, and saw many more fresh signs of caribou crossing the island. Vegetation was not conspicuous in quantity. From the head of the bay we set out directly for Cape Mudge keeping well out from the coast. It was obvious that the ice here had not broken up for several years. It was very ridgy and covered by a considerable depth of granulated snow, which made very heavy pulling for the dogs and hard walking for us. We camped late in the evening about midway across the bay. That night the sun did not go below the horizon.

Joy: May 31 -- It would be difficult to compute the mileage of this patrol with any accuracy owing to the necessity of our following almost every indentation of the coast line for hundreds of miles, and making great detours in the rough ice to take advantage of the best travelling conditions available. From the number of hours spent on the trail each day and the consistency of our daily marches, I would estimate the distance covered to be well over 1,700 miles. Time occupied -- 81 days.

Assembled by Tom Crawshaw

[1] Firearms had to be left outside or they would frost up and could jam.
[2] The flour would have been from either 1850 or 1917.

* * * * *

Chapter Seven

Police Communications

A MATTER OF TIMING

Present-day radar has certainly saved a lot in manpower, but back in 1947 the RCMP hadn't progressed that far and a certain amount of ingenuity had to be employed.

I was stationed in Melville, Saskatchewan, at the time. We had a problem with speeders on one of the streets in town. The old police car, a 1946 maroon coach with white lettering on the sides, was known to everyone, so it was useless for speed enforcement. Fortunately, most of the speedsters operated after dark, so we devised a system to catch them in the act.

One member would climb up a tree armed with a flashlight. A measured distance away another constable would climb up another tree with a flashlight and a stop watch. A third member stationed himself at the end of the street with the ticket book. As a suspect went by, Number One shone the flashlight and Number Two would start the stop watch and time the speed attained between the trees. If the speed was in excess, Number Two would shine his flashlight and Number Three would step out and do his thing. The reason I recall this so vividly is we had to borrow a flashlight to complete the patrol.

H.K. Coulter

*   *   *   *   *

THE SQUELCH NETWORK

These new-fangled talking radios we have had in police offices for the past few years have certainly livened things up. Today, with a radio in the office you are hooked right into a global party line. You can listen to policemen, housewives, oilmen, ranchers and whoever else can get the line, from all over the world, holding forth in a profusion of chit-chat on subjects ranging from crime to croupy kids, gas pressures to runaway steers.

Our radio network has widened its scope mightily from a modest two-station start, back in 1949. I can well remember when the radio technician arrived at our detachment to install the first police radio in the division. After scrambling all over the building from cellar to roof, stringing lead-ins and outs, blowing all the fuses in the place and electrocuting the family cat, the gentleman departed, leaving a big metal monster standing silently in a corner of the office, staring unblinkingly at us with one green eye.

The technician installed another of the same at the next detachment and then halted construction for a time. Our two-station network went on the air without any fancy speeches or ribbon cutting. The system operated very informally and broadcast started when one party called: "Hey, you there?" The occupants of the other station either acknowledged the call or a feminine voice came on the air to say, "The men are all out."

Finally, every larger detachment in the division had a radio set with a regular operator keeping order from a control station. The ether started to vibrate then. The air waves stirred from wild wiggles to convulsions as "Rogers", "Wilcos", "Go aheads", and "Overs" fanned the air. Experimenting reached new heights when the police cars got sets. Everybody drove their cars to the tops of the highest peaks in their areas to find out how far this new contrivance would throw their voices.

Some personnel had difficulty adapting to the mobile-radio age. One man was heard calling a car to ask the driver whether or not he was in a radio-equipped car. Another told a party to phone him so they could talk in peace. A corporal with a dead set asked the radio technician for three tubes and a pint of squelch -- although it was rumoured that he knew more about pints and squelch than he let on.

When the first cold, windy day went by without knocking the control station off the air, the radio technician looked up at the 100-foot tower and declared the network in operational order. With the system working on all kilocycles you could now keep close tab on your neighbour. This sometimes came in handy for correcting him if he tried to tell you he was busier than you were.

Our detachment was somewhat out of the way, radio-wise. Ordinarily, we only heard the control station and two detachments. In our corner everyone had time to have his say without treading on the other fellows' ears. When I moved to another detachment which was in the geographical centre of three control stations and about ten detachments, the well-mannered radio I had known now sounded like a play-back of a ladies' club meeting.

At this cross-roads of the air waves the antenna snagged everything in the air and rolled it out of the loudspeaker in a mulligan stew of bulletins, messages and static, leaving us to sort the discord into something we could make sense out of. It took practice before we could catch what was meant for us and let the rest go on over our head to the other fellow.

Messages that arrived a bit the worse for transmission were hard for a green man to decipher. We left the new junior man to take down a bulletin one day and when we returned to the detachment office he had the following posted up:

Bulletin No. 20

During the night of the 14th instant a breaking, entering, occurred in the Q.M. stores and the following items are missing;

3 pay cheques stamped NSF

10 pairs of women's nylon stockings,

50 booklets on crime prevention,

1 deck of cards and a crib board,

1 dog sled equipped with 2 h.p. electric motor loaded with two kegs of nails and a condemning board.

A suspect is Charlies Uncle Zebra 54" in height, wearing 3 khaki shirts, 2 pairs of drawers long, black mitts and 4 buckle overshoes. If located return with old shirts and drawers express collect to Ottawa.

We were glad when this gentleman was finally caught.

Despite these hybridizations of radio messages we were able to get a working system good enough to trust the radio most of the time. However, the day it kicked over the wave length and leaped out of the province we were caught with our kilowatts down. We called the number of our neighbouring detachment to the west. There was a prompt answer.

"When will you have a car coming down this way?" we queried.

"A what?"

"A car -- poleese c-a-r."

"You must be crackers, bye, we just has the dory here -- this detachment is Forget-Me-Not, Newfoundland."

That was just the start of an interprovincial line tangle. We resolved to watch for the Newfoundland accent and not to be caught like that again. But the next time the radio jumped its air lane, we fell hard again. Every fall, in this division, a man was assigned to go around the province assisting in the enforcement of the game laws as laid out in the Lands and Forests Act. We were trying to locate this man by calling around the detachments. A voice answered one signal.

"Is the Lands and Forests man at your detachment?"

"The Lands and what man?"

"Lands and Forests -- you know."

A long silence -- then -- "Has this anything to do with the Wheat Board?"

This time we had Manygophers, Manitoba.

We knew without asking that we had Quebec on the radio one morning. Our junior man began turning prematurely gray when the bulletins came in both French and English. At that, he was lucky he was not at the next detachment where one morning the NCO entered the office and found his radio spouting Gaelic. Two women had possession of the air and stubbornly warded off every attempt made to wrest it from them. The frustrated NCO, not having the Gaelic, had to admit defeat and leave the airways to the victorious housewives. He finally called the radio technician to help him out. The technician found that the line to the radio tower had crossed with a rural telephone line, so the NCO regained the use of his radio without a headlong clash with the two Highlanders.

We began to get more accustomed to the radio's frolicking, such as skipping several thousand miles or switching languages on us. Everyone noticed immediately the day it slowed down to a Texas drawl. An oil company joined the network and we began to follow the daily activities of a crew drilling an oil well. Now we started getting oil and some gas in our bulletins.

The next one to join the hook-up was a Texas rancher. Now we had westerns on our daily program. It was inevitable that the radio would gallop across the border into Mexico. A hombre started pouring Spanish out our loudspeaker. No one ever found out whether this guy was an oil man, rancher, a sheriff, or the bad guy.

One day, just when the programs were at their best, the chief radio technician came into the office. Newfoundland was booming in. A dispatcher at a town was urging a car to hurry to the corner of Rumpus and Whacko streets to break up a fight. Up in Quebec, three French-speaking members were trying to corner a smuggler. The Texas oil man was chewing out somebody, the Mexican was yelling and in the background the rancher's steers could be heard.

"Interesting, eh?" we asked the chief.

We expected he would be proud of his network. This was the man who had started the system with its first 50 little watts. He had climbed every high windy hill in the province, testing or putting up towers. He had painfully gathered shingle splinters off every detachment roof in the division, while putting up aerials. Now, eight years later, he could sit back in comfort and enjoy the product of his pioneering hardships.

But instead of beaming with paternal pride, he grimaced; "It's slowly driving me nuts," he said.

We tried to point out to him what he had accomplished. A far-flung network broadcasting in four languages from three different countries. Broadcasts, direct from the scenes of crime, from oilfields, ranches and farm kitchens. Drama, comedy, variety, static, everything a radio network could have.

"But it's doing everything the books said it couldn't do," he groaned. "It has me all mixed up. Why, they're even passing messages direct from Halifax to Regina. That's not supposed to be possible. I feel all off the beam."

We tried to reason with him. "Look," one of the detachment men said. "We on detachments get to think we're the only ones in the world with troubles. Your network has broadened our outlook. When we think that everyone in the world is getting along fine except ourselves, just flick up the squelch on the radio. Then all these other stations come in and we hear that other people have troubles too. If you have the Gaelic you learn that over in Cape Breton, little John Rory, big Alex's son, has the shingles; in Newfoundland the herring are not running; in Quebec they're having trouble with tourists who forget to stop at the Customs; out west wheat is disappearing; down on that Texas ranch the herd stampeded; something must be wrong over in Mexico the way they're yelling; in short, everybody has their troubles. When we hear that it helps us to carry on."

We couldn't convince him. He was a real headquarters man when it came to trying to get him to see a viewpoint from detachment level. He left abruptly, muttering about sunspots and skips. We felt anxious about letting him go out alone.

The next time we met him, he was his old self again. He was elated by a recent technical break-through in the communications field, made by a detachment man's wife. It seemed that one Sunday night, at 7:22 p.m., to be exact, this lady was trying to relay a message to her husband in the police car. She called the car, missed it by 14,000 miles and startled a man in Sydney, Australia, with the sound of her Canadian voice. A lively two-way conversation followed. Later investigation, made with the help of an observatory, disclosed that she had ricocheted her signal off "Sputnik II" which was passing over Australia about that time.

"Don't you see the possibilities," the technician cried. "I'll build an RCMPnik, economy-size of course, which will orbit from Newfoundland to British Columbia. Why, it will be tremendous. Every police office in Canada can be linked up. All you need to do is turn up the squelch on your radio and ..."

"It might need a radio technician in it to act as a control operator," ventured the junior man who had been listening intently.

We haven't heard about the plan since. It got the squelch all right.

H.G. Searle
RCMP Quarterly - Volume 24, Number 2

* * * * *

PROBLEMS WITH RADIO COMMUNICATION

Editor's Note: The RCMP has reached into high technology in the communications field. Radios in police cars have been in existence for many years. In the near future, if not already in some areas, the police car will be able to contact the computer centre and obtain the record of the owner of the car they are following, just through the car licence.

*

It was not always thus. When I was on detachment in Nova Scotia in the 1940s, though the telephone operator was a definite boon as an informant, the party line was a detriment to long-distance communication within the detachment area. A complaint phoned in was open to everyone on the system, with the result that by the time I arrived at the scene, all evidence had been erased or disposed of in some other manner. I was able to solve this problem in a unique way. My informant at the northern end of my detachment area was a Roman Catholic priest. When he had some information he thought I should know about, he phoned me and spoke in Latin. I was able to understand him, but none of the subscribers on the party line could. My information was thus secure, proving there is more than one way to skin a cat.

Bill Fraser

*

I was on a duty visit to Newfoundland in 1967 and was required to take a day trip out of Gander. The country was somewhat mountainous and the FM police-car radio went out of range for a couple of hours. When it came back into range later in the day, the dispatcher came on the air with the query, "Car 4, where are you? We've been looking for you for two hours."

The reply from the young Newfoundland constable at the wheel was "I don't rightly know."

George Fleming

*

FM radio was unpredictable, particularly at certain times of the year when "skip" was prevalent. One day in 1953 when I was stationed in northern New Brunswick, I was travelling in the police car from Jacquet River to Bathurst. I attempted to raise Bathurst on the radio. I was unable to contact them despite the fact that there were no hills to speak of between Bathurst and me. I was about to give up when suddenly a voice came over the radio: "We can hear you loud and clear. What is your message?"

I didn't recognize the voice so I said, "Where are you calling from?"

The answer came, "On Highway 2 just south of Wetaskiwin. This is Red Deer, Alberta Highway Patrol." To say I was astonished was the understatement of the year. I thanked them very much and passed on my message which they relayed to Bathurst with no difficulty at all. I tried to pick them up again a couple of days later with no luck. The other men within radio range thought I was out of my mind.

Donovan Saul

*   *   *   *   *

"SKIP CONDITIONS" -- A LIFESAVER

At 11 a.m. on October 19, 1971, while on duty at Brandon RCMP Detachment, I received a call from Corporal James Prentice at Canadian Forces Base Shilo, Manitoba. He advised he had picked up a distress signal on his citizen's band car radio from a vessel stranded on the rocks off the west coast of the Queen Charlotte Islands in British Columbia. Corporal Prentice was attempting to reach the vessel on the more powerful set in his home.

Half an hour later Corporal Prentice called back. He had made contact with the vessel, a pleasure craft, the *Vernon Bay*, and discovered she had run aground in Sialun Bay on Graham Island. This information was passed by telex to "E" Division RCMP at Victoria, B.C. They alerted the Canadian Armed Forces rescue coordination centre which immediately began search operations.

About five p.m., "E" Division advised that two adults and a seven-year-old boy had been flown safely to their home at Masset, B.C., by a United States Coast Guard helicopter. Despite the fact the *Vernon Bay* was well stocked with food, the trio could not have survived much longer. The rugged coastline is entirely cut off from civilization and fierce storms often strike hard there. They had been attempting to contact the outside world for ten days -- they had run aground October 9, 1971.

The phenomenon known as "skip conditions" causes radio signals to bounce off ionic layers in the atmosphere and carry for thousands of miles. Countless citizen's band stations across western Canada and the United States had received the distress calls from the *Vernon Bay* on October 19 but Corporal Prentice was the only one to get through and obtain the vital information which led rescue craft to the spot.

C.F.B. Shilo is 20 miles east of Brandon and the *Vernon Bay* was marooned about 2,000 miles northwest of Brandon with the formidable Rocky Mountains in between. Masset, the home port of the *Vernon Bay*, is on the northeast corner of Graham Island, about 100 miles from Sialun Bay. A U.S. Coast Guard helicopter was used since it was closer than any Canadian craft, Alaska being only about 300 miles north of the Queen Charlottes.

Corporal Prentice received a letter of commendation from the Commander, Canadian Maritime Forces Pacific, for his role in bringing what might have been a tragic misadventure to a happy conclusion.

S.G. MacBeth
RCMP Quarterly - Volume 37, Number 4

*   *   *   *   *

MOBILE COMMUNICATIONS

With the advent of cellular phones, instant communications are now a factor in everyday life. It is interesting to look back at the primitive but effective measures that were used before the arrival of these modern communication marvels.

In the late 1940s, depredations by the Sons of Freedom sect of the Doukhobours were rife in the Kootenay region of British Columbia. Extra manpower was brought in and 24-hour patrols were in effect. Our detachment had no radio communication.

Detachment members happened to mention this while having coffee one day at the B.C. Telephone warehouse. As a result, a telephone, a tall crank type, was placed in the back of the police car. This type of manual telephone was still in general use at that time in that area. Two long wires were attached to the instrument, with spring clamps attached to the free ends. The police members were then asked to identify locations from which they would like to have access to the telephone system. At the locations indicated, wires were placed running down the poles to two terminals. By driving up to these poles, clipping on the leads from the telephone and giving the crank a turn or two, members had access to the operator and the telephone system.

To the best of my knowledge, no billing was ever made for this service and it continued until police cars were provided with two-way radios.

George Reed

*   *   *   *   *

COMMUNICATIONS AT FORT RELIANCE

In 1937 or 1938 when I was stationed at Fort Reliance, NWT, our radio quit operating and we were without news of the outside world for several months until we were able to get repairs.

Later on in the year a plane landed at the post and before departing, the pilot loaned us a two-way radio equipped with phone and key. Shortly afterward, the phone went out of commission and our only hope of contacting Yellowknife radio station was by using the key and transmitting by Morse code.

None of the detachment members could transmit by key so Special Constable Archie Larocque and I began practising the code with the use of a buzzer, transmitting and receiving to each other until we became fairly proficient and were able to contact Yellowknife by key. The radio operator always came back by key and at first we found it very difficult to read the message because he transmitted too fast for us to pick up every word. However, in due time we were able to transmit and receive messages from the Yellowknife operator. This was a real godsend to us all as this was our only contact with Yellowknife and the "Outside".

Prior to this, our only contact was by mail which we picked up at Fort Resolution about 250 miles away. We were fortunate enough to get mail four or five times a year; twice by dog-team patrol and two or three times by police schooner patrol.

Robert W. "Tommy" Thompson

*　*　*　*　*

Chapter Eight

Dogs and the Force

A TRIBUTE

In May 1961, I became the master of a rock-rolling, log-hauling, bird-chasing bundle of energy, who went by the name of Police Dog Sultan. At the time I did not know whether I had acquired an earth-moving machine or a horse, but when I put him in harness, I found I had a tracking machine and a loyal companion who was to work with me for six years, come rain or shine.

During those six years, Sultan found children lost in the woods, missing hunters, strayed mental patients, stolen goods and culprits who had broken into stores or houses. He found children who had run away from home and tracked murderers from the scenes of their crimes.

Once Sultan was called upon to search for four children reported missing from their home. The children, aged four to seven, had disappeared while playing in the woods. They had wandered six miles over blueberry barrens and through swamps during the night. Sultan searched all night and at dawn came upon them on an old woods road, still holding hands. Four very tired and happy children were returned to their parents.

One of his first cases involved several safecrackers who arrived in the city of Sydney, N.S. Sultan was being used to keep track of their whereabouts without their knowledge. These men spent their days in their hotel room and their nights wandering about the city, casing business premises. Sultan, cooperating with city police and members of the RCMP, was used to track the routes taken by these men. After several nights of surveillance, his tracking connected them with the breaking and entering of a garage. They were picked up, charged and convicted, and received several years in penitentiary. Sultan's tracking was all on the main streets of the city, used by hundreds of people each day.

One early spring morning we were called to a small settlement to investigate a break and enter into a cottage. Sultan was successful in following a track from this cottage through the fields and along the ditch of a main road for about a mile and a half, where he turned off the road and tracked to the front door of a house. I knocked on the front door which was opened by a young boy. Upon seeing the dog, he admitted that he had entered the cottage and had stolen some food two days earlier. The interesting part of this case was that, besides the track being two days old, approximately two inches of snow had fallen, covering it, and the boy had been riding a bicycle!

One Christmas morning, Sultan and I were called to investigate a break into a small store in Sydney. At the scene he picked up a track which led across the street and down several back alley-ways, where he stuck his nose into a garbage can. I was about to chastise my friend when I happened to look into the can and discovered the stolen goods. A short wait produced the culprit, who returned for his Christmas dinner. An extremely surprised young man received his Christmas dinner in gaol.

In April 1967, Sultan, due to sickness, was put to sleep.

D.F. Marston
RCMP Quarterly - Volume 33, Number 1

*   *   *   *   *

DALE OF CAWSALTA

Bassano, Alberta, a small town about 90 miles southeast of Calgary, has a unique niche in the Force, being the home of the first dog employed by the RCMP in police work. In the early 1930s, a German Shepherd pup was born on a farm near the town of Duchess, Alberta, policed from Bassano Detachment. Sergeant Jack Cawsey, in charge of Bassano Detachment, had always been interested in dogs and was seeking a suitable animal to train for police work. The pup's reputation as a superb animal reached his ears and it was purchased by him to train for police work.

This pup, named Dale of Cawsalta, was destined to become one of the most dedicated and valuable "members" of the RCMP to have served the Canadian prairies. During his service Dale's accomplishments won him fame throughout western Canada. Sergeant Cawsey's senior officers were especially impressed and thus the Force's Dog Section was formed.

Sergeant John Nicholson Cawsey was born at Halifax, N.S., and joined the old Alberta Provincial Police on February 15, 1917. He became a member of the RCMP on April 1, 1932, when the APP was absorbed, and retired to pension February 13, 1944. He passed away on March 31, 1964, at Calgary. Dale of Cawsalta "retired" from the Force on July 31, 1939, and died September 6, 1941.

An interesting conclusion to this story is that the town of Bassano and district chose to honour the late Sergeant Cawsey and Dale of Cawsalta as an Alberta Century Celebrations project. In memory of the team and to represent the Force's Dog Section in general, a life-sized cairn of a dogmaster and his dog was unveiled in Bassano on September 15, 1974. Present to accept the honour on behalf of Sergeant Cawsey were his widow, Mrs. Florence Cawsey, and his sons, Lorne Cawsey, an ex-RCMP staff sergeant from Vancouver, B.C., and Provincial Judge Allan Cawsey from Wetaskiwin, Alberta, with their families.

J.M. Herman
RCMP Quarterly - Volume 40, Number 3

* * * *

A HEAVY DAY FOR SERGEANT CAWSEY'S DOG DALE

On the night of August 17, 1935, word was received at the Calgary Detachment that little Eileen Simpson, whose parents resided some ten miles from Carstairs, had been missing since about 1:30 p.m. and that the country had been scoured by numbers of neighbours in an unsuccessful search to locate her. The weather was cold and wet and the little child was only 2 1/2 years of age. Sergeant Cawsey left Calgary Detachment with two constables and his dog Dale just after midnight.

Eight miles from Calgary the patrol came upon an old model T Ford coupe which attracted their attention. There was one man in the car. He was interrogated and it was noticed there were a lot of articles piled up in the car which looked as if they might have been stolen. The occupant was R.A. J...... He denied there was anyone else with him but his explanation was not satisfactory and Sergeant Cawsey set Dale to work. Dale very quickly led them to a man crouched down in a wheat field with his coat over his head. His name was T..... M..... He was taken back to the car and denied any knowledge of it or the occupant. He was searched but nothing was found on him.

Thinking he might have disposed of some articles, Cawsey commanded Dale to search and he soon came back with a fountain pen sticking out of the end of his mouth like a cigar and a pleased expression on his face. To make sure there was nothing else, Dale was commanded to search again and before leaving the scene recovered another pen and pencil in the wheat field. The wheat at this point was about four feet high and there had been an extremely heavy rain for several hours prior to this; in fact it was raining at the time. The patrol returned to Calgary with their prisoners and, after checking over the property, returned on the road again to continue their original mission.

Arriving at the Simpson farm, where there were many neighbours present, the dog was given the scent of the child and shortly before seven a.m. gave tongue violently in the middle of a wheat field. At the scene the patrol found Dale licking the face of little Eileen who was crouched with her head on the ground. Constable Rasmussen immediately carried the child to the house and applied first aid. The patrol had the satisfaction of hearing Eileen talk in a cheery manner before they left, and she made satisfactory progress, no complications having set in.

On returning to Calgary, Sergeant Cawsey continued his investigation into the case of the two men arrested, and ascertained that the leather coats, ladies' purses, jack knives, flashlights, etc. etc. and even a .22 rifle had all been shoplifted at Red Deer the previous day. The prisoners were taken back there for trial. Both had lengthy records.

From the papers of the late Superintendent Bavin,
donated by his daughter, Gladys Adams

*   *   *   *   *

DOG DISARMS DESPERADO

Publicity concerning police service dogs of the Force generally centres around missing persons, searches for escaped prisoners, trailing criminals from the scenes of crimes, and the rare occasions when they successfully sniff out valuables lost by farmers while working their lands. Their attacking ability does not usually come into the limelight, but probably only because this is generally used as a last resort.

Police Dog Warrior of Westlock, Alberta, earned the plaudits of three of his two-legged comrades on October 15, 1958, and the healthy respect of a gunman who, earlier that morning, had broken into the post office at Bruderheim, Alberta, with two companions.

Later that day one of the culprits was spotted near Fort Saskatchewan, Alberta, and after being chased to a nearby farmhouse, began to exchange pistol shots with three members of the Force. It was about this time that Warrior and his master arrived at the scene.

The pair got in behind a shed where the fugitive was taking cover, and then the dogmaster suddenly gave the command "Attack!" As soon as Warrior rounded the end of the structure, the dogmaster heard two close shots ring out and Warrior started to yelp and whine. However, a few seconds later, Warrior came trotting proudly around the side of the shed carrying a .32 calibre pistol in his teeth, apparently none the worse for wear. The still nerve-wracked gunman was taken into custody, and later admitted that upon seeing the police dog rushing towards him, he had shot twice at point-blank range, but had missed on both occasions and the animal was upon him.

Anonymous
RCMP Quarterly - Volume 24, Number 3

* * * * *

KLIA'S TRACKING ABILITY

During the evening of October 7, 1963, the RCMP dogmaster at Kamloops, B.C., received a call from the Force's detachment at Enderby to the east, requesting the urgent assistance of Police Dog Klia

Victor, a resident of the Mabel Lake district east of Enderby, had reported that his twin 14-year-old daughters, Donna and Dianna, had not arrived home after leaving the school bus about a mile from their home. A search party had been organized and Victor had found a pencil beside what appeared to be scuff marks on the road a quarter of a mile from his home.

The dogmaster and Klia reached the area at 11:20 p.m. and 25 minutes later the dog picked up a scent on some leaves near the scuff marks. Closer inspection by the dogmaster turned up what appeared to be blood on the leaves. The spot was a few feet northwest of the driveway to Victor's home. Searching on the other side of the road, Klia found more bloodstains and, tracking from that spot, he located a pair of girls' shoes, some school books and parts of a broken forestock of a rifle.

At 12:35 the following morning, Klia started digging beside a rotten log and partly uncovered another girls' shoe. When the debris was sifted, police found another shoe, more school books and a girls' coat. The search continued for an hour and a half and Klia led his master to the beaten and stabbed body of Dianna. This was about 100 feet northeast of the driveway in thick bush. Searching continued through the night.

With the aid of daylight, police found the bolt and other broken forestock parts of a rifle. At 8:05 a.m. on October 8, Klia dug out the broken butt of a rifle with bloodstains, which had been buried under leaves and bark about 60 feet from where he had turned up the coat and books.

About this time, X was taken into police custody after he walked out of the bush into a mill yard about a mile from where Dianna's body had been found. Klia was taken to the mill yard and the dogmaster started him tracking where X had emerged from the bush. The dog followed a northerly direction, roughly parallelling the Kingfisher River. About a quarter of a mile into the bush, the police dog sniffed and pawed the side of a log and his master produced a flashlight in good working order.

Tracking again, Klia twice led his master to the edge of the river and back to the bush again; after another quarter of a mile he started pawing between two rotten logs. The dogmaster picked out a bloodstained shirt. The dog continued in the same direction and then swung up a steep sidehill and went directly to a campfire still burning. Nearby were some boughs which looked as if they had been used as a bed.

While Klia was thus engaged, X had made statements to the police and had drawn maps, with the result that the body of Donna was found in an area not worked by the police dog. A careful search by police and civilians to locate the missing rifle barrel was made but without result.

All searchers were then taken from the area and the German Shepherd continued the probe. On October 11 -- after four days of searching -- the dogmaster noticed Klia sniffing and pawing the end of a hollow log. Nothing was visible, but when the dogmaster reached into the log he could feel the front sight of a rifle, and after tearing the log apart, he turned up the bent barrel of a .22.

X was charged with the murder of the two girls and after a preliminary hearing, was committed to stand trial. He appeared at

Kamloops on February 24, 1964, and was convicted on March 6 of the capital murder of Donna. He was sentenced to life imprisonment for the non-capital murder of Dianna.

In his direction to the jury, the judge stated that to his knowledge, this was the first time that the total evidence of the dogmaster and the police dog had been accepted. He asked the jury to consider the qualifications of the dogmaster and the latter's interpretation of the actions of the dog.

K.W.MacKay
RCMP Quarterly - Volume 30, Number 2

* * * * *

THEY CALL ME MAJOR

Well, here it is in early February 1973 and I'm at the Society for the Prevention of Cruelty to Animals in Ottawa. Only three weeks old and still wondering how I came into this world.

I just heard a rumour from one of my fellow canine friends that there is a Mountie in here looking for someone like me. Can't remember doing anything that bad in the past few weeks. Little did I realize he wanted me as a mascot for the world-famous RCMP Musical Ride. In addition, I would be part of the Centennial Review celebrating the 100th anniversary of the RCMP, heading on a cross-Canada tour travelling from St. John's, Newfoundland, to Victoria, British Columbia, be on national television, meet thousands of people, have my picture taken many times and eat some of the best foods.

My introduction to my new home at the stables at "N" Division was a trifle unfortunate. I didn't mind sharing my new home with those huge black horses, but I did mind the old mother cat. She let me know pretty fast who wore the pants around here and I was just a newcomer. Kind of embarrassing to sit and wait for her to finish eating before I got my turn. You see, we both ate and drank out of the same bowls for the time being. I hope none of my canine friends see this.

The next group I met were all the fellows I would be working with. I'll admit I was pretty shy at first. Have you ever been attacked by 40 pairs of hands, all picking you up over and over again? However, confusion starts when everyone is calling me at the same time -- not knowing whom to go to. Still haven't figured that out yet although my name has finally been decided: Major.

My trip across Canada was quite enjoyable. I travelled in the horse truck with one of the guys and, of course, the horses. I managed to spend a little time riding in the cab. Ah! There isn't anything better than cruising down the highway on a sunny day with your nose stuck out the window and ears flapping in the breeze, unless it is sitting on the bridge of the *Steiner Carrier* from North Sydney to Port aux Basques, Newfoundland, being fed boiled Atlantic salmon by Captain Peter Drake.

There was a bit of work to my travel -- I had a spot in the Centennial Review to act out. It was up front on the prairie schooner with an Indian called Bill. All the fellows had to put on make-up for the performance, but I managed to evade that except for the one time they attempted to put woolly eyebrows on me.

Another of my tasks started as soon as the fellows finished unloading the horses and equipment. I was placed in charge of equine security looking after the stables in their entirety. If any unauthorized persons came around during the late hours I would sound the alarm. Mind you, there were two big Mounties to back me up if I couldn't handle the matter alone.

I think the most trying experience had to be in Kitchener, Ontario. One particular morning I went for my early stroll, as always, in the nearby area. It was a beautiful day so I decided to wander a little farther away than usual. Let me tell you, I sure was surprised to get back to the stables to find all the men, equipment and horses had left for our next show at St. Catharines, Ontario.

What was my next move? The Mounties realized I was lost and immediately put out an All Persons Bulletin through the local communications media for the most "wanted" canine. Luckily for me a thoughtful little boy recognized my description and the identification on the collar and turned me in to the local detachment. While I was waiting to be claimed, a pretty secretary offered me a delicious helping of spareribs to make my day.

The next thing I knew two of my buddies were coming through the door to claim me and we were headed for St. Catharines. Imagine that -- two of the fellows driving all the way back just to get me. After all, we had travelled together from coast to coast and to forget about me just 400 miles from Ottawa wouldn't seem right. The remainder of the tour went quite well, and we were back in Ottawa on October 10, 1973.

I am back to familiar grounds now, guarding the horses and still playing second fiddle to that old mother cat. Should any of you good people I met on the road be coming through Ottawa, please drop in to see me at "N" Division.

H.B. MacDonald and B.A. Guzda
RCMP Quarterly - Volume 39, Number 2

* * * * *

SEA DOG

The following incident occurred when I was NCO in charge of Patrol Boat *M.L.6*, stationed at Ganges, B.C. We had just returned from a routine patrol through the Gulf Islands, and engineer Bob Dodds, having satisfied himself that all was secure in the engine room, departed for home. I remained aboard a little longer to "clew up" a few odds and ends of office work, then left for my cottage, which stood on a rocky point a stone's throw from our mooring place.

At that time the small-boat dock at Ganges consisted of a long float extending into the harbour, well secured to pilings driven into the mud. From this, three smaller floats extended at right angles to provide mooring spaces. These were made of large cedar logs capped over with planks.

The shoreward side of the innermost float was reserved for small rowboats, since there was insufficient water to float larger craft at low tide. The location was very sheltered and the rowboats were moored by a single rope from their bows to the float, their sterns being left to swing freely in the harbour. From the inner end of the main float a ramp extended upward to a landing above tide level.

As I climbed the ramp I was passed by a young dog. Obviously hardly out of puppyhood and busily intent upon the business of exploring the world, he trotted past me and out onto the innermost float. There he paused for a moment to consider the rowboats moored alongside and apparently thought them worthy of closer inspection.

He jumped into the nearest boat, trotted aft and stood briefly with his forepaws on the after seat, but soon realized that unless he was prepared to leap into the icy water, he had certainly come to the end of that particular road. At once he decided to return to the float, but this was easier said than done.

Instead of leaping down he must now leap up, and instead of the broad, steady platform of the float he must now jump from an unsteady footing in the narrow bow of the boat. Moreover, he was a fairly large dog, and as he trotted from the stern to the bow the momentum of his weight moved the light boat away from the float to the full three or four foot length of its tie rope. I paused to see if and how he would solve his dilemma. He next attempted to climb up and balance on the narrow sides of the boat, but this resulted in disaster and with a flailing, sprawling splash of legs and tail he found himself in the water.

Since it is instinctive for an animal in danger to return to the last safe position it occupied, I knew the dog would attempt to return to the float rather than swim to the shore some 12 yards away. He had no hope of climbing the straight high side of the float, so I started down the ramp to lift him aboard when he broke surface. I suddenly realized that something was very wrong. The dog should have put in an appearance, but was nowhere in sight. I just as quickly realized that he must have gone under the float and if he was to be saved, speedy action was called for.

Forage cap, tie, watch and wallet were shed as I ran, and then I was in that cold, cold water along with the dog! I dove beneath the float, but in the tangle of seaweed and streamers which grow so abundantly in Gulf of Georgia waters, I was unable to see the dog. My air supply exhausted, I was obliged to surface and had no better luck on a second dive. I now concluded that the unfortunate animal was doomed and climbed onto the float, but a series of woeful wails assured me that the terrified creature was still very much alive. By the greatest good luck he had somehow found an airspace under the float.

Fortunately, the proceedings had been observed, and a gang of men began to assemble on the run. As if by magic a peavey appeared. (I swear that B.C. loggers carry them in their pockets!) Two or three planks were ripped away and the pup's plight could now be observed. By a whim of providence he had surfaced where two protruding knots on adjacent float logs had left a narrow space.

He was able to get most of his head through this and he had further managed to grip one of the logs with his forepaws. But not by any measure was there space enough to lift him through, and the diminished volume of his terrified howls seemed to reflect the hopelessness of his situation. There was but one way to get him, and now with a safety rope about my waist it was back into the icy water. I was able to grasp firmly onto two brown dog legs instead of handfuls of waving kelp. One mighty heave to break his desperate grip on the log and we were both surfacing, to be lifted aboard the float by willing hands.

I was now prepared for the razzing of my life from the local gentry, but strangely, the good people of Ganges seemed to think it not at all peculiar that a Mountie would dive fully clothed to the rescue of a mongrel dog. Only one grinning engineer seemed to find the whole proceeding hilariously funny, but since I had my share of fun at his expense during our close association, I merely grinned back.

B.G. Boutilier
RCMP Quarterly - Volume 45, Number 2

* * * * *

Chapter Nine

Highlights of the Past

DICKENS' WATCH

Most visitors to a museum will find themselves drawn to certain artifacts. They may be entranced by the beauty of a piece, its age or its design. At times they may simply be surprised that a particular item survived at all. An eavesdropper might hear, "Look at that. I wonder how that got here?" or "If it could talk I'll bet it could tell quite a tale." An object from the past can link the observer with distant events and absent participants.

So it is that the story of a gold pocket watch that once belonged to the beloved creator of Tiny Tim and Scrooge finds itself in a book devoted to the exploits of Canada's national police force. It is at once incongruous and poetically just that Charles Dickens, one of the English language's most respected writers and a commentator on the inequities of London's society, can be linked by a timepiece to the likes of Louis Riel, the Earl of Dufferin, Big Bear and NWMP Commissioner French.

Dickens' watch was carried into western Canadian history by his third son, Francis Jeffrey (Frank). Frank was something of a disappointment as a son. Although he had won prizes when sent to school abroad and had shown ability in languages, he did not enter the fields that his father would have liked -- medicine, diplomacy, writing or business. With his father pulling some strings, Frank obtained an appointment in the Bengal police. There he remained for seven years. When he returned to England after his father's death, rather than supporting his family in their grief, he disappeared for a time. When found again he was ill, broke and dejected. He had also overstayed his leave and lost his Bengal appointment. Perhaps his only remaining possession of value was his father's pocket watch.

At this point Frank was assisted by his aunt, Georgina Hogarth, who put him in touch with his father's friends. One such friend was the Earl of Dufferin, Governor General of Canada, who suggested that he might have a commission in the newly formed NWMP. It was now the summer of 1874 and the police had started their march west from Manitoba. Shortly after the march began, Commissioner

French, in command, dismissed an inspector. This left an opening and when Frank appeared in Ottawa he was given a police commission and ordered to hurry west.

Frank lived the life of an NWMP officer. He rode patrols in bitter weather. He took prisoners, chased whisky smugglers and U.S. bad men who had strayed across the border. He helped maintain the uneasy peace when the Sioux, Sitting Bull, led his warriors into the refuge of Canada -- "Grandmother Land". By 1884 Frank Dickens had done well enough to be posted to command Fort Pitt in the territory of Big Bear.

It was in this same year that the Metis leader, Louis Riel, returned to what was then the Northwest Territories from his exile in Montana. Tensions mounted during the winter of 1885 and by spring the rebellion had begun. Big Bear's men had already attacked at Frog Lake and were poised, 350 strong, to take Fort Pitt with its detachment of 24 men. Three police scouts tried to ride into the fort to warn of the impending attack. One was shot dead, one was wounded and the other escaped.[1] Although Frank was prepared to fight, the fur traders and settlers at the fort decided to accept Big Bear's assurances of safe passage and went to the Indian camp. The police, badly outnumbered, and no longer having a reason to remain, undertook the cold, 100-mile voyage down the North Saskatchewan River to Battleford. Perhaps Frank was able to see the plumes of smoke from the fort as it burned, when he realized he had left his father's watch behind.

The watch survived the fire and was found, in a trunk, by one of Big Bear's men. We can imagine that he was probably pleased to have found such a prize. He may have wondered about its function, may have been puzzled when it ceased ticking. A dent in its casing suggests he may have tried to remedy the situation with his rifle butt before he traded it to a half-breed acquaintance. It was then offered for a price of $15 to the men who had been taken prisoner at Frog Lake. This piece of the watch's history became known almost 60 years later, when the lone white survivor of the Frog Lake ordeal, W. Bleasdell Cameron, heard a broadcast about Frank Dickens given by James McCook.

The captured loot, including Dickens' watch, was recovered by the NWMP at the conclusion of the Northwest Rebellion. Frank Dickens, in ill health and increasing deafness, could no longer serve as a police officer. Assisted at times by a hospital orderly, he travelled first to Swift Current, then Regina, and eventually to Ottawa where he made application for a government grant for his services, as pensions were not then being paid. He stayed in Ottawa at the Russell Hotel awaiting the slow mechanism of the government. He got into debt and was forced at one point to borrow money from a Toronto friend, F.W. Midford. In exchange for this loan he offered his father's gold watch.

Frank Dickens died of a heart attack in June of 1886 in Moline, Illinois. He had travelled there with a friend from the Russell Hotel, Dr. A.W. Jamieson, who had persuaded him that he could lecture about his experiences. He was buried in Moline and a monument was raised to mark his grave.

The story of the watch arouses curiosity and the obvious questions: "Then what happened? Where is it now?" One interested historian, Sergeant G.S. Howard, a former editor of the *RCMP Quarterly*, was fortunate to learn at least part of the answer to those questions after mentioning the watch during a recent broadcast interview. The present owner appeared at his office with the watch in his hands.

Based on a story by James McCook, *Ottawa Journal,* and published in the *RCMP Quarterly*

¹ The three in the scouting party were Constable D.L.Cowan, Constable C. Loasby and Special Constable Henry Quinn. Cowan was killed, Loasby was wounded and taken prisoner and Quinn escaped. He was captured later by the Indians.

*   *   *   *   *

REMINISCENCES OF ONE OF THE ORIGINALS

He is Regimental Number 41, Staff Sergeant John A. Martin. He was a member of "A" Battery under Lieutenant-Colonel French. When he heard the North West Mounted Police was being organized he purchased his discharge and went to Toronto where he engaged on October 8, 1873. He was assigned to "B" Troop. His story, told to Constable W.J. Monoghan in the first issue of the *RCMP Quarterly,* July 1933, follows:

We started on the morning of October 9 for Collingwood on the Lakes and took a steamer to Prince Arthur Landing at the head of the Lakes. There arrangements were made for boats and guides, and we traversed the Dawson route through 13 small lakes and over portages from a half to two miles long until the prairies were struck and the march on foot commenced. We proceeded to St. Boniface which we reached on Halloween. Ice was making in the Red River and the ferry boat was unable to cross so we made ourselves comfortable in the Catholic college for the night. It was so cold that we were able to walk across the river on good firm ice the next morning to Fort Garry. From there we went by teams to Stone Fort (Lower Fort Garry), where we stopped for the winter.

At Stone Fort we bought a lot of native ponies and started to drill and kept it up until the last of May, when we broke camp and started for Pembina, near Dufferin, 60 miles southwest of Winnipeg.

While on the line of march not a house or camp was seen all summer. The Indians were about but kept out of sight. Scarcity of water was one of our chief troubles. Buffalo wallows were plentiful and the men often drank the water so there was quite a lot of intestinal trouble. I noticed that the rivers were small and shallow and very scarce.

About the middle of September, when we were north of the Cypress Hills, a severe snowstorm started and lasted two days and two nights. We were advised by our guides to cut our blankets in two, put them on the horses and put them in the shelter of a coulee. In spite of this precaution some of them died.

Thousands of buffalo were seen at this time and the assistant commissioner was so impressed that he said he thought it would be a splendid idea to have the buffalo head on the buttons. In his report that fall he made this recommendation to Headquarters and it was adopted.

When we reached the Old Man's River, near the Rocky Mountains, we pitched our tents and called the place Camp Macleod after the assistant commissioner. But we would never have reached the place except for the ox teams as our horses died or became played out, nearly all of them.

Log cabins of cottonwood were built on a small island in the river. They were partly finished when we moved in on Christmas Eve. They had mud roofs and floors and there was a small chimney in the middle. We lived in them for about three years.

The assistant commissioner had us put the motto "Pioneers of a Glorious Future" on the inside wall of the mess cabin, and at dinner on Christmas Day, he proposed a toast to absent friends with cold water. Dinner was mostly buffalo meat, and was for the next three years, along with sour pork, beans, tea, flap-jacks, but no potatoes.

The barracks surrounded a square with the officers' quarters on one side, stables and stores opposite, and the men's quarters on the other two sides.

When we left Stone Fort in the spring each man was allowed only one suit of clothing, so that by the time we reached Camp Macleod they were pretty well worn out; lots of them were in tatters.

When burning the grass off the island, preparatory to building the cabins, one of the men, in stooping down to light a torch near the assistant commissioner, had the misfortune of having his pants split right across the seat. The assistant commissioner when he saw this became very much worried and wondered what he was going to do to save the men during the winter. As I was a tailor by trade and had made a suit for him the winter before, I told him I had been down the river and had seen the squaws making moccasins out of buffalo hides and that I thought I could make clothes for the men. "The very thing. You have saved our lives", said the assistant commissioner.

So hides were bought from the Indians. They were plentiful and cheap. The first outfit made was for the guard -- moccasins, cap, pants, coat and mitts. Very soon the whole outfit was clothed.

The Indians, not used to seeing a man sewing, were very much taken up with me and called me *"Howichanackie"*, which means "The man with the needle".

W.J. Monoghan
RCMP Quarterly - Volume 1, Number 1

*   *   *   *   *

TRUMPETER FRED BAGLEY

During my service at Banff I was fortunate to meet and become close friends with Major Bagley. He shared his memories, his diary and mementos with me and I value the opportunity I had of being acquainted with him.

In 1874 Fred Bagley, a strapping youngster just 15 years of age, escaped from the humdrum of Toronto for adventure in the wild west. He signed on as a trumpeter with the North West Mounted Police and for 75 cents a day endured danger, hunger, thirst, sweltering heat and freezing blizzards. He was a survivor in a dangerous age who managed to place his name and achievements in the history books.

Regimental Number 247 was the youngest member of the famous march of 1874, and was probably the last survivor. He rose to the rank of sergeant-major, served at both Fort MacLeod and Calgary and was active during the Northwest Rebellion of 1885. After serving for 25 years he took his pension and went to South Africa where, as Major Bagley, he commanded "C" Squadron, 5th Canadian Mounted Regiment, Imperial Yeomanry.

One of the experiences he shared with me was the time he decided to get a mount of his own prior to the trek west. Bagley had been riding any horse that was handy, but the great march was ahead and he wanted the security of a good horse. During his first weeks of service the young trumpeter had picked up some smarts from days on the train with old soldiers, a memorable stop in Chicago where he saw Frank James, brother of the famous outlaw Jesse, and other adventures that few of today's recruits experience. At Fort Dufferin Bagley proved himself equal to the task.

They had a muster parade of horses and he strolled innocently through the lines in a determined frame of mind, studying the mounts in each troop until he pulled up behind "B" Troop. There it was, a buckskin that suited his fancy, tough enough for the trials ahead. With the prescience that foretold a remarkable military career, the kid worked out his strategy. There was a grog shop set up temporarily just outside the camp and the constable holding the buckskin looked as though he could use a booster. After a friendly exchange the trumpeter offered a loan of 50 cents and volunteered to hold the horse while his new friend slipped away for a drink.

As soon as the coast was clear Bagley sneaked through the lines with the buckskin to "D" Troop where the horse was quickly mustered and assigned to Regimental Number 247 by his officer commanding who just happened to be Major Walsh. "Old Buck" became known as "the Bagley Pony" throughout the Force and survived for 32 years. What happened at a reunion of the Originals 50 years later when "that damned horse thief" and the original owner met is another story. (Bagley said he asked for the return of his 50 cents.)

Another story not contained in history books that he related to me was the time in October 1874 when Colonel French, the first commissioner, was leading a small detachment from Fort Benton with emergency supplies. The Force was in dire straits and he was hurrying to the main body with oats for starving horses, fresh mounts, necessary rations and even boots for the troops. They ran into a war party of Assiniboines on their way to raid Blackfoot country with at least the intention of stealing horses, not to mention taking scalps and women. What to do in such a situation? The commissioner did the sensible thing. He sent them on their way with gifts of coffee and tobacco. Law and order were yet to be defined.

Gray Campbell

*   *   *   *   *

SERGEANT FURY

William Fury was born in Ireland in 1847 and came to Canada with the British army in the late 1860s. Upon his discharge from the army he joined the NWMP at Fort Walsh on July 4, 1879, taking Regimental Number 333.

During his service he was stationed throughout the northwest including construction sites on the railroad through the Rockies. He also served in the Northwest Rebellion, receiving a serious wound that eventually caused his early retirement from the Force. Fury was made corporal on February 24, 1882, and on September 5 the same year was promoted to sergeant. For short periods in 1886 and 1888 he held the rank of staff sergeant. He was invalided to pension on August 6, 1888.

Sergeant Fury, who stood only five feet eight inches tall, seems to have been a very determined man with a fine disregard for his personal safety. An example of this occurred during January 1884, near Calgary. Fury, with a constable and an interpreter, went into an Indian encampment and arrested one of them for horse stealing.

The arrested man's friends -- 190 strong -- surrounded the police party and attempted a rescue. At one point the bridle of Fury's horse was seized by Whitecap, one of the leaders. However, the police party was able to break free and bring in the prisoner. The next day a troop of 45 men under Inspector Steele went to the encampment only to find Whitecap had fled and the other leaders could not be identified. The consequences of obstructing an arrest were explained and the police left. Some days later Whitecap and one of the other leaders were arrested at Calgary and brought before a magistrate. After being severely warned they were released.

The spring of 1884 saw labour problems at construction sites along the CPR line through the Rockies. Inspector Steele was charged with keeping order in the area and in preparation for moving his headquarters from Golden, opened a small detachment at Beaver with Sergeant Fury in charge. The situation was unsettled, with some violence already committed and more threatened.

At one stage a group of demonstrators, armed and inclined to violence, was preventing tracklayers from working. Fury took a small party of police to the scene and, placing his men in a line in front of the demonstrators, warned them he would fire if they attempted to force the line. In spite of their superior numbers the demonstrators reconsidered and withdrew.

Inspector Steele was suffering from mountain fever and was confined to his bed when Sergeant Fury reported to him. At the same time it was learned that Constable Kerr, who had been in town, attempted single-handedly to arrest a man who was inciting a group of strikers to storm the police barracks. However, the crowd overpowered him, took his prisoner and forced him to leave.

Upon hearing this Inspector Steele instructed Fury to take a few men and recapture the prisoner. They returned some time later, tunics in tatters and bearing other evidence of a struggle. Once again the crowd had rescued the prisoner. Drastic situations call for drastic actions and Fury was told to return and secure the prisoner, using his revolver if need be.

Sergeant Fury and three constables went back into town. Two of the constables grabbed the prisoner while Fury and the other held off the mob. At one point the mob charged and Fury carefully shot one of them in the shoulder. The police and their prisoner retired to the barracks with the mob following, but keeping a little more distance between them. As they approached the barracks, which were across a bridge, Inspector Steele rose from his sickbed, took a rifle and joined his men, eight in number.

The mob was warned not to attempt to cross the bridge and after the Riot Act was read, told to break up. While this was going on some of the local citizens took up arms and joined the hard- pressed police. The mob broke up and left. Inspector Steele reported that the next morning the town was as quiet as a country village. The ringleaders were arrested without further difficulty and fined $100 each. From then on the area was considerably more peaceful.

On June 3, 1885, Fury was involved in the fighting at Loon Lake where a group of rebels had dug in at the top of a ridge. He led a charge against their position and just as he gained the top of the ridge was felled with a bullet through the right lung. He was moved to Fort Pitt for emergency treatment and later to Battleford. Although he survived his wound, he never recovered fully.

On August 1, 1888, Surgeon A. Jukes and Assistant Surgeon H. Dodd reported it was their opinion "that his present condition of permanently impaired health and vigor which renders him unfit for active service is mainly due to the injuries he received in the discharge of his duty and while recommending that he be invalided as unfit for further service, we strongly recommend him to the favorable consideration of the Department for as liberal a pension or allowance as his long and meritorious service in this Force entitles him to receive."

Later that month the comptroller, F. White, added to that recommendation. "In consideration of the fact that prior to the wound received in action Sergeant Fury was one of the most efficient NCO's in the Force, the undersigned recommends that he be granted the maximum pension allowed for the third degree of injury, namely 60 cents per day from August 7, 1888, to be continued to the term of his natural life."

On September 5, 1888, the Governor General-in-Council acted on the recommendation and Sergeant Fury retired to a small farm near Richmond Hill, Ontario. The government, on June 17, 1932, granted $300 to each of the surviving veterans of the rebellion, including Sergeant Fury. William Fury passed away at Richmond Hill on April 19, 1936. Two days later he was borne to his grave at Killean, Ontario, by a party of eight members of the RCMP in review order.

J.R.Henry
RCMP Quarterly - Volume 38, Number 3

* * * * *

FORT CARLTON 1885

Fort Carlton is situated about 16 miles west and north of Duck Lake, Saskatchewan. The fort is in a valley with the North Saskatchewan River on one side and high hills separated by a gully trail on the other sides. This is the beginning of the Prince Albert Trail, from which the Duck Lake Trail branches off at the top of the hills.

The first sight of the fort today almost takes one's breath away. The Union Jack will be seen first, waving jauntily in the breeze. The fort itself is in the centre of a meadow and has the appearance of permanence and bustling activity. This look of commerce is only an illusion, added to by the presence of school buses in the spring and fall with their loads of excited, interested and exploring children brought from near and far to this real live fort.

On the top of the hill to the east one can sit beneath the huge cross. It signifies the burial place of the white settlers who died as a result of a smallpox epidemic when the fort was a Hudson's Bay trading post. It also marked the site of the fort to weary travellers paddling up the river from Cumberland House and to less hardy souls arriving with the gentle flow of the river from the Battlefords. Not only can the inside of the fort be seen from either of these two high vantage points, but all roads to the fort can be kept under surveillance, including the all-important river highway. The fort was rebuilt in 1968 after considerable research by the Saskatchewan Department of Natural History.

It was this fort, defended by a small detachment of NWMP under Superintendent S. Gagnon that drew the attention of Louis Riel. It would be necessary to lay siege to the fort and bring the occupants to their knees before marching on to greater victories at Prince Albert. Riel was protesting his innocent intentions to the government and at the same time advocating the overthrow of the yoke at Ottawa.

Evidence of this treachery was discovered by Sergeant H. Keenan, stationed at Batoche. Superintendent L.F.N. Crozier's decision to reinforce Carlton may have been due in part to this intelligence. As there was no indication of the trouble to follow at Battleford and Frog Lake, Superintendent Crozier departed for Carlton with a patrol to augment the defending forces.

Fort Carlton was a difficult place to defend and was vulnerable to siege. This must have been foremost in the minds of Superintendents Crozier and Gagnon. They had an increased strength of police and a militia unit from the Prince Albert Volunteers to provision. They decided to detach Sergeant Alfred Stewart and 17 men to Duck Lake to obtain supplies hidden there for the police by Hillyard Mitchell when he realized his store would be seized by the rebels. As it was thought most of the rebels were at Batoche, on the east side of the South Saskatchewan River about 30 miles from Duck Lake, no trouble was anticipated.

Sergeant Stewart's party had ridden only half-way to Duck Lake when it was accosted and held at bay by a larger party of rebel Metis. Stewart managed to extricate his men from this dangerous position and retreated to Fort Carlton without mishap, but also without the much-needed supplies.

Superintendent Crozier, after conferring with the militia officers, decided to mount a party large enough to deal with the handful of rebels believed to be at Duck Lake and to obtain the supplies. Fifty-five policemen, 43 Prince Albert Volunteers, 20 sleighs and wagons and one seven-pounder gun departed. They marched and rode up the winding trail to the top of the hill, then struck across country toward Duck Lake.

They were within two miles of Duck Lake when the trap was sprung. The government forces were caught in an ambush and surrounded. The sleighs were quickly placed at right angles to the road, but they offered scant protection. The Metis, having the advantage of surprise, were hidden on a wooded ridge to the east of the road and in an abandoned cabin in the trees on the west.

This was no small party of rebel Metis, but the full complement under the direction of their military commander, Gabriel Dumont, and their commander-in-chief, Louis Riel. Their intentions were unknown. They may have already committed themselves to outright war by proceeding to Fort Carlton to lay siege. In any case, acts of war were perpetrated and all hope of a peaceful settlement to the troubles in the Northwest seemed lost. Various sources put the number of rebels at from 150 to 400.

In any event they were superior to Superintendent Crozier's force and could have annihilated the meagre army had they pursued their advantage. That they did not was probably due to one expeditious act by Tom McKay, a Scottish Metis and interpreter for the police.

Shortly after the battle was joined, McKay put Gabriel Dumont out of action, albeit temporarily. Dumont suffered a head wound that looked much worse than it actually was and probably knocked him unconscious for a time. Riel declined to pursue the fleeing army back to Fort Carlton.

In their defeat -- and it was a defeat -- the bodies of the soldiers and one member of the Force were left on the field of battle. Constable Thomas James Gibson was killed and eight policemen were wounded, two of whom died the following day: Constable George Knox Garrett and Constable George Pierce Arnold. They were buried temporarily behind Fort Carlton and eventually moved to Prince Albert for proper burial at St. Mary's Cemetery. The militia suffered nine killed and five wounded.

The Metis had four killed, with one Indian killed, and only four wounded. Had Riel capitalized on his advantage and followed the troops back to the fort he would have found demoralized opposition. He did not choose to do so. Riel claimed to have divine powers; could it be that he was aware that Colonel Irvine, Commissioner of the NWMP, was en route to Fort Carlton from Prince Albert with volunteers?

Some gains resulted from the outbreak of open warfare in the Northwest Territories. When the electrifying news was received in the nation's capital, that old war horse Cornelius Van Horne, general manager of the CPR, placed the full services of the railroad at the disposal of the government to transport troops to the front. The only other means of transportation was through the United States, but international law prohibited an armed force from one country entering another.

An army was quickly raised and en route. They were shopkeepers and tradesmen from Toronto, orchardists and farmers from the Maritimes. They suffered hardships before reaching Qu'Appelle. Stretches of the railroad along the northern shores of the Great Lakes were not finished and the army had to march with all equipment in freezing temperatures on the slush and ice of the lakes to reach another section of railroad.

Van Horne said he would feed them en route and he did. Otherwise, many would have perished from the cruel cold which was not relieved by the open slats of the cattle cars in which they had to ride. However, it was better than walking.

The Canadian Pacific Railroad obtained the funds needed for completion from the Government of Canada as a direct result of the Northwest Rebellion. The fledgling province of British Columbia no longer trumpeted annexation to the United States.

When peace finally arrived after the last-ditch battle on May 12, 1885, the lessons must have been painfully clear to all concerned. The government in far-off Ottawa must have realized it could no longer force its will on the population of the fledgling country, and the Metis, sorrowfully, found that if the system must be changed, it had to be done within the law, not by rebellion.

D.F. McLeod
RCMP Quarterly - Volume 38, Number 2

*   *   *   *   *

THE FIRST MUSICAL RIDES

It is not widely realized that the RCMP Musical Ride was 100 years old in 1987. Although it is sometimes said that the first ride was organized in 1876, no evidence has ever been found to support this claim. There seems little doubt that the first musical rides performed publicly by the North West Mounted Police took place at Regina in the winter of 1887 as Constable John Stewart, who participated in those original performances, described them many years later in an article in the *Scarlet and Gold* entitled "How the Musical Ride Started." Known today throughout the world for its skill and appeal, the RCMP Musical Ride traces its humble beginnings back to the Canadian prairies.

Mounted tournaments and displays of horsemanship go back through the centuries and usually involved a mounted troop being put through its drill movements; this was often followed by a mock battle on horseback or contests in swordsmanship and the use of the lance. In July 1885 the NWMP held a field day at the barracks in Regina which included several mounted events organized by Sergeant George Kempster, who was to be a key figure in the presentation of the first musical ride two years later.

What distinguished a musical ride from these exhibitions of cavalry movements and tactics was the substitution of a brass band for a drill instructor. Instead of words of command, the change from one formation to another was signalled by a change of tempo or tune in the accompanying music. The result was a non-stop harmonious blend of music, movement and horsemanship. The first known public performance of what was from the start "a musical ride" was given by the First Regiment of Life Guards at the Royal Military Tournament in London, England, in June 1882.

It was the fortunate conjunction of several factors which brought about the first Mounted Police musical rides. Strangely enough, Louis Riel and the rebellious Metis of 1885 had a large part in it. It was the unrest of that year and the possibility of further trouble that prompted the government to expand and reorganize the NWMP on a more permanent footing. The strength of the Force was increased from 500 to 1,000 men and the annual budget was doubled to over one million dollars. Among the organizational changes was the establishment of a "Depot" Division at Regina as a permanent training centre.

As part of the building program an indoor riding school was built. Commenced in the summer of 1885, it was not completed until May of the following year. It was 60 metres long and 36 metres wide with a gallery at one end for spectators and a band. It was described by *The Regina Leader* as being "one of the finest riding schools in the country."[1]

The riding school provided the necessary accommodation. Three key individuals now entered the scene. The first was George Kempster who took his discharge from the Life Guards in London in 1884 and joined the Mounted Police in December of that year. Whether he was involved in the first musical rides in London from 1882 to 1884 is unknown, but it is unlikely that he would not have known about them. He turned out to be an outstanding horseman and by 1886 was the senior riding instructor in Regina with the rank of sergeant-major.

Next to appear was Jacob "Jakey" Farmer, a short, stout man with an unmistakable cockney accent. He joined the Force in May 1885. He had spent ten years in The King's Own Regiment and had considerable experience with military bands. Commissioner Herchmer was a strong supporter of bands in the Force and in 1886 he appointed Farmer bandmaster with the task of reorganizing the mounted and dismounted bands in Regina.

Finally, and probably most important, there was Inspector William George Matthews, a 40-year-old former lieutenant and riding master of the Third Hussars, a regiment which played a prominent part in presenting mounted displays at the Royal Tournament. Matthews had also spent several years of his life with the regiment stationed in India. He was commissioned as inspector in the NWMP on October 20, 1886, and Herchmer appointed him riding master in Regina. He took up his duties just as the men of "B" Division returned from summer detachments to spend the winter at mounted and dismounted drill. Exactly what Matthews and Kempster knew about musical rides at this point, no one will ever know for sure. They were certainly experienced and accomplished horsemen, and it was their expertise, together with the new riding school, the men of "B" Division and Jakey Farmer and his band, that put together the first musical rides of the NWMP.

There were five public performances of the ride during the winter of 1887. The records of the NWMP reveal very little as to the nature of them. Although they sometimes comprised 16 men instead of 32 (a full troop), from the descriptions of them in the local newspapers they appear to have had most of the elements which are to be found in the RCMP Musical Ride today. The first performance took place in the riding school on Saturday afternoon, January 15, 1887. In the spectators' gallery were Commissioner and Mrs. Herchmer, several other officers and their spouses, as well as a number of guests from town who braved a blizzard and sub-zero temperatures to attend. The reporter from *The Regina Leader* described the scene:

"The band, under Mr. Farmer, was playing a spirited march, and sixteen Mounted Policemen, with lances at rest... were putting their equines through a series of geometrical and other figures with remarkable accuracy and skill, with a most pleasing effect.

"After going through a number of interesting gyrations, radiating circles and other odd figures, now walking, the next minute trotting, and then breaking into a gallop, the horsemen formed into a line at the opposite end of the pit from the gallery, and as the band struck up 'Bonnie Dundee', cantered forward to the other end, keeping exact time with the music, halted abruptly, broke in the centre, wheeled sharply to right and left, formed fours and cantered back along the sides."[2]

Apart from the number of riders it sounds very similar to the present RCMP Musical Ride. Interestingly enough, the ride still performs to the sound of 'Bonnie Dundee.'

The second performance took place on Wednesday, January 26, but the newspapers did not cover it. The third occurred a month later on February 26. This time it was a state occasion with His Honour the Lieutenant-Governor and Mrs. Dewdney in the gallery, and there were 32 riders instead of 16. The newspaper's brief account describes it as being "Heartily applauded by the spectators," and reflecting "great credit on the drill officers."[3]

The only illustration depicting these first musical rides is a drawing by the well-known American frontier artist Frederic Remington, which appeared in the December 24, 1887, issue of *Harper's Weekly*, a New York magazine. It shows 16 riders charging. The scene, however, is set on the barrack square rather than in the riding school. Whether Remington actually witnessed one of the first performances is not known, although he certainly was in western Canada about that time. The editor of *The Regina Leader*, who did see the rides, described the drawing as "pretty accurate."[4] Indeed the detail of the uniform and saddlery is so good it is hard to believe that Remington was not working from real life. If Remington is correct, these first musical rides used western saddlery.

Stan Horral, RCMP Historian
RCMP Quarterly - Volume 49, Number 3

[1] *The Regina Leader*, May 11, 1886
[2] *The Regina Leader*, January 18, 1887
[3] *The Regina Leader*. March 1, 1887
[4] *The Regina Leader*, January 10, 1888

* * * * *

THE ARCTIC ISLANDS — THE RCMP AND 100 YEARS OF CANADIAN SOVEREIGNTY

Another milestone in Canada's history was marked in 1980 with ceremonies held in the north to observe the centennial of the acquisition of the Arctic islands. This was the last frontier acquired by Canada and it was to be many years before it was indisputably Canadian in sovereignty and administration. The RCMP was an important agent in bringing this territory under control, as it had been earlier in the frontiers of the west and the Yukon.

For 300 years after the voyage of Martin Frobisher in 1576, British explorers and commercial adventurers had staked claim to the vast regions of the Arctic archipelago, north of Hudson Bay. After Confederation, Britain was anxious to turn over most of her North American possessions to the new Dominion of Canada. In 1880,

Britain transferred the Arctic islands to Canada by means of an imperial order-in-council, kept deliberately vague in wording to avoid inadvertently alienating any territory in that poorly charted area. Simply holding title inspired little desire in the Canadian government to assert its control of the region. Pressures of national development to the west were already taxing Canada's financial resources.

By the turn of the century, threats to or rivals of Canadian possession of the Arctic began to make their claims. American whaling ships were visiting the region more and more frequently, often wintering in Hudson Bay or off Baffin Island. Moreover, American and Norwegian scientific and exploration parties made extensive forays into the area without reference to the Canadian government. One Norwegian expedition conducted by Otto Sverdrup between 1898 and 1902 went so far as to claim several islands west of Ellesmere Island. Fortunately for Canada, Sverdrup's pretensions did not receive the official support of his government.

By 1903, these activities had caused justifiable alarm to the government of Sir Wilfrid Laurier. Canada had just lost a bitter dispute over the delineation of the border between Alaska and the Yukon, and learned that it was important to assert Canadian control in the north. Laurier decided to send expeditions to the north to explore, patrol and establish the authority of the Canadian government. With the first expedition in 1903 went Superintendent J.D. Moodie and a six-man detachment of the NWMP. Their instructions were to bring notice to both the natives and the visiting white men that the laws of Canada would be enforced in the Arctic.

On the voyage north, Moodie stopped at Baffin Island's Cumberland Sound to inform Scottish whalers that the Canadian government was extending its authority to the area. Moodie then took the detachment to Fullerton Harbour in northwest Hudson Bay where American whalers were wintering. Setting up a post here, the police soon made their influence felt. American vessels were required to submit to Canadian Customs and licence regulations. Patrols were conducted along the west side of Hudson Bay, visiting the Inuit and reporting on their condition and relations with white traders. A ban was imposed against exporting hides of the endangered musk-ox. The Mounted Police were soon covering an area of 1,000 square miles, which constituted the jurisdiction of the newly-created "M" Division based at Fullerton Harbour and at Fort Churchill. Both natives and whites acknowledged police authority, even if they did sometimes try to evade the regulations imposed by the under-strength force.

Although the police made a strong assertion of Canadian sovereignty in Hudson Bay, this did not stop challenges to the title of the islands farther north. During World War I, considerable exploration took place among these islands, and Denmark seemed anxious, by 1920, to stake a claim. The situation arose out of an instruction that the Canadian government delivered to Knud Rasmussen, leader of a Danish scientific expedition, not to kill the protected musk-ox on Ellesmere Island. Rasmussen refused to heed the warning, claiming that the northern islands were a no-man's land. The apparent support of Rasmussen's position by the Danish government caused Canadian officials to examine the sovereignty issue. They concluded that to solidify, emphasize and maintain Canada's title to the region, more effective control would have to be established. One important means of emphasizing Canada's authority was to place RCMP outposts on the islands.

In 1921 Staff Sergeant A.H. Joy was sent to establish a post at Pond Inlet on Baffin Island. The next year another post was set up at Craig Harbour on Ellesmere Island and, in years to follow, other detachments were placed on Devon and Cornwallis islands. Control of the area was also asserted through long and arduous dog-sled patrols performed by Joy in 1927 and 1929 and by Constable Anstead in 1929. These patrols travelled across Ellesmere Island and the islands to the west, putting an end to any question of the territory's ownership.

These outposts and patrols were not simply symbolic of sovereignty, but bore a heavy responsibility for governing the Arctic. The RCMP brought law enforcement and the administration of justice. In addition, the Force was required to perform the work of many other departments, with a variety of duties ranging from the welfare of the native people, to tax collection, to scientific observations.

Perhaps the most impressive example of RCMP control of the Arctic came in 1942 and 1944 with the voyages of the *St. Roch*. Built in 1928, this vessel served as an RCMP supply ship and floating detachment. In June 1940 the *St. Roch* left Vancouver bound for Halifax, in an attempt to be the first vessel to cross the Northwest Passage from the Pacific to the Atlantic. Encountering heavy ice, Captain Henry A. Larsen and his crew spent two winters frozen in the Arctic before arriving at their destination in October 1942. Then, in the summer of 1944, the *St. Roch* became the first ship to traverse the Arctic in both directions when she crossed via the Northwest Passage again en route to Vancouver.

The RCMP were not alone in asserting Canadian sovereignty in the Arctic islands. Canadian explorers, scientists and other government officials shared in the hardships and the success. However, as in the previous frontiers subdued by Canada, the government turned to the Mounted Police when it needed a consistent authority in the Arctic.

William Beahen, RCMP Historian
RCMP Quarterly - Volume 45, Number 3

*   *   *   *   *

THE MOUNTED POLICE AT WAR

The battle honours of the RCMP are reflected on the guidon which is maintained in a glass case at Headquarters in Ottawa. One of the few times it is carried is when the Musical Ride escorts the Governor General to the Parliament Buildings, at which time it is borne by the corps sergeant-major.

The beginnings of the guidon are unique. An older *Encyclopedia Britannica* provides some insight into the origin: "The principal varieties of flags borne during the middle ages were the pennon, the banner and the standard. The 'guydhommes' or 'guidons' 'banderolls', 'pennoncell', 'streamers' or pendants, may be considered as minor varieties .... Every standard or guidon to have in the chief the cross of St. George, and to be slit at the end .... The guidon, a name derived from the French Guyd-homme, was somewhat similar to the standard, but without the cross of St. George, rounded at the end, less elongated and altogether less ornate. It was borne by a leader of horse, and according to a medieval writer 'must be two and a half or three yards long, and therein shall no armes be put, but only the man's crest, cognisance and devyce.' "

The only further reference to the guidon is found in an old dictionary: "guidon -- a small guiding flag or streamer, as that usually borne by each troop of cavalry or mounted battery of artillery, or used to direct the movements of infantry, or to signal with at sea. It is broad at the end next the staff and pointed, rounded, or notched at the other end." These characteristics describe the guidon of the RCMP and provide an insight into the shape of our guidon.

The original guidon of the Force bore our battle honours, specifically Northwest Canada 1885, South Africa 1900-02, France and Flanders 1918, Siberia 1918-19 and the badge of the Canadian Provost Corps. This guidon was retired to the RCMP in 1973 and replaced by Queen Elizabeth with the modern guidon. The Canadian Provost Corps badge was replaced by the battle honours of Europe 1939-45.

Our Force has many traditions, most of them built around accomplishments in maintaining and in enforcing the law or in storied patrols of the west and north. A few of those traditions that are especially inspirational are founded upon gallant but fatal attempts to finish a job at all costs.

There is also a bright, if for the most part unwritten, chapter of tradition which concerns the Force's association with Canada's armed services in times of war. This chapter of our story, though never stressed, comes more and more into focus as effort is added to effort and sacrifice to sacrifice. Every time Canada has gone to war, the Force has shown an eagerness to serve which, of necessity, was tempered by a genuine and reluctant realization that all could not go. Only a lucky and envied few were privileged to carry the name of the Force into action in the two world wars.

Back in 1885, in the Northwest Rebellion, almost the entire Force was committed in one way or another. Squadrons, troops and details fought under their own officers as components of the North West Field Force, while smaller parties acted as scouts for other units.

The North West Mounted Police, as the Force was then designated, was represented in the South African War by an outstanding body of officers and men. Though unable to serve as a unit -- for normal police work must continue even in time of war -- the Force contributed 245 officers and men to the Canadian cavalry. The commissioner himself, Lieutenant-Colonel L.W. Herchmer, took command of the second Canadian Mounted Rifles, and Superintendent S.B. Steele, already famous for his work in the Yukon during the gold-rush days, became Colonel of the Lord Strathcona Horse. Colonel Steele achieved further distinction in World War I when as Major-General Sir Sam Steele, he commanded the Second Canadian Division in England. He died in 1919.

Another member of the Mounted Police who served gallantly in the Boer War and subsequently won fame and promotion during the 1914-18 conflict was Inspector A.C. Macdonell, who became

Major-General Sir Archibald Macdonell, Commander of the "Old Red Patch". Another was Trooper J.H. MacBrien, who for several years after the Boer War was sergeant-major in the South African Constabulary, became a brigade commander in the Canadian Expeditionary Force, a major-general and Chief of the Canadian General Staff after World War I and finally, in 1931, rounded off his unique service record by becoming Commissioner of the Royal Canadian Mounted Police. Knighted by King George V in 1936, Sir James MacBrien's brilliant career was brought to a close with his untimely death, at 59 years of age, in 1938.

Many other members of the Force gained distinction for bravery and leadership in the South African War. Two were awarded the C.M.G., three the D.S.O., and one, the late Sergeant A.H. Richardson, the highest award of all, the Victoria Cross. Richardson was a sergeant-major in the Force. Seven gave their lives in this, the first Empire war in which Canadian soldiers fought side by side with troops from Great Britain, Australia and New Zealand.

On the outbreak of hostilities in 1914, Commissioner A. Bowen Perry sought authorization for a Mounted Police unit to serve as cavalry overseas. The government, however, turned a deaf ear: the C.E.F. had more than sufficient cavalry, and the Force was needed to maintain order in Canada. Nevertheless, in the course of the war several hundred members of the RNWMP were permitted to join the army individually when their term of service in the Force expired, and served with different units in France and Flanders. Among these stalwarts was Constable G.R. Pearkes who left the Force, time expired, to gain fame and fortune. Later Major-General Pearkes, V.C., D.S.O., M.C., at the outbreak of war he had been stationed in the Yukon as a constable. He won the V.C. at Passchendael while a major in the Canadian Mounted Rifles.

Finally on April 6, 1918, the Royal North West Mounted Police were authorized to form a draft to reinforce the Canadian Cavalry Brigade in France, and when recruiting began, the Force enlisted almost to a man. Only 15 officers and 231 other ranks, however, were permitted to go overseas, while an additional 495 new recruits were taken on strength. The Officer Commanding was Major (Superintendent) G.L. Jennings, later to become deputy commissioner.

Leaving Regina -- until 1920 the headquarters of the Force -- on May 30, 1918, the police contingent of four squadrons sailed from Montreal on June 3. On arrival in England, drafts were sent to reinforce Canadian units at the front, especially the Royal Canadian Dragoons and the Fort Garry Horse, while others joined the newly formed Canadian Tank Corps. On October 7, "A" Squadron, commanded by Major Jennings and comprising the original officers and most of the other ranks, was ordered to France, retaining its designation "Royal North West Mounted Police." For a short time the squadron was attached to the Canadian Light Horse, which also comprised the 19th Alberta Dragoons, the 16th Saskatchewan Light Horse and the First Hussars. Later, the unit was placed directly under the Canadian Corps Headquarters. It served with distinction in the battle area throughout the final stages of the pursuit to Mons, and one troop, under Lieutenant A.E. Ackland, proceeded with the Canadian Corps to Germany as part of the Army of Occupation. The squadron returned to Canada in May 1919, and nearly all its personnel, on demobilization from the army, resumed their normal work in the police.

In July 1918, Commissioner Perry was instructed to furnish another squadron to serve as the only cavalry unit with the Canadian Expeditionary Force which, under the command of Major-General J.H. Elmsley, was being sent to Siberia. Six officers and 184 other ranks, with 181 horses, were specially trained for this undertaking, and on October 1, an advance party sailed from Vancouver for Vladivostok. Although November 11 saw the termination of the war on the Western Front, hostilities in Siberia continued for many months, and the main body of the RNWMP squadron left Vancouver on November 17. The Officer Commanding was Major (Superintendent) G.S. Worsley. The squadron rendered good service in the Vladivostok area, where the presence of trained and trustworthy troops was of considerable value under the chaotic and lawless conditions which then existed in Siberia Several members of the Force served on special missions in the interior. One, Sergeant E. Margetts, M.M., of Ottawa, went as far as Ekaterinburg in European Russia, where he inspected the cellar in which Czar Nicholas and other members of the Imperial family were shot by the Bolsheviks and brought reports of the murder back to the British headquarters in Vladivostok. In the summer of 1919 the Mounted Police unit recrossed the Pacific Ocean and returned to its regular duties in the Force.

A large number of Imperial Reservists, moreover, took their discharge in 1914 from the RNWMP when called back to their original units, and many of those who survived re-engaged with the Force after the armistice. A famous warrior among these reservists was Constable Michael O'Leary, V.C., one of the earliest winners of the Empire's highest military award in the 1914-18 conflict. Incidentally, a member of Number 1 Provost Company (RCMP) met him in 1943, again in uniform. O'Leary proudly mentioned that his seven children, both sons and daughters, were in the armed services.

L.H. Nicholson and Donovan Saul

*   *   *   *   *

BATTLE-DRESS PATROL

In 1939, when war threatened, it was a tradition that the RCMP should seek the privilege of participating with Canada's armed forces. However, Commissioner S.T. Wood, who had served with the RNWMP in World War I, offered the services of the Force in any capacity at home or abroad. There would be a heavy load to carry at home during the war and the minister in control of the Force made it clear that he would not consent to granting leave or discharge by purchase to members of the RCMP to serve overseas. It was decided that the Force could best contribute by providing a provost company.

Number 1 Provost Company (RCMP) became a unit of the First Canadian Infantry Division. Its history must always be regarded as belonging to the larger story of that formation, but it was the first of Canada's Provost Corps and was unique in the Canadian army.

Volunteers were selected from all divisions of the Force. The first group assembled at "N" Division, Rockcliffe, in November 1939. Commissioner Wood inspected the unit and saw with pride that the men were to carry the name of the Force again into action. They left for Halifax and in December 1939 arrived at the garrison town of Aldershot in southern England.

The Provost Corps always had to enforce discipline but the troops soon realized that it aimed at fairness and impartiality, and that part of the job was to help any soldier who was lost or in trouble. The need for trained investigators within the army became apparent and, early in 1941, a Special Investigation Section was created in London to investigate all matters with which uniformed provost personnel could not cope.

Many of the original members of Number 1 Provost Company went to strengthen the whole fabric of the Canadian Provost Corps abroad. As the Canadian army grew, a few selected NCO's were drawn from the divisions, granted commissions and posted to infantry regiments.

At Aldershot the days were spent acquiring and testing the vehicles and other equipment a modern provost company takes to war. The hazards of shepherding a convoy over narrow, unmarked, unknown roads in almost total darkness are difficult to visualize. The full story of those waiting years in besieged Britain cannot be told here.

In the spring of 1943, the First Canadian Division concentrated in Scotland and was guided by the company up the length of the British Isles in what was thought to be just another of the many exercises. It was not long before they realized that their sojourn in Scotland was not merely to enhance the historic friendship of that land with Canada, and when they water-proofed their vehicles, drew tropical kit and began assault exercises, they scented adventure on a strong wind from the Mediterranean.

Ahead was the invasion of Sicily, the first "break-in" by the Western Allies on occupied Europe. Before the assault, the troops were loaded in the sequence of their landing on the beaches. Each detachment of provost had a definite part to play in keeping the well-ordered mass moving efficiently on D-Day, July 10, 1943.

The men first experienced traffic work under mortar and shell fire in Sicily and this experience paid big dividends later. When vehicles needed guidance past danger spots, the provost's responsibility was to "keep 'em rolling". When enemy fire or the weight of traffic destroyed a bridge or road -- and they frequently did -- the provost had to find a way around or hold up traffic until the damage was repaired. In Sicily, those members who participated in the landing were given the 1939-43 Star which required six months active service prior to the end of 1943. All members also had the volunteer medal. The latter was called the EBHO (Everybody Has One) and the former called the NEBHO (Nearly Everybody Has One). As there were many members who participated in the Italian campaign but did not arrive within the six-month period before December 31, 1943, they changed the medal to the 1939-45 Star.

On September 2, 1943, the Italian campaign opened. Number 1 Provost Company, equipped with field telephones to control traffic through lengthy detours and bottlenecks, had to keep moving forward, "leap-frogging" in sections as new ground was taken. Sharp engagements were fought. Pointsmen were stationed at the forward end of vehicle movement to prevent drivers from running blindly into danger and drawing enemy fire on forward troops. Pointsmen and patrolmen were frequently under shell fire.

Provost personnel experienced major traffic problems with the concentrated assault on Cassino. Miles of ground back of the gun positions were crowded with units and formations waiting their turn to advance, supplemented by the vast dumps of ammunition, stores and equipment needed to sustain such an operation. A 24-hour census on one route 20 miles to the rear, showed that 9,000 vehicles moved up and 5,000 down in that period.

For all provost personnel, the pursuit towards Rome was a nightmare of narrow, one-way tracks, desperately heavy traffic, long hours of duty and short snatches of rest in temporary, ever-changing bivouacs. Occasional trouble arose with Polish Corps drivers who persisted in going the wrong way on one-way routes, and with the Greeks who thought looting should be permitted. The answers had never been given at Depot Division, Regina, nor were they in any army text-book. They were furnished on the spot, with provost personnel using tact and persuasion and sometimes more forceful measures. And through it all, the roads were kept open and looting to a minimum.

Early in February 1945, all Canadian troops in Italy were ordered to northwest Europe. They left from Livorno near Pisa and landed at Marseilles, travelling non-stop through France and Belgium to Holland. Provost set up its headquarters in Holland, and on May 4, 1945, the fighting stopped. Provost members still had to man patrols, road-check stations and traffic points. They did not come under the general scheme for repatriation and had to continue their duties until the bulk of the troops were cleared homeward.

Disbandment came on October 18, 1945, after almost six years. The battle-dress patrol ended in September when the last remaining RCMP members started home on a priority draft. With the departure of the last remnant, the badge of the Force was seen no more in the unit it had sponsored.

Discharged from the army, the men reported back to the Force and again donned the uniform they had doffed for khaki. They were, in the cold official language of General Orders, "retaken on strength of the R.C.M.P. for pay and allowances".

Of the 213 members of the RCMP who served in Number 1 Provost Company, 12 gave their lives in the service of their country,

13 were wounded and one became a prisoner of war. Fourteen received special honours and there were 17 Mentioned in Dispatches. The men of Number 1 Provost Company take their places with the men of Cutknife Hill and Battleford, the South African veldt, Siberia, France and Flanders. Their spirit and example are a credit to Canada and the Force.

It is important to recognize a further group of men who left the Force when their term of engagement expired and joined other branches of the army, navy and air force. In 1939 some members who had a considerable time to serve before their term expired took the extreme course of getting married without permission and thus were discharged. This happened so often that the commissioner ruled that any other such malefactors would be kept in the Force and given a heavy fine. It is interesting to note that many members in pre-war days who were discharged for marrying without permission were invited to return to the Force and several of them attained high rank.

There are so many who left time expired to join the armed forces that they cannot all be named. The following members are but a fraction: Fred Andrishak and Ivan Rolstone are two who left to join the Canadian navy; Bob Poole went into the army, won the Military Medal and returned to the Force after the war; some members joined other provost companies such as Len Jones, Al Foster, Jack Brown, Jack McAthey (accidentally killed), Bill Neff and Tom Crawshaw; Gray Campbell joined the Royal Air Force. The above men represent the many others who also served in the armed forces during wartime and whose names are unavailable.

L.H. Nicholson and Donovan Saul

* * * * *

HISTORY OF THE MARINE DIVISION

In 1932 the RCMP absorbed the provincial police forces of the three maritime provinces and at the same time acquired from the Department of National Revenue the ships which were being operated in the Customs and Excise Preventive Service. This segment of the Force then became known as the RCMP Marine Section. The personnel wore the uniform and held ranks similar to that of the Royal Canadian Navy.

The Marine Section played a very important role in sea search and rescue as there were no rescue centres in Canada at that time.

Working in close cooperation with the land divisions, the Marine Section carried out police duties on the Atlantic seaboard and has to its credit some very interesting cases involving the smuggling of liquor on the high seas.

At the outbreak of the war in 1939, the Marine Section was suspended. By prior agreement between the RCMP and the Department of National Defence, the ships were transferred to active service with the Canadian navy and the RCAF. The personnel were allowed to volunteer and some 155 officers and men entered the navy with the remainder going to the RCAF Sea Search and Rescue Section and the Canadian army. They served their country well and many were decorated for outstanding service. Many Marine Section members such as R.A.S. MacNeil performed outstanding service during hostilities. His son, Robert MacNeil, in his book, *Wordstruck,* describes MacNeil's well-known corvette, the *Dauphin,* which had a crest on its turret showing a Mountie riding a German submarine like a bronco buster. This got a lot of attention when Lieutenant Commander MacNeil was decorated by King Haakon of Norway for rescuing the crew of a freighter torpedoed in very stormy conditions in the Atlantic.

Another member, Ken Hall, born in Ireland, joined the Force on November 15, 1932. Shortly after he completed training he transferred to "H" Division where he served with the Marine Section. He achieved the rank of able seaman when he joined the Royal Canadian Naval Reserve and had achieved the rank of lieutenant commander by the time he rejoined the Force on October 21, 1945, as a corporal. His ultimate rank in the Force when he retired on January 14, 1966, was chief superintendent.

After the war the Marine Section was reorganized and the majority of the pre-war personnel returned to take up the positions they had held prior to dissolution. In 1947 the Marine Section was renamed and constituted a division of the Force.

In 1949, when Newfoundland entered Confederation, the RCMP took over the federal police duties and on August 1, 1950, the Newfoundland Rangers. The island of Newfoundland with Labrador is an area of 154,734 square miles, which gave the Marine Division a larger patrol area and eventually, detachment-class patrol boats were stationed "on command" in "B" Division, with the larger vessels carrying out numerous patrols in the waters surrounding Newfoundland, Labrador and the French islands of St. Pierre and Miquelon.

In 1950 the Force took over the British Columbia Provincial

Police and again acquired a number of older patrol vessels. These, along with the fleet of ships acquired from the Canadian navy after the war, eventually had to be replaced. In 1952 a program was started to upgrade the existing fleet with new construction. In 1958 the first large patrol vessel to be commissioned was the *Wood* followed by the *Fort Steele*. This construction program replaced approximately 35 detachment-class patrol units in addition to the *Wood* and *Fort Steele*. A further addition was made in 1967 with the construction of seven patrol boats, in operation at Expo 67, and later placed on command in different divisions.

One of the last patrol vessels acquired from the navy was the motor launch *Blue Heron*, which, after serving with the Force for approximately 11 years, was replaced in 1967-68 by detachment-class boats, the *Nicholson* and *Standoff*. These two 75-foot patrol boats help to make up a fleet of 41 patrol units entirely RCMP owned. Each is equipped with the most modern navigational and police communications equipment.

Prior to the establishment of the Canadian Coast Guard, the Marine Division was called upon at all times to assist the air-sea search -and-rescue centres across Canada. The division has now been relieved of total responsibility in that field, but is still called upon to assist in many instances.

On the Atlantic and Pacific coasts and the Great Lakes, the Marine Division works in close cooperation with the land divisions. In isolated towns and villages on the west coast, patrol boats act as floating detachments and provide the only police service in many areas.

M.R. McKay
RCMP Quarterly - Volume 34, Number 4

* * * * *

THE AMERICAN CONNECTION

It is of interest to note that the original Force had a close connection with our neighbours to the south. Many members of the NWMP came from other nations and conditions of life. Notable among these were men from both sides of the American Civil War, or those who were descended from such veterans. One of the first six officers chosen to command the original NWMP was one Jacob Carvell, an ex-Confederate Army officer.

After the Civil War, the family of John Taylor Wood, commander of the Confederate blockade runner *Tallahassee*, moved to the Canadian Maritimes. A son, Zachary Taylor Wood, named for the American President Zachary Taylor, joined the NWMP as an inspector, later assistant commissioner. In turn, his son, Stuart Taylor Wood, was commissioned in the RNWMP and rose to become commissioner of the Force. He was also named for his grandfather and perhaps for Confederate General Jeb Stuart.

George B. McLellan joined the RCMP and rose to the rank of commissioner. He was the grandson of General McLellan of the United States Union Army.

Finally, Floyd Sherman Anderson served for some time in the RCMP. He was the grandson of General Sherman of the Union Army.

Tom Crawshaw

* * * * *

INDEX